Liquid Landscape

EARLY AMERICAN STUDIES

Series editors: Daniel K. Richter, Kathleen M. Brown, Max Cavitch, and David Waldstreicher

Exploring neglected aspects of our colonial, revolutionary, and early national history and culture, Early American Studies reinterprets familiar themes and events in fresh ways. Interdisciplinary in character, and with a special emphasis on the period from about 1600 to 1850, the series is published in partnership with the McNeil Center for Early American Studies.

A complete list of books in the series is available from the publisher.

Liquid Landscape

Geography and Settlement at the Edge of Early America

Michele Currie Navakas

PENN

UNIVERSITY OF PENNSYLVANIA PRESS

PHILADELPHIA

Published by
University of Pennsylvania Press
Philadelphia, Pennsylvania 19104-4112
www.upenn.edu/pennpress

Printed in the United States of America
on acid-free paper

10 9 8 7 6 5 4 3 2 1

Library of Congress Cataloging-in-Publication Data

Names: Navakas, Michele Currie, author.
Title: Liquid landscape: geography and settlement at the edge of early America / Michele Currie Navakas.
Other titles: Early American studies.
Description: 1st edition. | Philadelphia: University of Pennsylvania Press, [2018] | Series: Early American studies | Includes bibliographical references and index.
Identifiers: LCCN 2017013303 | ISBN 9780812249569 (hardcover : alk. paper)
Subjects: LCSH: Landscapes—Political aspects—Florida—History—18th century. | Landscapes—Political aspects—Florida—History—19th century. | Land settlement—Florida—History—18th century. | Land settlement—Florida—History—19th century. | Florida—Description and travel—To 1865.
Classification: LCC F314 .N38 2018 | DDC 975.9/01—dc23
LC record available at https://lccn.loc.gov/2017013303

For Gene Navakas

Contents

Liquid Landscape

Introduction. Porous Foundations

What does it mean to take root on unstable ground? Ground that shifts, seeps, expands, and erodes cannot sustain the familiar practices of settlement that British colonists brought to North America's Eastern Seaboard in the early seventeenth century. Enclosure, demarcation, and improvement—in the form of fixed dwellings, sturdy fences, and cultivated fields—defined landed property according to John Locke and many Enlightenment philosophers. These practices also marked ownership in British colonial America, and later they enabled political participation in the United States. Yet these practices, which have historically signaled and secured belonging in much of North America, are difficult to imagine, let alone pursue, on shifting ground. For such ground cannot bear fixed markers of possession.[1]

People have taken root in Florida for thousands of years, despite the fact that Florida's liquid landscape challenges crucial notions of land, space, and boundaries that underlie familiar British and Anglo-American forms and practices of founding. The Calusa, one of Florida's many indigenous societies, established themselves on the shifting shoals of the southwest coast by way of wooden dwellings that floated above shell mounds when the waters inevitably rose. Florida wreckers, who salvaged distressed ships, made the Florida Reef their permanent home and source of income during much of the colonial and antebellum period by moving continually over coral terrain in small boats. Seminole Indians, who migrated south to Florida and there joined many Africans who escaped slavery during the eighteenth and nineteenth centuries, maintained communities on the spongy flatlands of the Everglades by constructing homes of thatched palmetto raised above the earth on poles made of cypress logs, and by planting crops on natural rises of dry ground known as hammocks. And the challenges of taking permanent hold on elusive, porous, and shifting ground continue to inform architectural choices in twentieth- and twenty-first-century Florida, from coastal homes on stilts built to withstand hurricanes that alter the shoreline to the offshore dwellings of Stiltsville, a group of houses constructed on Biscayne Bay east of Miami in the 1930s, and still standing just above the shallow coastal waters of the Atlantic. These historical examples of living in the absence of solid, stable ground reveal that Florida's porous landscape has always necessitated modes of settlement, attachment, and belonging that differ from, yet are no less durable than, those that developed on firmer ground.

Recognition that Florida's unstable land required different modes of use and possession infuses a broad archive of imaginative reflections on root-taking in Florida that circulated widely in North America from the late colonial period through the late nineteenth century. This archive attests that many people living across the continent during the eighteenth and nineteenth centuries were aware of and interested in local, Floridian forms of taking root—forms that did not depend on the stable ground that a Lockean tradition of landed property required. A different narrative of U.S. founding and expansion emerges when we focus on widely read accounts of settling a particularly unsolid part of the continent. Reflections on Florida from Revolution through Reconstruction reveal that, from the moment of founding onward, the United States was a nation deeply interested in imagining roots, and thereby personal and collective identity, in the absence of solid ground.

A large number of early observers of Florida and other southern parts of North America felt these spaces could never be founded, and thus dismissed them as "problems" for an expanding settler empire. Early maps, settlers' guides, travel narratives, novels, and other texts characterized these spaces as "undeveloped," "deviant," "retrograde," "uncultivable," "degenerate," and even "impenetrable."[2] But Florida's porous foundations frequently elicited another type of response as well. To many early Americans the liquid landscape appeared not as an obstacle to settlement, but rather as a provocation to think beyond more familiar ideals of land and boundaries that made it possible to imagine the United States as settler nation and empire in the first place.

While Florida's local topographic features have always raised pronounced physical challenges for those who pursued long-term settlement there, this study focuses on the many conceptual possibilities the prospect and process of Florida settlement raised, particularly for those living in other areas of the United States during the eighteenth and nineteenth centuries. Sometimes this involved imagining how an individual or community might best take root on Florida's shifting foundations. At other times, it involved the larger political and cultural task of envisioning unstable Florida's incorporation into the United States, an event that many struggled to imagine long before Florida's official annexation in 1821, and struggled to pursue thereafter, during Florida's long Territorial period (1821–45). But whether personal, national, or imperial in scope, founding Florida challenged fundamental understandings of land and possession. Florida's founding mattered well beyond its liquid landscape, exposing how some of the nation's most politically significant concepts of self, nation, and empire rested on assumptions that were as contingent as its topography.

*   *   *

Florida's indeterminate, shifting ground contributed to the complex history of U.S. founding by raising large conceptual questions about root-taking that had wide-ranging political and cultural implications for a country seeking to expand over and beyond the continent. First and foremost, for a significant number of U.S. observers more familiar with stable, contiguous, solid ground, Florida proved difficult to imagine as *land*. This initial difficulty, in turn, frequently prompted a reconsideration of root-taking. And, across a vast time span and many forms of representation, Florida's shifting ground gave rise to new ways of imagining roots, and thereby personal and national identity, that did not depend on solid ground.

This does not mean that Florida prompted *all* early observers to ponder the difficulty of settling there personally or incorporating the land and populations politically. After all, some people who reflected on Florida had no difficulty establishing themselves in familiar ways. In fact, a thriving plantation culture developed in certain parts of the panhandle (known then as "Middle Florida") and the east coast near Jacksonville; during several decades of the antebellum period, these places looked no different from the rest of the U.S. South.[3] Furthermore, some who wrote about Florida had no interest in settling there at all—indeed, this study includes many texts by people who had no plans to live in Florida or develop it as an extension of the United States.

Yet this study unearths a widely circulating, though largely unexamined, archive demonstrating that local Floridian features—such as saturated swamps, shifting shorelines, coral reefs, tiny keys, and various native and non-native populations—frequently provoked people throughout North America to engage with pressing questions about place, personhood, and belonging that animated U.S. culture and literature during the eighteenth and nineteenth centuries. This archive includes settlers' guides, captivity narratives, military accounts, images such as woodcuts and lithographs, continental maps, natural histories, tales of adventure, and coastal and inland surveys, as well as works by canonical authors such as William Bartram, James Fenimore Cooper, and Harriet Beecher Stowe. Importantly, published texts provide nearly all the evidence for this study's claims. A number of these texts were extremely popular among their original readers and viewers. Many were reprinted during the period, and many more proved valuable to Americans long after the date of initial publication. In fact a large number of texts about Florida that were published prior to the founding of the United States exerted significant influence in the new nation after the Revolution. Especially during the decades after the 1821 U.S. annexation of Florida, U.S. readers and writers relied on information about Florida from earlier accounts produced for and by naturalists, government officials, explorers, and prospective settlers during Florida's First Spanish period (1565–1763), its British period (1763–83), and its Second Spanish period (1783–1821). Telling the story of what Florida settlement meant to those living in North America between Revolution and Reconstruction thus requires analysis of the large variety of materials published on both sides of the Revolution that circulated in the eighteenth and nineteenth centuries.[4] These materials establish that Florida's local land and populations were more than local in meaning.

Too frequently, Florida remains a topic confined to regional studies because of a persistent notion that it somehow had its own, separate, self-contained history that was only occasionally part of a more familiar national historical narrative or literary history.[5] Yet Florida's fundamental porosity and dispersal made it part of North American thinking about personal, national, and imperial identity even before there was a coherent nation. From the early sixteenth century onward, reflections on Florida capture the region's resistance to containment, borders, and regulation, and its influence on other places and peoples on and beyond the continent. This historical context is the basis for *Liquid Landscape*'s central claim that the farthest southern reaches of North America already mattered to people in many other places on the continent at the moment of the founding of the United States, and thus that these seeming peripheries of early America should matter more centrally to our own scholarly understanding of early U.S. literature and culture.[6]

*　*　*

The Florida known to North Americans at the time of the nation's founding had already challenged European and American thinking about the very nature of land, boundaries, and foundations for centuries. From the first Spanish landing on its shores in the sixteenth century, Florida's topographic, geographic, and demographic indeterminacy shaped maps, travel accounts, surveys, and other texts. Ponce de León, who landed near present-day St. Augustine and claimed "La Florida" for Spain in 1513, recorded his discovery of the "island" of Florida, while immediately subsequent explorers affirmed Florida's attachment to the continent. These conflicting geographic descriptions confused European mapmakers: some chose to map Florida as an island, and others as a peninsula.

By about 1520 some of the initial geographic uncertainty about Florida's location and contours gave way. But just as more maps began featuring Florida as a peninsula rather than an island, another spatial discrepancy emerged. Spain began to apply the name "La Florida" to an area that stretched far beyond the peninsula to include much of the present-day southeastern United States. Thus, alongside maps of Florida as an island and maps of Florida as a peninsula, maps locating "La Florida" along the entire southeastern portion of the North American continent appeared. This designation for the region persisted among many European mapmakers and even American colonists for nearly two hundred years.[7]

Complementing Florida's early spatial fluctuation among island, peninsula, and continental Southeast is the mobility of its indigenous and nonnative populations. Reports penned by Spanish missionaries who founded Catholic missions during the sixteenth and seventeenth centuries frequently characterize Florida's variety of mostly nonagricultural Indian societies—including the Calusa, Guale, Tequesta, and Timucua—as "scattered" and nomadic. Such descriptions probably emerged from the difficulty of converting indigenous peoples who moved seasonally from place to place, and even lived offshore in fishing villages.[8]

Indigenous populations, along with a variety of newcomers to Florida during this period, both contested and enabled Spanish rule, which lasted until 1763.[9] Imperial rivals from France sought to establish a colony near present-day Jacksonville. Pirates of many nations attacked the Florida coast seasonally, sometimes capturing Spanish forts and seizing vessels.[10] Some indigenous Indian groups helped sustain the Spanish mission system, but missionization was always a contested process, and by the early eighteenth century many converts began to flee, Indian revolts had challenged the authority of the missionaries, and Spanish-borne diseases ravaged the population.[11] Further challenges arose when Indians in other parts of the Southeast began coming to Florida. Yamasees and Lower Creeks, armed and sometimes led by the British, raided the peninsula for Indian captives to use and sell as slaves.[12]

Yet not all populations drawn to Spanish Florida (1565–1763 and 1783–1821) contested colonial rule. Many became allies in exchange for freedom. African slaves, who began escaping to Florida from British colonies during the late seventeenth century, gained sanctuary and liberty in Florida upon conversion to Catholicism.[13] And during Florida's Second Spanish period, when civil war broke out among the Creek Nation of the Southeast during 1813, many of these Indians—today known as Seminole—began streaming southward onto the peninsula, where Spain recruited them to protect the colony from other Native groups and European imperial competitors. African and Creek migration to Florida would long outlast the end of Spanish rule in 1821, for Africans continued running south to freedom until the Civil War, and Creeks arrived in waves until the 1830s. By and large the two groups lived as allies, and the Seminole augmented their Florida chiefdoms by absorbing outsiders. They granted African newcomers protection in exchange for tribute, and welcomed some formerly missionized "Spanish Indians," the U.S. name for Florida's indigenous populations who had been almost entirely decimated by warfare and disease by the mid-eighteenth century.[14]

Early encounters and alliances among various populations in Spanish Florida produced new cartographic understandings of the region on European and American maps. During the early eighteenth century many of these maps began to represent Florida as multiple islands. The islands of Florida likely originated when slave raiders from the British colonies solicited topographic information about the Everglades from local Indians who may have described the southern part of Florida as a flat expanse of water studded with innumerable rises of dry land.[15] A cartographic conception of Florida as islands persisted on some of the most popular maps of North America from the early eighteenth century until well into the nineteenth century, while other popular maps featured the region as a peninsula. These competing spatial representations of Florida influenced geographic conceptions of the whole continent, for on many maps of the continent the islands of Florida are scattered so widely that they blend with those of the Caribbean, making it difficult to tell where North America ends.

An inaccurate sense of Florida's location and terrestrial shape exacerbated the enormous challenges to colonial rule that Great Britain faced upon gaining Florida from Spain in 1763 at the end of the Seven Years' War.[16] The British Board of Trade quickly launched a massive cartographic project to survey and map the peninsula, reef, and keys. This project was the first step toward defending Florida from imperial and Native rivals and enticing British settlers who would render the region a southern extension of Great Britain's continental empire. The British divided Florida into two provinces: West Florida included the panhandle and adjacent parts of present-day Alabama, Mississippi, and Louisiana; East Florida consisted of the entire peninsula stretching south of the Georgia border.

British planters from the Carolinas came to East Florida enticed by generous land grants, and soon "Florida fever" spread through New England, producing new maps, surveys, and natural histories, such as Bernard Romans's lavishly illustrated *Concise Natural History of East and West Florida* (1775).[17] British plantations exploiting the work of slaves and indentured servants spread along the St. Johns River near Jacksonville, where agriculture flourished until the outbreak of the American Revolution.[18] Briefly during the war this area became a stronghold for Loyalists who fled south from Charleston and Savannah along with their slaves. Yet as fighting disrupted plantation labor and slaves escaped to Seminole villages in the interior, British planters fled Florida for good.

Many early U.S. political figures were intrigued by the prospect of including Florida within the new nation. From their point of view, U.S. control over the region would bolster the emerging nation's claims to the continent by guaranteeing mastery of the Gulf of Mexico and adjoining commercial waterways such as the Mississippi River.[19] For this reason John Adams, Benjamin Franklin, and James Madison urged claims to the Floridas from the moment independence was declared. Soon these and other U.S. observers had additional cause to do so: upon the war's conclusion in 1783, Great Britain retroceded the Floridas to Spain, which immediately revived its sanctuary policy, drawing to the Floridas an ever larger number of slaves from plantations across the U.S. South.[20]

For a newly emergent, slave-holding nation with expansionist designs on the continent, Spanish Florida was an unavoidable topic of concern and debate. The unstable borderland harbored populations both black and white from across and beyond the country, and many of these groups were averse, or even hostile, to the prospect of U.S. rule.[21] After the American Revolution Spain opened a generous land grant policy to foreign and non-Catholic immigrants, encouraging planters with their slaves and servants from all over the Caribbean and North America to settle in Spanish Florida alongside Cuban planters and homesteaders.[22] And although in 1790 Spain yielded to U.S. pressures to rescind the sanctuary policy, Africans and Creeks continued migrating to Seminole country. The savannahs and swamps of the Florida interior would remain a stronghold of black freedom for many decades to come.[23]

Spanish Florida's threat to U.S. chattel slavery compelled Madison, Thomas Jefferson, and James Monroe to pursue the Floridas during the first decades of the nineteenth century. In 1812 agitated planters, who lived north of the Florida-Georgia border and called themselves "Patriots," independently invaded East Florida in an attempt to overthrow Spain. Although Seminoles and Africans joined together and repelled the planters, this unprovoked invasion caused fighting that destroyed what little plantation culture had developed in Spanish Florida after the Revolution. It also provoked Spain to bring a militia of Africans from Cuba to defend the peninsula.[24] Soon the British also armed Africans in Florida. During the War of 1812 British troops engaged both Seminoles and Africans to build a fort near Tallahassee and enticed additional Africans to Spanish Florida by offering freedom for loyalty to the British crown.[25] Unable to tolerate an ever-enlarging population of Indians and free, armed blacks from the Caribbean and the U.S. South on the nation's borders, Andrew Jackson invaded Florida in 1818. With the tacit approval of some government officials, Jackson seized Florida for the United States, intensifying local border skirmishes into what we now call the First Seminole War (1817–18), and compelling Spain to relinquish Florida for good.[26]

By the time the United States annexed Florida officially in 1821, its local populations and landscape were already infamous subjects of national interest. Florida had long challenged plantation slavery as well as control of the Gulf of Mexico, border security, and the burgeoning project of Indian removal. The new U.S. territory of Florida thus raised challenges to national cohesion and imperial expansion over and beyond the continent—challenges that only intensified as expansionist ambitions burgeoned. For this reason the federal government sponsored several costly interventions in antebellum Florida to prepare the territory for statehood. Government officials believed that Florida's settlement by a landholding populace loyal to the United States would peacefully expel maroon communities, discourage additional Africans from arriving, and guard the coast from imperial opponents and independent profiteers.

Yet Florida's populations and landscape continued to complicate efforts at U.S. settlement and sovereignty. A territorial survey, required for public land sales, began in the mid-1820s, though it was delayed for decades by bad weather, swampy ground, preexisting Spanish land grants, and conflicts with the Seminole. A reliable map including the Florida interior south of Lake Okeechobee was not available until the mid-nineteenth century.[27] Military officials began surveying the Florida Reef and Keys during the 1820s, and plans for lighthouses and coastal fortifications soon developed, but difficulties of weather and topography stalled these projects also. Although some lighthouses appeared along the reef during the 1830s, there was no complete reef survey until 1851, and coastal forts proved altogether impractical. In fact, on tiny Florida islands that were supposed to become the U.S. "Gibraltar of the Gulf," the remnants of one partially built fort still stand. The construction begun by slaves in the 1840s was abandoned after four decades of struggle during which hurricanes, waves, and sinking sands continually undermined the fort's foundations.[28] Plans to drain Florida's interior swamps also ran aground. This initiative garnered national interest and funding on a number of occasions, beginning when Congress sponsored an expedition to the Everglades for reclamation in the late 1840s. But the sponge-like flatlands repeatedly confounded such projects.[29]

While federally funded initiatives propelled Florida's swamps, shores, reefs, and keys into national discussion and debate, the most costly and galvanizing issue during this period was war. The United States waged a series of military conflicts with Florida's populations of Africans and Seminoles that erupted into war on three separate occasions between 1818 and 1858. The second of these wars—the Florida War, or Second Seminole War (1835–42)—was the nation's longest and most expensive Indian war. It drew thousands of American troops into the swamp, where they battled Seminoles and Africans in an effort to establish U.S. control over Florida, for sovereignty over this contested space had become essential to the preservation of plantation slavery throughout the South. Not all inhabitants of the United States supported the war, which prompted debates about the use of federal funding to sustain slavery and pursue Indian removal.[30] In the end, the Florida War exterminated or expelled thousands of Africans and Seminoles. Yet it also pushed many maroon communities farther south onto the peninsula, where their justified hostility to encroaching American settlements initiated the Third Seminole War in 1855—a full ten years after Florida had become the nation's twenty-seventh state.[31] While all three Indian wars drastically reduced Florida's populations of Africans and Seminoles, many members of both groups remained, and their descendants continue to live in Florida today.

During the post-Civil War period, when this study concludes, Florida's porosity and dispersal continued to challenge key understandings of ground and founding that made it possible to imagine the country as a single entity that could continually expand, yet still cohere. Florida differed dramatically from other parts of the U.S. South. It was the region's poorest and most sparsely populated state, and the only area where plantation culture had never flourished on a large scale.[32] Decades of war against Seminoles and Africans had disrupted U.S. settlement and, while no decisive Civil War battles were fought there, Union troops repeatedly occupied and ravaged several cities after Florida seceded in 1861.[33] It was difficult to travel in and to Florida as well, for public roads were in deplorable condition, and an extensive railroad would not exist until the 1890s.

Nonetheless, post-Civil War Florida's lack of traditional foundations gave many populations a home in the post-slavery United States. Freedmen came south to live as squatters on unoccupied lands or purchase farms cooperatively. Poor white Southerners became owners of Florida's inexpensive, abandoned lands. And well-established white Northerners, including Harriet Beecher Stowe and her extended family, pulled up stakes and came to Florida by steamboat to found farms, churches, and schools.[34] As a place without a traditional plantation past, postbellum Florida accommodated Americans both black and white who could not manage—or did not desire—to belong in traditional ways on other parts of the continent. Even after Reconstruction, Florida's unfounded ground gave many people from other parts of the nation new and necessary ways to pursue and imagine roots.

*   *   *

The value of attending carefully to the large and largely underexamined variety of early American writings about Florida is twofold. From local surveys to classic works of literature, reflections on Florida offer new understandings of both the conceptual history of U.S. incorporation and the roots and routes of U.S. writing.[35] The case of William Bartram in eighteenth-century Florida provides a useful illustration of how this study's consideration of Florida simultaneously enriches the conceptual history of belonging in North America and U.S. literary history. Bartram's *Travels* (1791), a natural history of the Southeast, portrays Florida as a place where land and water continually combine and trade places with little warning, dissolving property lines and even geographic boundaries: "porous rocks" channel waters "by gradual but constant percolation" through "innumerable doublings, windings, and secret labyrinths" just beneath one's feet.[36] Fish "descend into the earth through wells and cavities or vast perforations of the rocks, and from thence are conducted or carried away, by secret subterranean conduits and gloomy vaults, to other distant lakes and rivers" (206); "vast reservoirs" of water "suddenly break through [the] perforated fluted rocks . . . flooding large districts of land" (226); "floods of rain" drive lake waters over their usual bounds and creeks "contrary" to their "natural course" (142); and "old habitations . . . [moulder] to earth" (95). There is a "deserted" British plantation, the "ruins of ancient French plantations," the "vestiges" of Spanish ones, and a functioning plantation that disintegrates when a hurricane flattens buildings and destroys fields of indigo and sugar cane (253, 407, 233, 143).[37]

Yet Bartram's Floridian ground fosters and rewards a model of permanent inhabitance nonetheless. Sailing along Florida's St. Johns River on "a fine cool morning," Bartram finds his small boat surrounded by "vast quantities of the *Pistia stratiotes*, a very singular aquatic plant" (88). This plant—commonly known as water lettuce—displays remarkable resilience in a volatile and watery landscape, a capacity for endurance that Bartram credits to its unusual roots. He writes that the water lettuce "associates in large communities, or floating islands" that, though tossed about by the wind and waves, remain "in their proper horizontal situation, by means of long fibrous roots, which descend from the nether center, downwards." Thus, in great storms, "when the river is suddenly raised" and "large masses of these floating plains are broken loose," "driven from the shores," and even "broken to pieces," the plant "communities" always "find footing" once more and, "forming new colonies, spread and extend themselves again" (89). In a place given to sudden, unpredictable fluctuations in the water level, rooting firmly to the earth is perilous; floating or moving continually best achieves stability.

Upon first consideration, the relevance of Bartram's liquid landscape to early debates about U.S. identity seems unclear. Yet for Bartram— as I show in Chapter 1—this land raised conceptual questions about human belonging that were politically significant to his North American readers, many of whom were members of a new nation seeking to establish itself and expand over new and untested ground. Implicitly, Bartram's reflections on Florida raise several pertinent questions. How can one imagine or pursue long-term settlement in the absence of solid ground? And how can one take root permanently on a foundation that seeps and shifts both endlessly and unpredictably? First and foremost, such questions expose the limits of a prevailing ideal of land as firm and divisible. To post-Revolutionary Americans familiar with founding documents that describe a nation of small farmers achieving political belonging by demarcating, cultivating, and remaining on a single plot of ground, these questions expose additional limits. They suggest that this founding version of the emerging republic—and the Lockean account of the subject subtending it—is provisional and highly contingent on the particularities of the landscape.

Ultimately *Travels* suggests that some parts of North America require another version of personal and political belonging, according to which one achieves permanent inhabitance by taking very shallow root, spreading continually over the earth, or even floating just above it. For it is precisely because the *Pistia stratiotes* refuses firm fixity that it remains ineradicable, and can always "find footing" and "spread and extend" itself once more. Bartram's reflections on local Florida roots may thus be read as an important contribution to the history of landed possession on the continent. Considered as such, these reflections also constitute one reason for including *Travels* more centrally in U.S. literary history alongside other reflections on local landscape, such as those by J. Hector St. John de Crèvecoeur. In *Letters from an American Farmer* (1782) Crèvecoeur's narrator moves across several American geographies and ultimately finds that different parts of North America produce different versions of character. In the frequently anthologized Letter III ("What is an American?"), for example, Pennsylvania fosters an idealized version of Jeffersonian agrarianism, but other parts of North America require a revision of this ideal.[38]

If scholars have no trouble accepting Crèvecoeur's Pennsylvania, South Carolina, Nantucket, and Wyoming as valuable contributions to the literature of North American place, personhood, and belonging, then we should also accept Bartram's Florida as such. After all, early Americans living in the United States easily could have read *Travels* alongside *Letters*: editions of each text were printed in Philadelphia during the early 1790s.[39] Furthermore, long after its initial publication, *Travels* inspired American artists, naturalists, travelers, and writers.[40] Bartram's Florida landscape reached an enormous U.S. audience in particular through the popular works of François-René Chateaubriand, who never visited Florida and draws extensively on *Travels* in the novel *Atala* (1801) and later in *Travels in America* (1828). In fact Bartram's Florida roots in particular captivated Chateaubriand, for "floating islands of pistia" populate the setting of *Atala*.[41]

If reflections on root-taking by both Crèvecoeur and Bartram supplied early Americans with metaphors of attachment to North American ground, then why not pair these authors in anthologies of American literature, in the classroom, and in our research and writing? Doing so establishes that the mosaic of U.S. imaginings of founding is richer than we have supposed. For Bartram provides what Crèvecoeur does not: a theory of landed possession in the absence of secure material foundations. Indeed, reading *Travels* as both a natural history of Florida *and* a complex theory of root-taking in North America paves the way for a consideration of other published and popular writers on Florida during the early national period—such as John James Audubon—as theorists of early U.S. identity no less fascinating than Crèvecoeur.[42] Throughout the following chapters of this book I take such an approach to all materials, from maps of Florida to novels by canonical U.S. writers: these texts establish both the *conceptual* relevance of Florida to discussions of American character and the *literary* value of Florida to our understanding of various themes and genres of U.S. writing as the nation's borders emerged and expanded.

*   *   *

Each chapter that follows centers on a different set of related, iconic features of the Floridian landscape—shifting shores, scattered islands, coral reefs, swamps and hammocks, and the roots of palmetto shrubs and orange trees, respectively—that provoked early observers to realize that founding required something other than firm fixity to a single section of ground. The cultural and political implications of this realization change, of course, as the book proceeds chronologically.

The first two chapters establish the influence of Florida's liquid landscape on early North American practices and perceptions of landed possession. These chapters show that the same shifting grounds that many observers declared "uncultivable" in fact generated ways to think in terms other than those of an emergent nationalist narrative grounded in terra firma. As the book proceeds into the mid-nineteenth century, it charts how reefs, swamps, and hammocks that many living in the United States dismissed as "impenetrable" prompted some writers to think otherwise. For authors of several popular antebellum genres—including captivity narrative, female picaresque, and frontier novel—Florida offered a way to see beyond the limits of plantocratic and imperial accounts of space and subjectivity that increasingly underpinned the intertwined projects of American slavery and expansion. This book then moves into the post-Civil War period. During this time many observers considered Florida's resistance to more familiar modes of root-taking to be evidence of the region's destiny to remain a "backward" periphery of the United States. Yet I show that some authors, such as Stowe, found that this resistance afforded productive alternatives to more familiar Reconstruction-era concepts of domesticity and reform. Altogether these chapters demonstrate that Florida's fluidity inspired a rich set of materials through which to observe something that scholars of eighteenth- and nineteenth-century U.S. literature and culture had already begun to suggest: imaginings of self, nation, and empire were more varied, conflicted, and contingent on the local particularities of various landscapes than many of the period's better-known philosophical, political, legal, and literary formulations of these concepts indicate.[43]

By restoring reflections on Florida to the history of U.S. imaginings of self, nation, and empire, *Liquid Landscape* continues the work of unsettling an overly solid historical, geographical, rhetorical, and theoretical conception of the United States that was not shared by everyone calling it home. Certainly the conception of the U.S. nation as rightfully coextensive with a stable, solid, contiguous, and sharply outlined landmass served many nationalist purposes during the eighteenth and nineteenth centuries. A number of literary, cultural, and historical studies have shown that this continental ideal fostered a much-needed sense of national independence at the time of the Revolution. It also signified the nation's destiny to become one people united under a single power during the post-Revolutionary period, and it sanctioned expansionist territorial claims during much of the nineteenth century.[44]

However, while many North Americans embraced this idea in a wide range of genres—including classic works of American literature, decorative arts, and influential political essays and legal documents—many contested the continental ideal, even from the earliest moments of the nation's founding. For it promoted a political and cultural definition of the United States as a self-enclosed, ever-expanding nation of settlers united under a strong federal government—a definition that not everyone shared.[45] As recent scholars of empire usefully remind us, the nation emerged from and never fully displaced a "variegated colonial world" of many peoples and polities with their own concepts and practices of space, place, and belonging.[46] This fact challenges us to question the iconic imperial image of an evenly shaded map and recover imaginative alternatives to a nationalist narrative that depends on stable and contiguous land.[47]

Liquid Landscape answers this challenge by turning to the farthest southern reaches of the continent, reasoning that no other North American ground combined topographic instability, geographic indeterminacy, and demographic fluidity as obviously and dramatically as Florida. Certainly other parts of the continent resisted agricultural development, compelled settlers to contend with changes in the land, posed geographic challenges, and hosted heterogeneous populations.[48] Yet no other part simultaneously shifted perceptibly because of hurricanes, sinkholes, and swamps; belonged to the U.S. South and the Caribbean; and harbored itinerant enclaves of ex-slaves, pirates, Spaniards, and Native Americans. Put another way, we already knew that continental ground was rarely as firm, enduring, arable, and divisible as the abstract ideal of land informing so many familiar philosophical and legal conceptions of property, settlement, and expansion in eighteenth- and nineteenth-century North America. But Florida tells crucial stories of U.S. space and place, settlement and belonging, territory and sovereignty, that emerge in the absence of secure foundations.

Chapter 1

Liquid Landscape:
Estuary, Marsh, Sink, Spring, Shore

The third volume of John James Audubon's *Ornithological Biography* (1835) contains a description of the Brown Pelican perched upon a mangrove in the Florida Keys, an image of which appears as Plate 251 in *The Birds of America* (1827–38; see Figure 1). While the bird is Audubon's primary interest, he is also fascinated by the "glossy and deep-coloured mangroves on which it nestles," for at the end of his lengthy description of the Brown Pelican is a short sketch entitled "The Mangrove."[1] "I am at a loss for an object with which to compare these trees, in order to afford you an idea of them," Audubon writes, but he settles on the figure of "a tree reversed, and standing on its summit" (386). Audubon asks us to imagine the Florida mangrove as an upside-down tree, the roots of which spread widely above ground while its trunk is submerged below. Unlike most trees, he means to say, mangroves grow low along the earth's surface and have roots that take hold by spreading outward over the ground rather than delving deeply into it. Such lateral roots present some rather unique spectacles. From the shores of the southernmost edges of Florida, Audubon observes, "the Mangroves extend towards the sea, their hanging branches taking root wherever they come in contact with the bottom" (386). He even notices islands "entirely formed of Mangroves, which raising their crooked and slender stems from a bed of mud, continue to increase until their roots and pendent branches afford shelter to accumulating debris, when the earth is gradually raised above the surface of the water" (386). As Audubon observes, the mangrove trees that cover Florida's coasts prosper because their roots construct their own solid foundations. As the roots

Figure 1. John James Audubon, Brown Pelican. *The Birds of America* (1827–38), Plate 251. *The Birds of America, Vols. I–IV*, Special Collections, University Library System, University of Pittsburgh.

spread outward, sand clings to them, and it is not unusual for a small islet to form where before there was only water. This is why the mangrove tree is sometimes described as "nature's way of converting water into land."[2] Interestingly, the mangrove cannot take root in dry and stable earth; its shallow, lateral roots require wet and unstable ground in order to establish themselves.

I begin with Audubon's reflections on the mangrove because they belong to a large archive of widely circulating materials in which Florida's shifting ground generates ways to imagine roots in the absence of secure material foundations. During a time when many familiar Anglo-American practices and perceptions of landed possession depended on terra firma, Florida's shifting ground prompted Audubon and others to speculate on forms of permanent attachment that did not require enclosure, demarcation, and improvement. Such speculation attests that early Americans did not exclusively imagine Florida's resistance to fixed dwellings, sturdy fences, and cultivated fields as evidence of the region's destiny to remain an undeveloped, retrograde periphery of an expanding settler empire. In some cases Florida's fluidity gave Americans useful ways to think beyond concepts of land and attachment that underpinned settler colonialism more broadly.

A number of important studies have documented popular early American associations with the South as a place of underdevelopment, slavery, poverty, and tropicality. After the Revolution, these associations indeed enabled those in more northerly parts of the emergent nation to define the United States as an independent, exceptional republic whose South was an unfortunate aberration in need of reform.[3] It was easy to include Florida in this "geographic fantasy" of the South: many visual and written representations produced during the eighteenth century described the region as an uncultivable borderland that was only tenuously connected to the rest of the North American continent.[4] These descriptions tend to emphasize Florida's fluid foundations and tropical weather as insurmountable barriers to familiar practices of Anglo-American settlement and habitation; as such they constitute one aspect of an early modern imperial ideology according to which the southern and Caribbean colonies were degenerative environments.[5]

Yet alongside this colonial perspective, Florida also provoked a different conception of the southern borderlands in which resistance to traditional ideals of settlement and cultivation generated useful modes and metaphors of roots and root-taking. While some early British maps and popular agricultural texts such as *American Husbandry* (1775) declare Floridian ground impossible to divide, enclose, and cultivate—and therefore unfit to join an agricultural empire dependent upon a landholding citizenry—other descriptions produced during this same period portray the region's instability as an opportunity to rethink landholding and settlement altogether. The first surveys of British colonial Florida, produced by William Gerard De Brahm for the British Board of Trade, suggest that the region's resistance to fixed boundaries and familiar practices of settlement could produce a version of possession amenable to changes in the land. To accommodate such changes, De Brahm drew on multiple discourses of land: the images of Florida in his *Report of the General Survey* (1772) are indebted not only to a familiar philosophical and legal genealogy of landed possession underpinned by solid ground and articulated most memorably by Locke, but also to geological and legal theories of a changing earth. By accommodating such changes in an official survey, De Brahm implies that incorporating Florida involves accepting that permanent ownership need not rely on stable foundations, and that some fluid southern spaces simply require a version of possession amenable to shifting ground.

This concept of Florida appears also in writing by Bartram, Audubon, and the late nineteenth-century ethnographer Frank Hamilton Cushing, who draws significantly on Bartram's *Travels* (1791) when reflecting on the early settlement of Florida's shifting ground in *Report on the Exploration of Ancient Key-Dweller Remains on the Gulf Coast of Florida* (1896). Collectively, De Brahm's shifting shores, Bartram's water lettuce roots, Audubon's mangroves, and the Indian mounds of *Travels* and of Cushing's *Report* signal that traditional understandings of land were not capacious enough for many North Americans to imagine either the history of settlement or the future of root-taking on and expansion over the continent. For, from the earliest moments of U.S. nationhood until well into the late nineteenth century, many people embraced versions of land and roots inspired by encounters with the local particularities of Florida, which required a form of ownership involving detachment and mobility, rather than demarcation and enclosure. The case of Florida vividly reminds us that the South had multiple meanings to North Americans across the continent: for while Florida seemed to many people a regrettable deviation from a more acceptable narrative of British colonial identity—and, later, early U.S. identity—to others it gave new and much needed metaphors for considering the variety of forms that founding and belonging could take.

Uncultivable Outpost

In 1763, when Spain ceded Florida to Great Britain on the conclusion of the Seven Years' War, the challenges posed by Florida's porous and shifting ground became obstacles to the southern extension of the British Empire in North America. A widespread impression of Florida as a sterile imperial outpost, more Caribbean than continental, prevented British settlers from emigrating to Florida and investing money and time to render it both agriculturally productive and safe from imperial rivals and internal enemies. Seeking to revise this impression, the British Board of Trade undertook a massive information-gathering project that produced new surveys, maps, and natural histories of Florida. The idea was to establish Florida's contours, describe its inland topography, and verify its connection to the North American continent once and for all, steps designed to attract a landholding populace to the region.[6]

The project had a dramatic effect on many popular images of Florida: during the 1760s and 1770s, on important maps of North America, the geographic shape of Florida altered, solidifying from islands to peninsula. The alteration is evident in a comparison of two maps by the same cartographer, the first created in 1755 (Figure 2), prior to British possession of Florida, and the second created after, in 1772 (Figure 3). Whereas the former map displays a region broken into elusive islands, as it had appeared on important European maps of North America since the beginning of the eighteenth century, the latter map, based largely on the board's surveys, communicates a new understanding of Florida as a solid, integrated, and cultivable region that materially resembles the rest of North America.[7]

Maps of Florida during this period are one of several discourses through which British officials sought to attract prospective settlers to Florida by assuring them that the new colony was on a developmental path from elusive, tropical edge of North America to integrated, contiguous extension of the continental mainland. In what has been called "the first campaign of publicity for Florida," promotional tracts and advertisements hailing Florida's fertility, and announcing a policy granting one hundred acres of land to every head of family, circulated widely in North American and British newspapers, books, and periodicals.[8] Challenging this narrative of progress, however, other writers perpetuated an idea of Florida as fluid ground irremediably resistant to settlement.

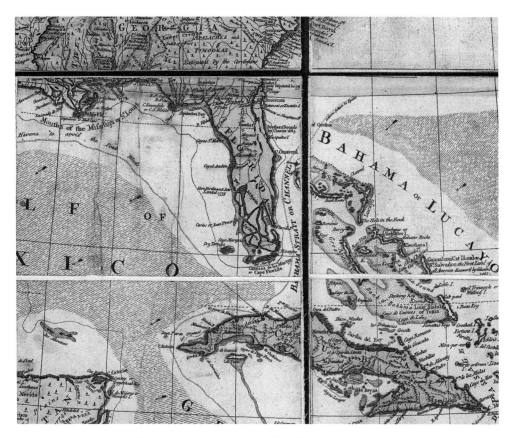

Figure 2. Emanuel Bowen, *An Accurate Map of North America* (1755), detail. Library of Congress, Geography and Map Division.

American Husbandry (1775), published in London "By an American" and purporting to offer objective evaluations of each American colony's agricultural capacity, is an especially memorable example of a popular text that casts Florida as a hopeless deviation from the rest of North America in its total resistance to improvement.[9] The author blithely approves of New England: "cultivated, inclosed, and cheerful," the place so greatly resembles Old England that, "In the best cultivated parts of it, you would not . . . know . . . that you were from home" (46). "The Floridas," however, are unique, even among southern colonies, for their hostility to the transformative

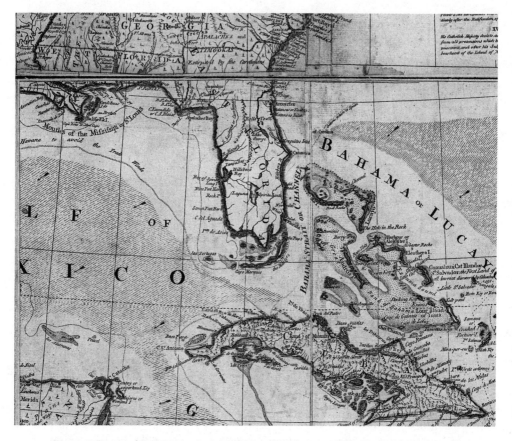

Figure 3. Emanuel Bowen, *An Accurate Map of North America* (1772), detail. Library of Congress, Geography and Map Division.

power of the plow. All southern colonies have some section of uncultivable land, typically in the form of a "flat sandy coast, full of swamps and marshes." Florida, however, is "nothing else but the flat sandy country"; it is all "maritime"—all coast (363–64). There is no "back country" to cultivate, no "proper soil" to enclose and plant with the useful crops that other colonies produce (364, 365). And Florida's geography enhances its fruitlessness: because Florida both "extends much to the south of any of our other colonies" and "forms a peninsula" that juts into the sea, "The rains . . . are almost incessant," making it "very unhealthy" indeed (363). "Fact, and not opinion," declares that Floridian soil is "such as no person would move to, from the worst of our colonies, in order to cultivate" (365). In Florida the plain facts of topography and geography combine, as they do nowhere else in the actual or prospective American colonies, to preclude cultivation, the basis of settler imperialism. At best, Florida may serve England as an outpost of empire where the "proper accommodations for shipping" may be stored; but "as to planting, none should be encouraged" (373). This description, though probably at least partly politically motivated, nonetheless accurately conveys a widespread British perception of Florida as a tropical backwater, topographically and geographically unfit for British citizens.[10]

Emanuel Bowen's maps and *American Husbandry* concisely capture both sides of a major debate about Floridian ground in the wake of Great Britain's acquisition of Florida from Spain: while some British observers championed the peninsula's capacity for improvement, others denigrated it as hopelessly retrograde. Yet it is important to recognize that a common perspective on land underpins and motivates both ways of responding to Florida: defenders and deniers of Florida's potential for cultivation alike idealize solid, stable, contiguous land as the only acceptable basis of a settler empire. This is not surprising, considering the ideologies of landed possession that were most familiar during the eighteenth century.

Some of the period's most highly regarded philosophical discussions of property and possession held that unvarying, solid, and divisible ground necessarily stabilized a polity, for such ground was the only kind that could be "subdued" and "improved," acts that were critical to demonstrating and sustaining possession. An especially influential formulation of this idea may be found in John Locke's *Second Treatise of Civil Government* (1690), in which Locke famously declares that "Whatsoever then [man] removes out of the state that nature hath provided . . . he hath mixed his labour with . . . and thereby makes it his property."[11] Through labor we "inclose [property] from the common," for otherwise land would remain as subject to ingress and egress as the sea, "that great and still remaining common of mankind."[12] Drawing on Locke, philosophers of the Enlightenment such as David Hume also rule out the possibility of possessing the sea, which is "incapable of becoming the property of any nation" because we cannot "form any . . . distinct relation with it, as may be the foundation of property."[13] Locke, Hume, and other well-known philosophers of landed possession prioritize subdivision, demarcation, and enclosure, pursuits that would be impossible in the absence of solid ground.

Within a context of thinking about land as the opposite of sea, which by nature prevents the "distinct relation" that permits property, it is no wonder that fluid ground appears inimical to settler imperialism: this project depends on a genealogy of land and settlement that excluded shifting foundations. It is instructive to keep this fact in mind as we read late eighteenth-century reflections on North American ground, particularly in texts that circulated widely in North America before, during, and after the Revolution. At the earliest moments of the founding of the United States, readers across North America were steeped in an intellectual tradition that could not accommodate unfirm ground. For example, in *Letters from an American Farmer* (1782), Crèvecoeur's Farmer James envisions British North America as a polity of autonomous and independent yeomen achieving "ample subsistence" by dividing and laboring on the land.[14] *Letters* is an idealized version of the agrarianism Jefferson espouses in *Notes on the State of Virginia* (1785), for Jefferson's own notion of the emergent United States as an expanding "empire of liberty" involves more mobility, exchange, and commerce than Farmer James endorses; yet even visions of a republic only partly sustained by small farmers still require a substantial amount of cultivable ground.[15] While of course North Americans always debated the importance and role of agriculture in the ideal political economy, it is safe to say that, well into the nineteenth century, unvarying, solid, divisible ground remained important to the political "stability" of the republic at large.[16]

This is not to say that North Americans were unfamiliar with ways to improve and profit from watery land. After all, roughly 41.3 million acres of wetland stretched from New England to Georgia, and North American colonists could easily find instructions for enclosing and draining swamps, such as those in Book III of Thomas Hale's *Compleat Body of Husbandry* (1756).[17] Southeastern swamps in particular provided resources including beaver and timber, and proved ideal ground for rice cultivation. Many swamps and wetlands were "redeemed": some of the earliest European settlers of North America transformed wetlands through agriculture, and tidewater planters learned to use tidal ebbs and flows to drain and irrigate fields.[18] Even surveying the swamp was sometimes possible, at least if we believe William Byrd of Westover, who conducted a party of surveyors through the Great Dismal in 1728 in order to mark the colonial boundary between Virginia and North Carolina. Although Byrd declares that "we found the ground moist and trembling under our feet like a quagmire," and that "every step made a deep impression, which was instantly filled with water," he reports that his surveyors carried the surveying chain "right forward, without suffering themselves to be turned out of the way by any obstacle whatever," successfully completing what Byrd has no trouble imagining as a line that "shall here-after stand as the true boundary."[19]

Yet these instances of swamp survey and cultivation took place on parts of the continent that, for all their fluidity, were more solid than most of Florida. We need only turn to the environmental history of the Everglades to perceive that eighteenth-century British and North American impressions of Florida as a liquid landscape, differing fundamentally from the rest of the continent, are based in reality. More than half of the peninsula's 20.3 million acres was once swampland.[20] While twentieth- and twenty-first-century developers have drained and filled in significant swaths of South Florida, prior to reclamation efforts the Everglades more or less began where water "overspilled [Lake Okeechobee's] south shore," and from there they "spread out, and then slowly crept in a sheet, fifty miles wide and six inches deep," constituting more than 2.3 million acres of slowly moving water.[21] And it was not just the sheer extent of the Everglades that made Florida unusually fluid; tidal erosion of the shoreline, seasonal fluctuations in the water table, an inordinate amount of rainfall, and frequent hurricanes also combined to render Florida all "maritime," in the words of *American Husbandry*.[22]

Both coastally and inland, Florida fluctuated as no other part of the continent. This fact was advertised with particular force during the nineteenth century by repeated failures of efforts to survey, drain, and enclose the Everglades, which mostly remained "a distant wilderness" to those living in other parts of the United States.[23] And settlers' guides to antebellum Florida attest that its status as an elusive borderland with a debatable connection to the continent persisted long after the British Board of Trade sought to revise this impression during the 1760s. One especially popular guide to Territorial Florida declares the nation's recent addition a "curiously shaped and curiously formed terminal appendage to the great United States," and includes questions that cannot but raise doubt about Florida's contiguity and connection: are the Keys "fragments of the continent, torn by the abrasion of the tide," or are they "additions, constantly increased" by the growth of coral reefs? Have the Everglades "recently risen from the ocean? Is the land still rising?"[24] Thus, even as the writers of such guides sought to draw prospective settlers to Florida, they questioned its capacity to sustain settlement because they could not help speculating that the region was formed by unique processes and materials other than unvarying, solid, divisible ground.

These and other texts attest that, to many eighteenth- and nineteenth-century observers, Florida never quite shed its status as an elusive, underdeveloped borderland. In this way such texts establish that people frequently responded to Florida in much the same way that they responded to other southern spaces as unfortunate exceptions to the culture developing on the rest of the continent. Yet such texts also reveal that, in the case of Florida, this familiar mode of response was largely conditioned by the fact that people lacked a language for describing and imagining radically shifting ground as an integral part of North America. For familiar Anglophone philosophical discourses of landed possession offered no vocabulary for thinking through the incorporation of ground that shifts, seeps, expands, and erodes.[25] Put otherwise, salient rhetorical, geographical, and historical conceptions of empires and nations as reliant on unvarying, solid, divisible ground provided a context within which Florida's porosity and liquidity signaled its tenuous connection to or total exclusion from North America.

And yet, to many people, Florida's liquid landscape meant something else. During a time when dominant discussions of settlement, private property, cultivation, political economy, and even swampland redemption afforded no way to describe Florida as land or property, some eighteenth-century observers did both. Though it required a conceptual leap, William Gerard De Brahm, first surveyor of British colonial Florida, devised a land survey that accommodates shifting, seeping, "changeable" ground. His surveys reveal that the same particularities of Floridian ground that resisted familiar practices of Anglo-American settlement and habitation also generated new ways to take root. De Brahm's Florida surveys provided British and U.S. observers one way to envision Florida as an extension of North America. And just as importantly they also provide scholars one set of materials through which to perceive early American interest in a version of landed possession that did not descend entirely from a philosophical genealogy inherited through Locke and Hume.

William Gerard De Brahm on the Florida Shore

In 1764, during the year following Great Britain's acquisition of Florida from Spain, the British Board of Trade appointed De Brahm to the position of surveyor general of the Southern District of North America. As such he would administer the massive project of surveying and mapping all British holdings south of the Potomac, though the board prioritized Florida, and particularly the area from St. Augustine south to the tip of the peninsula.[26]

Accordingly De Brahm moved from Georgia to St. Augustine, and the following year he began surveying East Florida by following the board's instructions to focus specifically on the coastlands they believed to have the most potential for settlement: those stretching along the eastern side of the peninsula from St. Augustine to Cape Florida at present-day Miami.[27]

De Brahm's surveys were to guide the board's decisions about precisely where "a loyal landowning citizenry" would thrive, though De Brahm was also personally invested in locating the most valuable lands. His position as surveyor general meant that British landholders could commission him privately for small-scale surveys of particular tracts they planned to develop.[28] In fact, without such commissions, De Brahm would not have secured the patronage necessary to complete *The Report of the General Survey*, a detailed narrative in which he describes the character of Floridian ground.[29]

The *Report*, which De Brahm personally presented to King George III in manuscript form during 1773, proved valuable not only to the board but also to private parties, including members of the Cape Florida Society, a group of European investors who met informally in London to plan a colony along the Florida coast near present-day Miami.[30] While the *Report* remained unpublished in its entirety until the twentieth century, a London publisher issued an excerpt of it in 1772 as an independent volume called *The Atlantic Pilot*. London reviewers hailed the work as a "small but elegant performance" and evidence of the author's "fidelity, accuracy, and diligence" in carrying out his commission, and an American bookseller at Charleston quickly imported a supply of the *Pilot*.[31] De Brahm's detailed descriptions of the Florida coast and Atlantic Ocean currents proved particularly useful to several subsequent eighteenth- and nineteenth-century surveyors, many of whom employed the *Pilot* in their own publications. As *The Journal of Andrew Ellicott* (Philadelphia, 1803) attests, the well-known surveyor of the boundary line between the United States and the Spanish colonies of East and West Florida preferred De Brahm's discussion of the Gulf Stream in the *Pilot* to Benjamin Franklin's more widely known work on this topic.[32] For our present purposes the *Pilot* indeed repays careful scrutiny, particularly with regard to two large foldout maps featuring South Florida and the Florida Keys: *Chart of the South End of East Florida and Martiers* (1772; Figure 4) and *The Ancient Tegesta, Now Promontory of East Florida* (1772; Figure 5). Funded by and produced for prospective settlers, these maps describe the same stretch of coast near Miami; yet upon first consideration they suggest that Florida as a whole could never sustain permanent settlement.

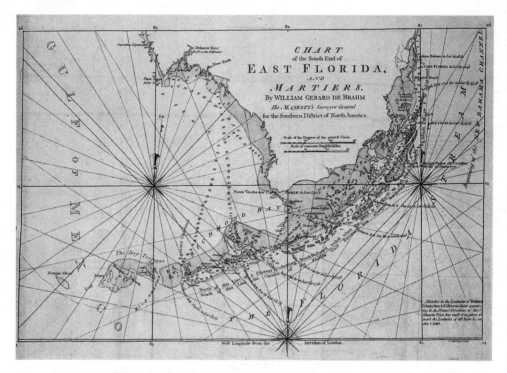

Figure 4. William Gerard De Brahm, "Chart of the South End of East Florida and Martiers" (1772). HM 121784, The Huntington Library, San Marino, California.

Images of Florida in the published portions of the *Report* depict a place that collapses the absolute distinction between water and soil. A comparison of two images in particular reveals land in flux. *Chart of the South End of East Florida* and *The Ancient Tegesta* describe the swath of coastland and shoals that stretches from Cape Florida, just barely visible in the upper right corner, to the Dry Tortugas, visible in the lower left corner. Yet ground shaded in dark gray as submerged shoal or sandbank in *Chart* (Figure 4) is outlined as a firm part of the peninsula in *Tegesta* (Figure 5). We can see the clearest example of this change when we compare the Dry Tortugas, depicted at the bottom left corner of each image. The Tortugas of Figure 4 are tiny islets, west of Key West, just as they accurately appear on twenty-first-century maps of Florida; yet those of Figure 5 are substantial landmasses. The "Tortuga Shoal" of each document strikingly illustrates the alteration, for the

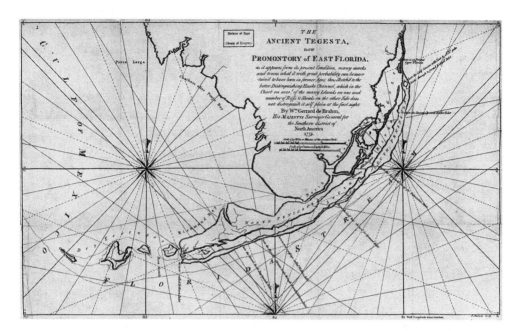

Figure 5. William Gerard De Brahm, "The Ancient Tegesta, Now Promontory of East Florida (as it appears from its present Condition, many marks and traces what it with great probability can be ascertained to have been in former Ages . . .)" (1772). Library of Congress, Geography and Map Division.

chain of islets that resembles an oval-shaped atoll in Figure 4 appears as a full-blown island of nearly the same shape in Figure 5.

De Brahm's title for Figure 5 partly explains the reason for the differences between the images: he calls Figure 5 *The Ancient Tegesta, Now Promontory of East Florida (as it appears from its present Condition, many marks and traces what it with great probability can be ascertained to have been in former Ages . . .).* Thus, whereas Figure 4 describes the land as it is, Figure 5 portrays it as it *formerly* existed.[33] In other words, using the remaining physical "marks and traces" of its former outline, De Brahm fills in the figure of the Florida "Tegesta," using a name for the peninsula that he derives from the Tequesta, one of Florida's many indigenous societies that the Spanish, along with internecine warfare, had largely decimated long before De Brahm's arrival in Florida.[34]

Whatever the reason De Brahm provides for Florida's substantially different appearances in each image, the effect of viewing both together is that mainland Florida appears to have dissolved; and the narrative accompanying the images reveals that this dissolution was ongoing at the time. For De Brahm explains that he considers coastal Florida evidence that "the Continent has been, *and is to this day* subject to yield its Limits foot by foot to the [Gulf] Stream."[35] During three years in Florida, he explains, he and his assistants "have observed many Places, where fresh Encroachments [of ocean on land] appear to this Effect," noting that trees growing in the water "between the Islands and the Main testify, that they lay on the Spot of the former Continent." Indeed, while all North America dissolves, Florida dissolves so obviously that it offers "Testimonies, if not evident Proofs, that the [Gulf] Stream . . . does not give up any of its Acquisitions, or exchange old Possessions in lieu, as Seas, and Rivers are well known to do *in all Parts of the known World*."[36] For although the surveying crew searched for places where the ground had expanded and "taken Possession of Limits deserted by the Stream," none could be found. In fact, the Florida Keys, once contiguous with the mainland, now represent the mere outlines of its "probable Ancient figure," which the sea continues to encroach upon, tearing the land "into so many Subdivisions" before one's very eyes. In short, what we see when we look at Florida is not permanent land, but ground in a state of dissolution, bound to erode and leave behind only traces of its former shape.

These observations on Florida set De Brahm apart from the typical surveyor because they suggest that he was interested not only in individual plots of land, but also in the larger whole to which they belonged.[37] His documentation of changing land within a survey was unusual enough that one fellow surveyor of Florida, Bernard Romans, looked unfavorably on *The Atlantic Pilot*: in the natural history of Florida that Romans published in New York in 1775, he declared that De Brahm's work bore "marks of insanity." Referring specifically to the images presented in Figures 4 and 5 above, Romans writes that "here we see an account of an unnatural change in the face of the country, which for many reasons never could have happened . . . ; he turns one peninsula into broken islands, another into sunken rocks; . . . in this unmeaning chaos he joins and disjoins, turns water into land, and land into water."[38] Yet a more likely reason for De Brahm's interest in recording exchanges of water and land is that he was not only an experienced surveyor, but also a polymath whose many interests included geography, engineering, botany, astronomy, meteorology, hydrography, alchemy, and even mystical philosophy.[39] Educated and widely read, he was keenly interested in the natural world and a range of religious and scientific discourses, and his

Report offers strong evidence that these interests directly informed his thinking about land.[40] Historians of geography have considered De Brahm more geographer than surveyor, and a careful reading of the *Report* reveals that De Brahm was also a "geotheorist"—the term historians now use to refer to the group of earth scientists who directly preceded the disciplinary rise of geology.

Of all the ways of thinking about land that De Brahm could have drawn on in Florida, geotheory was most useful because of its commitment to explaining and predicting changes in the land. Unlike geologists, such as Georges Cuvier and Charles Lyell, who would correctly hypothesize that earth was radically unstable and unpredictable in its changes, geotheorists, such as Horace-Bénédict de Saussure and James Hutton, held that earth operated according to a set of predictable Newtonian mechanical laws.[41] A brief comparison of De Brahm's *Report* and Hutton's "Theory of the Earth" (1788) suggests that De Brahm was geotheorizing in Florida. His perception of the Florida Keys as fragments outlining the peninsula's "probable ancient Figure" accords with Hutton's discovery that all discernible land exhibits "certain means to read the annals of a former earth."[42] Likewise, De Brahm's observation that the Florida shore "yields its Limits foot by foot to the [Gulf] Stream" matches Hutton's finding that "[all] land is perishing continually."[43]

And De Brahm's indebtedness to geotheory becomes especially evident when we perceive that his observations largely conform to a "uniformitarian" view of earth's changes. The well-known debate between theorists of "uniformitarianism," who asserted that earth's changes were uniform, and those of "catastrophism," who argued that changes were sudden, crystallized in the publication of the final volume of Lyell's *Principles of Geology* (1832), which supported a uniformitarian view.[44] However the debate began with the geotheorists long before the rise of geology. In fact, Lyell's belief that the earth was a "steady-state system" recalls aspects of Hutton's earlier contention that all land not only "[perishes] continually" but also revives proportionally, with the overall amount of land on the planet remaining the same.[45] In general, De Brahm believes with Hutton in both erosion and the "existence of . . . productive causes, which are now laying the foundation of land . . . which will, in time, give birth to future continents."[46] Florida, however, proves an exception to this rule; for De Brahm asserts that the peninsula's ever-eroding shores illustrate that the Gulf Stream "does not give up any of its Acquisitions, or exchange old Possessions in lieu, *as Seas, and Rivers are known to do in all Parts of the known World.*"[47] While geotheory offered the most useful language for describing Florida, even this science could not entirely account for a place where the sea fails to replenish what it continually wears away.

De Brahm's commitment to recording Florida's dissolution derives from his interest in geotheoretical speculation, yet it nonetheless appears antithetical to his explicit intention to attract investors and emigrants, a project that relied on portraying the ground as static, as historians of geography and property have shown. De Brahm was commissioned to produce both a large-scale survey of Florida and several smaller-scale "plats," documents containing a sketch and verbal description of an individual plot of ground. By and large, eighteenth-century land surveys aimed to stabilize the land record and thereby enable people to imagine themselves and their communities as firmly emplaced within national or imperial territory. And the plat served a particularly important role in this process: as Brückner explains, it was intended to facilitate an individual proprietor's "strong sense of personal geodetic emplacement."[48] The plat conventionally fostered this sense by representing land as immovable and personalizing the representation with an inscription of the proprietor's family name. In fact, the plat was an important discourse through which North Americans affirmed their ownership of "a particular locus in space and time"; a genre that became surprisingly popular in the eighteenth century in both Great Britain and North America, the plat placed individuals "inside a land- and map-based economy," and thereby fostered a Lockean version of "modern autonomous existence."[49]

As an experienced surveyor, De Brahm knew the conventions and objectives of surveys and plats. Furthermore, there is no reason to question his stated intention to attract settlers to Florida. Referring to an area he depicts at the right of Figures 4 and 5, De Brahm reports sincerely that "Settlers especially at Cape Florida will be much better off than all others on any Place I know upon the Eastern Coast of America."[50] Yet how is it possible that, in one description of Cape Florida, he suggests the entire cape dissolves, while in another he labels a plot of ground with a prospective settler's family name?

De Brahm's turn to geotheory within a survey ultimately suggests that Florida's dramatic dissolution did not suggest to him what it suggested to the author of *American Husbandry* and many other observers who declared colonial Florida inimical to British settlers. Rather than interpreting Florida as the doomed periphery of empire, De Brahm considers it an occasion to seek a new language to describe shifting ground as land and even as property. In other words, his commitments to surveying and geotheorizing were not antithetical; rather, geotheory gave De Brahm a much-needed vocabulary for portraying the liquid landscape in a genre committed to fostering a sense of "self-assertion" and "autonomous existence" in the service of possession, settlement, and imperial expansion. For De Brahm grasped that land is more constantly changeable than it appears, and he found Florida an especially obvious conceptual challenge to discourses that assumed land's stability. But by surveying obviously unstable ground, he indicated that land's instability did not have to compromise one's personal and permanent attachment to it. By furnishing a way to imagine the liquid landscape as *property*, his work resonates strikingly with another discourse in which possession did not require stability.

In riparian law, shifting, seeping, and eroding land had shaped the terms of possession since the Middle Ages. Just as the emergent discourse of geology did, this area of property law recognized that not all ground is made of the "sound good loam" and "proper soil" that *American Husbandry* overtly—and the founders implicitly—deemed land.[51] Additionally, riparian law demonstrated that there was a way to possess watery ground, although such ground demanded a different language and ideal of possession than did the terra firma of the founders.

Sir Matthew Hale's *De Jure Maris* (written in 1670 and published in 1787) and Sir William Blackstone's *Commentaries on the Laws of England* (1765–69) identify and discuss a variety of "incidentals," such as adjacent water and shores, that cannot be subject to the same laws of ownership that govern solid ground. In the language with which both legal theorists discuss shifting coastal lands in particular, instability alters the nature of proprietorship but does not prevent possession. For example, according to Blackstone, when the sea "make[s] *terra firma*"—that is, when the sea recedes so that the land increases—the individual riparian proprietor quite frequently gains whatever land the sea leaves behind.[52] On the other hand, as Hale explains, "If a subject hath land adjoining the sea, and the violence of the sea swallow it up," then the riparian proprietor does not suffer a total loss: particularly if he can show "reasonable marks" of where the land once was, then his full rights to the original space remain, and he may even regain it from the sea through ditching and draining if possible.[53] Blackstone's and Hale's reflections on riparian rights suggest that instability does not prevent possession, but merely changes the nature of it. For a proprietor who is aware that his lands may change as the waters increase or recede need not necessarily lose his livelihood thereby, as long as he is prepared to adapt to this eventuality. While, unlike De Brahm, theorists of riparian law assume that land both erodes *and* expands, the underlying logic is strikingly similar: in both cases, the recognition of land's impermanence does not compromise possession, although it may introduce new possibilities for and models of proprietorship.

Considered broadly, De Brahm's riparian and geotheoretically inflected reflections on Florida in the *Report* signal the limits of familiar political and philosophical discussions that did not recognize inherently unstable ground as land. They suggest that imagining how to stake claim to North American ground requires departing from these discussions, and in this way they differ significantly from those of many of De Brahm's contemporaries who, as we have seen, either explicitly or implicitly positioned Florida as resistant or threatening to settler colonialism on the basis of its instability. For by accommodating the liquid landscape with a language that could enable his readers to envision it as land and property, De Brahm offered a way to perceive Florida as part of North America. The *Report* attests that Florida prompted De Brahm to make mobility central to the survey, and thus to expand the very notion of what counted as "land"—that is, as ground that could stabilize and thereby count as politically significant.

De Brahm's survey signals that the material realities of Florida would prompt people to revise traditional thinking about how to achieve permanent possession, and about what kinds of land are acceptable bases of a polity dependent on such possession. Finally, however, it provokes questions that it does not entirely answer. For what would possession in the absence of stability actually look like? What new relation to land would it require of a proprietor? And how might these changes to the concept of landholding change the imagination of settlement and the pursuit of expansion on the continent? For fuller accounts of Florida roots and some of their larger prospects, we may turn to the work of two subsequent writers who also glimpsed the intersection of Locke and the liquid landscape in Florida.

William Bartram's Mobile Roots

In the Introduction to this book I discuss Bartram's encounter with "floating islands" of water lettuce, or *Pistia stratiotes*, along the St. Johns River. In *Travels* (1791) Bartram is struck by the plant's capacity to weather the sudden alterations of a landscape where water and land change places with little warning. Though jostled by winds and currents that continually drive the plants from shore and break their communities "to pieces," the water lettuce always manages to "find footing" and a place to "spread and extend" once more. Such resilience is the result of "long fibrous roots": rather than fixing the plant in place, which would guarantee uprooting, these roots enable mobility, and thereby ensure stability and longevity.[54]

I return now to Bartram's reflection on water lettuce to place it in dialogue with other passages on root-taking in *Travels* as a way of tracking the text's investment in the same topic that occupies De Brahm: human habitation of shifting ground. Human root-taking in Florida was never far from Bartram's mind, a fact that is especially apparent when he concludes his reflection on water lettuce with the following observation: "These floating islands present a very entertaining prospect; for . . . [in] the imagination . . . we . . . see them compleatly inhabited, and alive, with crocodiles, serpents, frogs, otters, crows, herons, curlews, jackdaws, &c. there seems, in short, nothing wanted but the appearance of a wigwam and a canoe to complete the scene."[55] The concluding vision of a wigwam complements Bartram's earlier descriptions of the plant as a being that "associates" in "communities" that "find footing" and form "colonies": such language encourages us to read the reverie as a reflection on human roots, an encouragement amplified by similarities Bartram suggests between water lettuce roots and Indian mounds.

Scholars have shown that eighteenth- and nineteenth-century interest in Indian mounds focused primarily on determining the mounds' origins. Thus the interest was not only anthropological but also deeply political.[56] For example, when Thomas Jefferson and others theorized that the mounds were made by a population of non-Indian "mound-builders" who mysteriously vanished before the arrival of the "savage" Indians currently occupying the land, they fashioned a "Mound Builder myth" that licensed Indian removal on the grounds that Indians were not indigenous.[57] This myth persisted as a way of invalidating Indian land claims until the late nineteenth century, though not without contest from writers such as Bartram, who claimed that the mounds were Indian in origin and should thus be considered proof of Indian indigeneity and rights to the land.[58]

While the mounds' origins certainly concerned Bartram, he was interested not only in *who* built the mounds, but also *why* they were built and *how* the original builders used them. At several points in *Travels* Bartram reviews existing theories of the intended purpose of the mounds. For example, he considers and then rejects the idea that the mounds were "sepulchres" for a funerary ritual; entertains the possibility that they were "designed . . . to some religious purpose, as great altars and temples"; and speculates that they were "raised in part for ornament and recreation," or simply as "monuments of magnificence, to perpetuate the power and grandeur of the nation."[59] Yet most persuasive to Bartram is another theory, which he derives from an encounter with a particular mound standing "in a level plain" near the bank of the Savannah River.

The mound, he reasons, must have enabled the community to remain on ground that could become water with little warning. For after puzzling over "what could have induced the Indians to raise such a heap of earth" in a place so frequently "subject to inundations," Bartram hypothesizes that the mound acted as an "island," "raised for a retreat and refuge" "In case of an inundation, which are unforeseen and surprise them very suddenly, spring and autumn" (325–26). In other words, rather than building "settled habitations" on frequently inundated land, the Indians established themselves by building temporary dwelling places that they could easily abandon for higher ground when the waters suddenly rose.

Bartram's claim that mounds enabled Indians to establish themselves on shifting ground is more than an assertion of Indian land rights on the basis of indigeneity; the claim also suggests that Indian inhabitance of the land was durable, and that this endurance resulted from a capacity to adapt to land's impermanence. This suggestion is important because it debunks the mound-builder myth in a way that resists co-optation by supporters of U.S. expansion. For, as Annette Kolodny shows, it was not always enough to prove that Indians had built the mounds, as scientists finally did during the 1890s.[60] For one thing, many observers interpreted the mounds as structures that enabled their builders to live nomadically, and nomads did not count as proprietors according to law. Yet Bartram's interpretation of mounds suggests a way out of this logic. By describing mounds as *both* the product of indigenous Indians *and* a sign of their capacity to endure on the land, Bartram fashions the earthen heaps as material evidence that Indians developed a complex form of land-based possession. Put otherwise, on the same ground where recently built British plantations lie in ruins, mounds endure as "monuments" attesting that prehistoric Indians, ancestors of those populating the land to this day, ably anchored themselves to the land via mobile roots.

While the broader political implications of mobile roots remain undeveloped in *Travels*, they were not lost on a late nineteenth-century reader of the text. Bartram's mobile roots enjoy an interesting afterlife in the work of ethnographer Frank Hamilton Cushing, who considered Bartram a fellow member of the American Philosophical Society and "the source of more definite information regarding the southern Indians than those of any other one of our earlier authorities on the natives of northerly Florida and contiguous States."[61] In Cushing's *Report on the Exploration of Ancient Key-Dweller Remains*, a narrative of archaeological discoveries about Florida's Calusa Indians, he uses *Travels* and another text by Bartram, "Observations on the Creek and Cherokee Indians" (1788), to imaginatively reconstruct the environment and daily lives of the Southeast's prehistoric cultures.[62]

Cushing's conclusion that Florida's early inhabitants remained on unstable ground by refusing firm fixity strikingly echoes Bartram's descriptions of Florida roots in *Travels*. For example, the language of Bartram's reverie on "floating islands" of water lettuce suffuses Cushing's descriptions of excavated architectural remains of Calusa Indian "pile dwellings," which Cushing calls "floating quays."[63] At "the Court of the Pile Dwellers," an archaeological site on Key Marco in Southwest Florida, Cushing finds the remains of Calusa homes that are floating islands for some of the same reasons that Bartram uses the metaphor. Each home, Cushing explains, consisted of a horizontal, "partially movable platform" of timber, to the bottom of which vertical "piles" or "pillars" were affixed (34). These piles extended downward into the water to support the timber platform and keep it above the sea's surface, much as the posts of a stilted house might. Yet, unlike stilts, the piles were not fixed firmly to the ground. Rather, they "rested upon, but had not been driven into" the top of artificial mounds or "benches" of "solid shell and clay marl" that the Calusa had built on the sea floor. The piles remained unfixed "so that as long as the water remained low, they would support these house scaffolds above it, as well as if driven into the benches." However, "when the waters rose, the entire structures would also slightly rise, or at any rate not be violently wrenched from their supports, as would inevitably have been the case had these [supports] been firmly fixed below." Cushing's description unmistakably recalls the roots of Bartram's water lettuce. Both pile-dwelling and plant remain upright by not being "firmly fixed" to the ground. Just as the water lettuce roots "descend from the nether center, downwards, towards the muddy bottom," the piles extend downward, yet "had not been driven into" the ocean floor. And Cushing's observation that, "when the waters rose, the entire structures would also slightly rise," echoes Bartram's statement that "when the river is suddenly raised" the water lettuce would rise and "float about."

Cushing's indebtedness to Bartram underscores the ethnographic and political implications of Florida roots in *Travels*. These implications emerge even more forcefully when Cushing draws on Bartram to describe Indian mounds.[64] According to Cushing, the Calusa eventually built mounds in Florida, and thereafter throughout much of North America, for the same reason that they originally built pile-dwellings on the sea: they needed to maintain stability on radically unstable foundations. Cushing's "theory of the origin of mound-building" holds that the mounds were built by the descendants of Indians living in "sea environments" to the "far south" of the continent. These Indians transmitted "ancestral ideas of habitation . . . down from generation to generation, and so, slowly up into the land" (81, 74). Over time, as the Indians moved north to inland Florida, they found that mounds suited Florida's "peculiarly unstable" ground, which Cushing describes as "soluble," "pervious limestone" that is "subject to undermining by . . . corrosive" rain and rivers; pocketed with sinkholes that "[fall] in" to form deep lakes and morasses; threaded by "subterranean rivers"; and ravaged by "the hurricane" that, "in a land so broken and low," causes "continuous change of shore-line" (67).

But the mound-builders eventually moved farther north than Florida. For "the great and regular mounds and other earth-works occurring in the lowlands of our Southern and Middle Western States, and celebrated as the remains of the so-called mound-builders, may likewise also be traced . . . to a similar beginning in some seashore and marshland environment" (15). Cushing imagines mounds throughout the continent as "islands . . . on high land" that prove his topographic theory that, until recently, most of the continent exhibited "conditions like those presented by the southern marshy shorelands" (76). In other words, Florida offers a good approximation of what North America was like: "the whole region"—by which he means most of the continent—was "suited to such modes of life as I have referred to, even well on toward modern times" (78).

Cushing's observations in the *Report* amount to the conclusion that mound-builders were the most able claimants of continental ground because of their capacity to remain on changing earth. This conclusion depends in part on Cushing's reading of Bartram on early Florida's landscape and the populations who managed to remain there. But even more importantly for our purposes, Cushing's conclusion elucidates the relevance of Bartram's mobile roots to later U.S. interpretations of the history and legacy of continental settlement and expansion. By suggesting that Floridian foundations reflect the character of the continent as a whole, Cushing suggests an alternate narrative of North America's settlement. His work signals that, both during and long after the last quarter of the eighteenth century that has been this chapter's historical focus, Florida provoked many North Americans to imagine those who managed to establish themselves on shifting ground as the rightful possessors of the continent.

*   *   *

While all the writers examined above recognize early Florida's dramatic dissolution, some perceive this solubility as something other than a threat to familiar Anglo-American settlement practices. For Audubon, De Brahm, Bartram, and Cushing, Florida provided useful metaphors for imagining land and inhabitance. Their reflections on mangrove trees, shifting shores, water lettuce roots, Indian mounds, and Calusa dwellings affirm the habitability of Florida's liquid land, albeit by way of alternate practices of possession according to which mobility secures longevity, stability, and endurance.[65] Collectively such work reveals that Florida provided many early Americans with a way to imagine roots that are no less secure for their lack of fixity.

The following chapter continues to chart the influence of Florida's fluidity on broader narratives of North American settlement, this time by turning to another set of materials: eighteenth-century European and American maps of Florida as islands. Such maps enable us to place Florida's topographic porosity in a broad geopolitical context, and to see that it disrupted a politically significant visual narrative of North America as a contiguous, self-enclosed, sharply defined landmass. By broadcasting Florida's soluble, corrosive, hurricane-swept, porous, and fragmented ground, maps of Florida as islands provide us with one way to see beyond the more familiar cartographic discourse of continental integrity that would underpin U.S. nationalism by minimizing or erasing the spatial fluidity and demographic heterogeneity of the early United States.

Chapter 2

Island Nation: Shoal, Isle, Islet

Amos Doolittle's *Map of the United States of America* (Figure 6), one of the first maps of North America to be published in the United States, first appeared in 1784 in geographer Jedidiah Morse's popular textbook, *Geography Made Easy*, which Morse hoped would inspire young readers to "imbibe an acquaintance with their own country, and an attachment to its interests" during the immediate aftermath of the Revolutionary War.[1] A staunch Federalist, Morse believed that "the United States, and indeed all parts of North-America, seem to have been formed by nature for the most intimate union."[2] Doolittle's map visually underscores this early precursor of the rhetoric of Manifest Destiny by illustrating the emerging U.S. nation-state as a contiguous territory stretching from British Canada to Spanish Florida, and bordered sharply on the west and east by the Mississippi River and the Atlantic Ocean, respectively.

As recent scholarship on the history of cartography has shown, early modern maps frequently "produced" space: by making ideological claims about the areas they represented, rather than reflecting the actual state of geographic knowledge, maps influenced the development of national and imperial identities, boundaries, population patterns, and power relations.[3] Doolittle's map is no exception, for it contributes to a widespread phenomenon in which North Americans of the Revolutionary period proclaimed North America's "continental status" in a range of texts—including maps, geographies, decorative arts, portraits, classic works of literature, and key political essays and legal documents—as a way of declaring the new country's independence, sovereignty, and destiny to become a culturally homo-

Figure 6. Amos Doolittle, *A Map of the United States of America* (1784). Beinecke Rare Book and Manuscript Library, Yale University.

geneous nation united under one government.[4] The figure of the continent continued to serve a range of nationalist purposes long after the Revolution, a fact prompting literary scholar Myra Jehlen's memorable claim that "the solid reality, the *terra firma*" of the continent was "the decisive factor shaping the founding conceptions of 'America' and 'the American'" from the early national period until the mid-nineteenth century.[5]

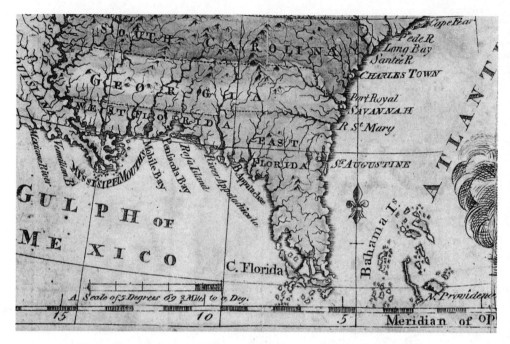

Figure 7. Amos Doolittle, *A Map of the United States of America* (1784), detail.
Beinecke Rare Book and Manuscript Library, Yale University.

Considering the continent's ideological significance during the early national period, it seems surprising upon first consideration that Doolittle's
map does not entirely sustain Morse's claim that "*all* parts of North-America"
encourage "attachment" and "union": one prominent part of the map does
not describe a solid, contiguous, and self-contained landmass. Morse's claim
falters at the lower right corner of the map, where Florida appears dramatically fragmented into islands that constitute a ragged, fractured southeastern edge of North America (Figure 7). The land is indented by vast harbors
and gulfs, broken into five or six large landmasses, and scattered in chains
of almost innumerable islets that extend into the Gulf of Mexico and the Atlantic, almost as though a gigantic wave had swept over the land and left it in
shards. Doolittle's depiction of Florida as islands was not unusual. It con-
forms to a cartographic convention through which many American and
European mapmakers described Florida before, during, and long after the
American Revolution.

While a familiar account of the cartographic tradition of Florida as islands suggests that this tradition was an antiquated fiction by the time of the Revolution, the maps themselves offer a different account. They show that this tradition began on the ground in Florida during an early eighteenth-century colonial encounter between English and Indians, and that maps participating in this tradition persisted in print long beyond the mid-eighteenth-century moment when North America ostensibly began to gain continental integrity. Furthermore, a sampling of maps in the island tradition conveys the sense that North American ground is not only fragmented, but also indeterminate, for mapmakers used a variety of different and even conflicting island configurations when attempting to describe the shape of Florida.

The persistence of Florida as indeterminate space on Doolittle's map and many others of the post-Revolutionary period reminds us that early modern maps frequently participate in multiple representational traditions. For many such maps are not only instruments of ideology, but also—and necessarily—the products of a host of interactions among professional cartographers, amateur mapmakers, and locals who provided information about the land in question.[6] Thus, while most of Doolittle's map endorses a popular ideology of the emerging nation-state, expressed through the figure of the continent, the Florida portion furthers another representational tradition that characterizes North American ground and boundaries quite differently.

The representational multiplicity of early national maps of North America depicting Florida as islands announces the contingent, provisional nature of U.S. geographic nationalism.[7] For the islands of Florida attest that a non-nationalist spatial understanding of North American ground and boundaries persisted into the early national period, and even on some of the same maps that otherwise asserted North America's continental status. During the same decades when the discourse of U.S. nation-building relied increasingly on North America's contiguity and self-containment—qualities prized in a range of widely circulating post-Revolutionary documents such as *The Federalist Papers* and the Northwest Ordinance—North Americans also pondered Florida's elusive island geography. And even though Florida was not officially U.S. ground until 1821, the islands of Florida encouraged some eighteenth- and early nineteenth-century observers to define the country as something other than a self-enclosed, ever-expanding nation of settlers that would cohere under a strong federal government. Ultimately, early reflections on the islands of Florida—in maps, settlers' guides, and popular tales such as "The Florida Pirate" (1821)—offer scholars of the early national period a chance to look beyond the spatial abstraction of the continent, which promoted a definition of national identity that was not shared by everyone calling the United States home.[8]

The Origin and Endurance of Islands

In 1775 Bernard Romans, an Anglo-American surveyor, mapmaker, and naturalist, explained that the cartographic tradition of Florida as islands resulted from an interpretive error long since corrected. In *A Concise Natural History of East and West Florida* (1775), the first natural history of Florida published in North America, Romans attributes the error to a misunderstanding of central Florida's Lake Okeechobee and the marshy flatlands surrounding it. "This lake," he writes, "has given rise to the intersected, and mangled condition in which we see the peninsula exhibited in *old* maps."[9]

Early Americans considered Romans an authority on Florida. His lavish two-volume natural history, featuring copperplate engravings by Paul Revere and financed by several prominent subscribers including John Adams and John Hancock, secured his election to the American Philosophical Society. In 1804 Charles Brockden Brown eagerly read the *Natural History*, writing that Florida's imminent incorporation into the United States rendered the work "uncommonly interesting to the present, and still more to the next generation."[10] Subsequent natural historians of Florida read Romans with interest, drew on many of the sources that he cited, and repeated many of his claims, including his explanation of outdated maps featuring an "intersected, and mangled" South Florida. One writer confirms in 1823 that the "immense body of low land" constituting the peninsula's marshy interior is to blame for the error that we see on "ancient maps": by echoing Romans, yet altering "*old* maps" to "*ancient* maps," this writer relegates the cartographic tradition of islands to an even more distant past.[11] Such works indicate that by the time Romans wrote in the mid-1770s, people generally classified a nonpeninsular Florida with other fanciful fictions of Floridian ground, such as the Renaissance idea of Florida as a large island, or the Creek legend, related by William Bartram, that in Florida fugitive Yamasee occupy a part of the Okefenokee Swamp made of "enchanted land . . . [that] seem[s] to fly before [one], alternately appearing and disappearing."[12] It seems that, by the last quarter of the eighteenth century, Florida, like the rest of the continent, had traded an antiquated, erroneous reputation as "fragmented, elusive territory" for a new and correct one of physical integrity.[13]

Yet this conclusion fails to account for several facts, including the relatively recent, early eighteenth-century origin of the cartographic tradition of Florida as islands; the persistence of this tradition well beyond the mid-1770s; and the circumstances that actually produced the tradition in the first place. The very first map of Florida as islands appeared in 1708, and thus not at an obscure moment in the distant past, as the terms "old" and "ancient" suggest. And, as Amos Doolittle's widely circulating map of North America published in 1784 (Figure 7) demonstrates, such maps persisted long after the moment when Romans declared them "old." In fact, Doolittle's map is one of at least seventeen maps of North America—of French, Italian, Dutch, Spanish, and English origins—first made between 1708 and 1799 that feature the islands of Florida, and some of these maps were consulted and reprinted long after 1799. Thus, for people in and beyond the United States throughout much of what we now call the early national period, the cartographic tradition of Florida as islands was not "old," but rather vibrantly ongoing and of recent emergence. And its emergence was not the result of European or American encounters with Lake Okeechobee or the marshes of Florida's interior; this explanation obscures the tradition's actual origins in native knowledge that was transmitted to the British conducting Indian slave raids on the Florida peninsula during the first decade of the eighteenth century.

The story of how Florida came to appear as islands on significant maps of North America that were made and circulated for well over a century begins when Thomas Nairne, first Indian agent of British South Carolina, participated in the British practice of leading Yamasee allies on raiding parties to Florida to capture indigenous people to sell at Charleston as slaves.[14] In 1702 Nairne and a party of thirty-three Yamasee took thirty-five captives from the Florida interior, and afterward Nairne described the experience in a map and legend for others who might wish to "go a Slave Catching" in Florida. The map, though now lost, informed Nairne's better-known 1708 map of the American Southeast that represents Florida in fragments so dramatically dispersed that they overlap the lower frame, as though the map could not quite contain them. The first extant map of Florida as islands, then, is Nairne's *Map of South Carolina Shewing the Settlements of the English, French, & Indian Nations from Charles Town to the River Missisipi* (1708/1711; Figure 8).

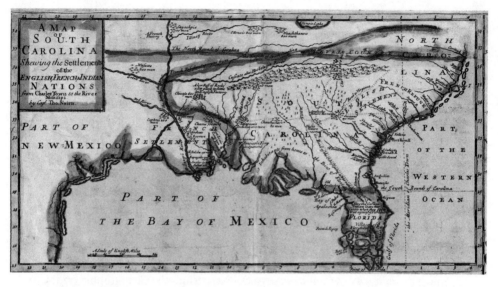

Figure 8. Thomas Nairne, *A Map of South Carolina Shewing the Settlements of the English, French, & Indian Nations from Charles Town to the River Missisipi* (1708/1711). Library of Congress, Geography and Map Division.

What compelled Nairne to describe Florida as no other mapmaker had? Nairne probably never saw the portion of Florida that he depicts as islands, for records indicate that his 1702 raiding party went only as far south as the northern border of the Everglades.[15] Yet a document accompanying Nairne's map of 1708 furnishes a clue to his understanding of Florida in fragments. In the document—a memorial to Charles Spencer, Earl of Sunderland, on British imperial strategy in the Southeast—Nairne laments that frequent raids on the peninsula have driven Florida's Indian population south "to the Islands of the Cape," such that the Carolina Indians pursuing captives in Florida must now "goe down as farr on the point of Florida as the firm land will permit."[16] Since Nairne himself had not been farther south than the "firm land," his information that "islands" lay below must have come from those who had: Carolina Indians, such as the Yamasee working with Nairne and other British colonial agents, or Florida Indians pursued or taken captive on the peninsula. Scholars have shown that it was not uncommon for American and European explorers to conduct "cartographic interviews" with Indians who knew the land more intimately, and one scholar of Nairne's map of the Southeast speculates that while much of it is based on personal observation, Nairne may have also derived significant cartographic knowledge from Indian informants.[17] He would not have been the only non-native observer to rely at least partly on Indians or other locally knowledgeable persons for geographic information about the southern reaches of Florida.

The northern edge of the Everglades is the point where many eighteenth- and nineteenth-century natural historians of Florida turned to locals for descriptions of the land to the south. Romans himself admits in his 1775 natural history that he had never explored "the far southern region of East Florida," though he knew about it from "a dark account . . . which the savages give" of Lake Okeechobee and its surroundings.[18] He also records that he gathered additional geographic information about this region from "a Spanish pilot and fisherman of good credit" who "had formerly been taken by the savages, and by them carried a prisoner, in a canoe" to their settlements on the banks of the lake.[19] Similar admissions appear decades later in the wake of Florida's annexation to the United States, in several texts that are part natural history of Florida and part promotional tract and settlers' guide designed to draw North Americans to the nation's newest acquisition.[20] In *Notices of East Florida* (1822) William Hayne Simmons relates that his knowledge of the southern region came from a fellow explorer's interviews of "many Indians and Negroes" who had crossed south over Lake Okeechobee to a place so swampy that "there was no spot sufficiently elevated to form a dry encampment upon."[21] And in *The Territory of Florida* (1837) John Lee Williams acknowledges consulting "the descriptions of Indian inhabitants" when attempting to draw "the outline south of Tampa Bay" because "the interior of this part of the Territory is wholly unexplored by white men."[22] This long tradition of turning to locals for information about South Florida increases the likelihood that Nairne did so in 1708 when creating a map that displayed Florida as no extant map had done.

Nairne's image of Florida immediately reached a wide audience because of the political significance of other portions of the map on which the image appeared. His map of the Southeast and accompanying memorial describing South Florida's lack of "firm land" are together regarded as "one of the most remarkable documents in the history of Anglo-American frontier 'imperialism,'" for these materials buttressed British claims to a part of North America held by the French, primarily by depicting British South Carolina as a territory extending west beyond the Mississippi River.[23] British observers eager to expand Great Britain's holdings in North America quickly embraced Nairne's map: its influence is readily apparent in London mapmaker

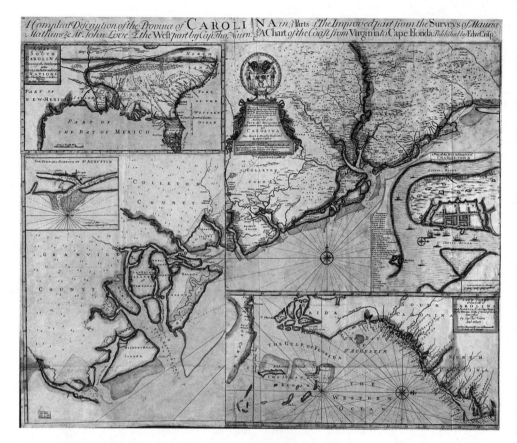

Figure 9. Edward Crisp, *A Compleat Description of the Province of Carolina in 3 Parts* (1711). Library of Congress, Geography and Map Division.

Edward Crisp's *Compleat Description of the Province of Carolina in 3 Parts* (London, 1711; Figure 9), which credits Nairne for the image of a fragmented Florida that appears twice on Crisp's map as an inset in the upper left and lower right corners, respectively. Crisp's map of 1711, bearing Nairne's image of 1708, was one of the most important maps of the Southeast during this period: because of its detailed information about British settlements and the general character of the backcountry, it was especially valuable to those eager to expand British holdings in North America.[24]

Since the British were not the only Europeans competing for land in North America, however, Crisp's map exhibiting Nairne's Florida almost

Figure 10. Guillaume de l'Isle, *Carte de la Louisiane et du cours du Mississipi . . .* (1718; repr., 1733). HM 52353, The Huntington Library, San Marino, California.

definitely gained an eager audience beyond Great Britain as well. The map is the most likely source for the image of Florida appearing on Paris mapmaker Guillaume de l'Isle's *Carte de la Louisiane et du cours du Mississipi* (1718; Figure 10), which quickly became one of the most widely circulated and highly influential maps of North America produced during the eighteenth century. De l'Isle, who is now hailed as the "founder of modern scientific cartography" for his efforts to rely on information gleaned from firsthand observation, clearly rejected the cartographic image of Florida most readily available to him, his father's portrayal of Florida as a peninsula on *Carte du Mexique et de la Floride* (1703).[25] It is likely that de l'Isle would have sought a more recent description of Florida, and even more likely that he would have been interested in a map such as Crisp's, which was widely praised for its wealth of detail.

The merit of de l'Isle's map bearing the image of a fragmented Florida was immediately apparent to his contemporaries, and the map's quality and political purpose made it an instant international success. It was particularly popular in France because it declared France's victory over England in an ongoing "cartographical war" for southeastern territory by aiming to invalidate English claims, yet English audiences also admired the map for its authority and excellence.[26] In North America, too, the map gained a large viewership: it appeared in atlases until after the Revolution, and its influence extended into the nineteenth century, for Thomas Jefferson owned and consulted it while planning the Lewis and Clark expedition in 1803.[27] De l'Isle's *Carte de la Louisiane* is also the source for subsequent maps of North America made all over the world, many of which were eagerly reprinted and consumed for several decades after their initial appearance.[28]

De l'Isle's 1718 map of North America ensured the nearly worldwide transmission of the image of a fantastically fragmented Florida for at least one hundred years, yet it did not do so alone. A list of eighteenth-century maps exhibiting Florida as islands includes Ion Baptista Homann's *Mississippi* (1717?; Figure 11), Antonio Arredondo's *Descripcion Geografica* (1742; Figure 12), John Gibson's *A Map of the New Governments, of East & West Florida* (1763; Figure 13), Thomas Wright's *Map of Georgia and Florida* (1763; Figure 14), and Isaak Tirion's *Algemeene Kaart van de Westindische Eilanden* (1769; Figure 15). The number of newly published maps featuring this arrangement decreases after the late 1760s, when, as I discuss in Chapter 1, British cartographers sought to revise Florida from islands to peninsula in the wake of Great Britain's 1763 acquisition of Florida from Spain. Yet long after this moment the tradition of representing Florida as islands persisted on maps published for the first time—such as Doolittle's map of 1784—and on those that circulated as reprints or in manuscript.[29]

A familiar account of this cartographic tradition—such as that provided by Romans and the writers of nineteenth-century natural histories and settlers' guides to Florida—thus conceals a more accurate story that emerges from the maps themselves: information provided by indigenous peoples on the ground in Spanish colonial Florida during early eighteenth-century encounters between Indians and English gave rise to the cartographic tradition of Florida as islands that discernibly shaped significant maps of North America for well over a century. The tradition outlasted the moment when Florida began to solidify on some important British maps, and it persisted beyond

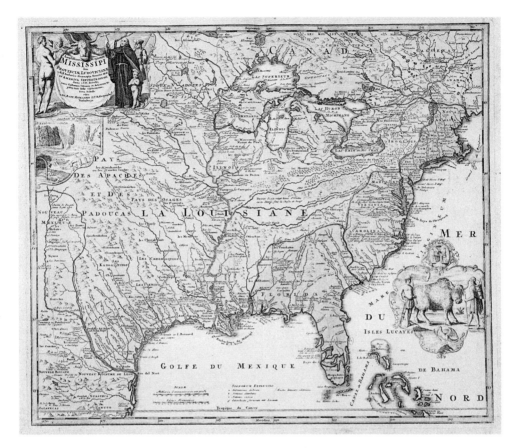

Figure 11. Johann Baptist Homann, *Amplissima regionis Mississipi seu Provinciae Ludovician* (1717?), detail. HM 44194, The Huntington Library, San Marino, California.

the formative period when other parts of North America gained continental integrity and solidity during the mid-eighteenth century. In fact, Florida's history as islands, and its endurance as such on several maps circulating during the early national period, suggest that many people of this period imagined the continent's southern edge as fragmented and even indeterminate. A sampling of maps in the island tradition shows Florida in a multiplicity of arrangements of islands varying in number, size, shape, and location. When we view some of these maps alongside one another, as

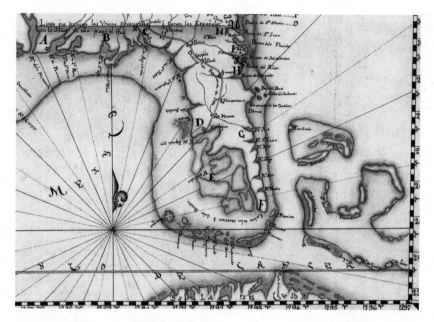

Figure 12. Antonio Arredondo, *Descripcion Geografica* (1742), detail. Library of Congress, Geography and Map Division.

many early Americans could have done, the variety of island configurations emphasizes the difficulty of discerning Florida's contours, and thereby of determining exactly what constitutes the ground and boundaries of North America (Figures 11-15).[30]

American Archipelago

Maps showing Florida as islands directly support a theory of North American geography that, though less well-remembered today, gained traction among many early Americans during the late eighteenth and early nineteenth centuries—namely, the theory that North America was naturally attached to the Caribbean and parts south via a chain of submerged mountains, the tops of which were, in the words of British geographer John Aikin, a "range of Islands extending from the southern point of east Florida to Guiana."[31] In his textbook, *Geographical Delineations* (1807), which was published in Philadelphia and well regarded in the United States, Aikin pro-

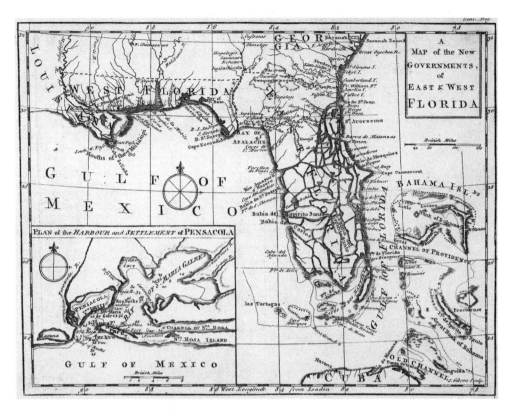

Figure 13. John Gibson, *A Map of the New Governments, of East & West Florida* (1763). HM 093:388 S, The Huntington Library, San Marino, California.

ceeds to explain that the islands "of this terraqueous region" are probably evidence that "at some remote period the ocean had made a violent incursion upon the North American continent, and had torn away a vast mass of land, leaving in an insular state all the elevated spots which were capable of resisting its fury."[32] The theory also captivated no less than Jedidiah Morse: one wonders whether Morse had in mind the islands of Florida that appear on Doolittle's map in Morse's *Geography Made Easy* (1784; see Figure 6) when in an 1805 edition of his work he reflects that "In the Bahama channel are many indications that the island of Cuba was once united to Florida."[33]

A fuller elaboration of this prospect comes from Charles Thomson, secretary to the Continental Congress: in an appendix to Thomas Jefferson's *Notes on the State of Virginia* (1787), Thomson more or less wonders why

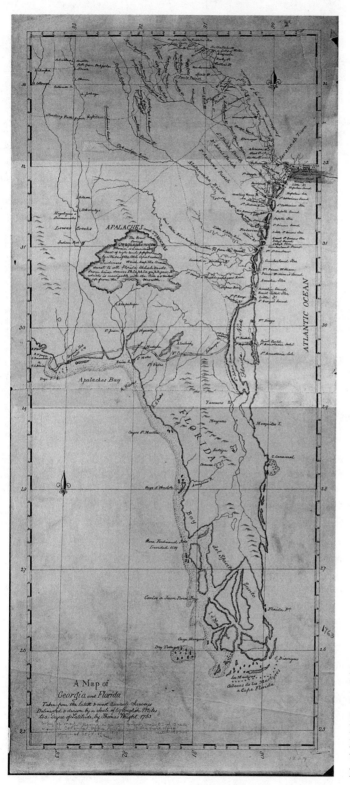

Figure 14. Thomas Wright, *A Map of Georgia and Florida* (1763). Courtesy of Hargrett Rare Book and Manuscript Library / University of Georgia Libraries.

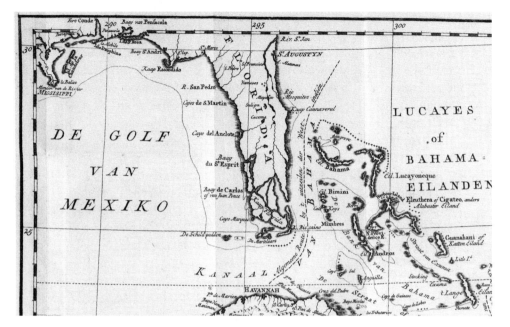

Figure 15. Isaak Tirion, *Algemeene Kaart van de Westindische Eilanden* (1769), detail, in Thomas Salmon, *Hedendaagsche historie, of tegenwoordige staat van Amerika . . .*, 3 vols. (Amsterdam, 1766–69). HM 222554, The Huntington Library, San Marino, California.

South Florida should be considered the edge of North America.[34] The thought occurs to him while reading Jefferson's famous description of a landscape-altering phenomenon that ostensibly occurred in the distant past at the point where the Potomac and Shenandoah rivers meet and run through the Blue Ridge Mountains: "at this spot," Jefferson muses, the two rivers, which had risen and "formed an ocean which filled the whole valley," broke over and "[tore] the mountain down from its summit to its base."[35] This "disrupture and avulsion," as Jefferson describes it, directs Thomson's mind farther south than Jefferson's Virginia. "While ruminating on these subjects," Thomson writes, "I have often been hurried away by fancy, and led to imagine that" the Gulf of Mexico was once a vast plain bordered on the east by "a range of mountains" running "from the point or cape of Florida . . . through Cuba, Hispaniola, Porto rico, Martinique, Guadaloupe, Barbadoes, and Trinidad, till it reached the coast of [South] America, and formed the shores which bounded the ocean, and guarded the country behind." Yet "by some convulsion or shock of nature," he continues, the Atlantic Ocean broke through this mountain range; the sea then "deluged that vast plain," turning it into the Gulf of Mexico, before receding "through the gulph between Florida and Cuba, carrying with it the loom and sand it may have scooped from the country it had occupied. . . . But these are only the visions of fancy."[36] Essentially, then, Thomson imagines that Florida's tip is part of a mountain range that joins the continents.

Scholars have speculated that North American geographic fantasies of Florida's connection to the Caribbean and points south either voice imperial ambitions to annex Cuba and other parts of the West Indies, or express anxieties that the Caribbean was already too close and could "contaminate" U.S. bodies, culture, and politics.[37] Yet if we read such fantasies more literally, they express first and foremost uncertainties about where the boundaries of the nation actually are and even what constitutes a boundary and a continent—uncertainties that Florida inspires across a broad range of texts. When Thomson and other writers fancy an American archipelago consisting of North America, the Caribbean, and points south, then, they describe a spatial possibility in play on many maps that show Florida as islands. Tirion's *General Map of the West Indian Islands* (1769; Figure 16), for example, centers on a chain of islands stretching from the tip of Florida, southeast through Cuba and Hispaniola, and nearly to the coast of South America. The map's geographic schema resonates with Morse's claim that Florida "was once united" to Cuba, and with Thomson's observation that a submerged, "continuous range of mountains" joins Florida, the West Indies, and South America. Ultimately, then, the maps underscore an existing sense of the artificiality of setting North America's southern edge at Florida, to which nature joins so many other places.

Reflections on Florida as islands strikingly remind us that a geographic understanding of North America as a sharply bounded, contiguous, self-contained landmass was not as universally embraced as we might imagine were we to focus exclusively on well-known political documents of the post-Revolutionary period that emphasize the importance of continental integrity and contiguity. For example, the Federalist project depended on solid, contiguous, self-contained ground, which would permit a "serialized" society: the goal was to organize communities all over the continent according to the same set of principles, so that people in all places, and with different and competing interests, could be managed and directed from afar.[38] Early

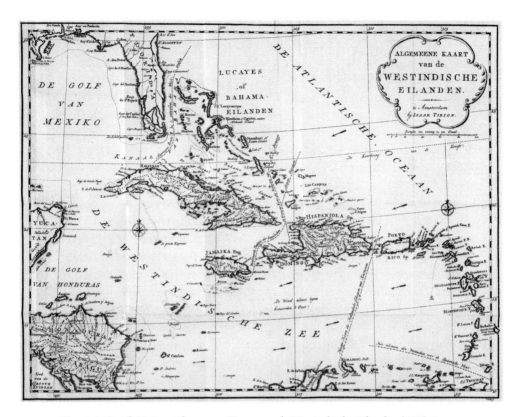

Figure 16. Isaak Tirion, *Algemeene Kaart van de Westindische Eilanden* (1769), in Thomas Salmon, *Hedendaagsche historie, of tegenwoordige staat van Amerika . . .* , 3 vols. (Amsterdam, 1766–69). HM 222554, The Huntington Library, San Marino, California.

federal land ordinances announce Federalism's dependence on a specific set of geographic assumptions about the North American continent. The Northwest Ordinance of 1787, for example, assumes that continental ground is universally fixed and integrated when requiring that the Northwest Territory be divided into five states, each composed of townships of six square miles that contain thirty-six one-mile-square sections to be auctioned to prospective settlers.[39] This requirement depends on the capacity of the entire continent to bear the sharp outlines of a permanent grid, without which the nation could not simultaneously cohere and expand. Indeed, proponents of the land system asserted that it would sustain federal authority over all prospective

parts of the United States and thereby prevent the expanding country's social and economic "disunion" and "disintegration."[40]

Federalism required not only a solid and integrated continent, but one
that was insulated as well. In fact, many early Americans expressed their fer-
vor for the continent by praising another landform: the island. Several political figures contended that the North American continent was actually a
single island, a form that philosophers and artists had long considered ideally suited to the nation-state.[41] Montesquieu, for example, had held that "the
inhabitants of islands have a higher relish for liberty than those of the continent," for "the sea separates them from great empires . . . and the islanders,
being without the reach of [their enemies'] arms, more easily preserve their
own laws."[42] Echoing this sentiment after the American Revolution, Alexander Hamilton expresses his affinity for the island in Federalist No. 8 when
praising the perfect form of Great Britain because of its "insular situation,"
which has "contributed to preserve the liberty which that country to this day
enjoys."[43] Hamilton continues: "if we are wise enough to preserve the Union
we may for ages enjoy an advantage similar to that of an insulated situation . . .
but if we should be disunited, and the integral parts should either remain
separated or . . . be thrown together into two or three confederacies, we
should be, in a short course of time, in the predicament of the continental
powers of Europe."[44] John Jay observes of England that "it seems obvious to
common sense that the people of such an island should be but one nation,"
and James Madison urges Americans to imagine the continent as a single
island, and accordingly to embrace the opportunity of "deriving from our
[geographic] situation the precious advantage which Great Britain has derived from hers."[45] Compact, integrated, and self-contained, the continent-
as-island is the ideal federal geographic form.

However, while the rhetoric of many of the period's iconic political
documents emphasizes the U.S. nation-state's dependence on a solid, contiguous, and enclosed landmass, we know that some continental ground
could not be geographically systematized. Certain peoples or polities demanded (or negotiated) spaces of autonomy, and certain environments such
as desert regions and riverine zones thwarted expansionist design by preventing familiar versions of settlement, agriculture, and surveillance.[46] In
reality, then, the evenly shaded map of the republic served as an abstraction
that belied a "politically fragmented," "legally differentiated" world "encased
in irregular, porous, and sometimes undefined borders."[47] Florida brought
this reality into sharp relief by prompting many early Americans to ob-

serve and reflect on multiple—and sometimes competing—understandings of the nature and boundaries of continental ground.

But how might we document narratives of U.S. identity that emerged from recognition of the continent's resistance to geographic systematizing? For, while maps and other descriptions of Florida as islands confirm early American awareness of the continent's capacity to fragment and disperse, they tell us frustratingly little about how people *interpreted* this capacity during a period when "the solid reality, the *terra firma*" of the continent underpinned so many important conceptions of individual and national identity. For that interpretation, we must turn to early nineteenth-century narratives of real and imagined encounters with Florida's elusive, shifting ground.

Mapping "The Florida Pirate"

John Howison's "The Florida Pirate" (1821) was instantly beloved by its U.S. audience. After the tale's initial appearance in *Blackwood's Magazine* (August 1821), a large number of U.S. editions were published as independent volumes.[48] Given the popularity of the tale among North Americans and the timing of the tale's publication just a month after Florida officially became U.S. ground, it seems natural to conclude that "The Florida Pirate" is about Florida, and that it answers American curiosity about the nation's newest territorial acquisition, as did so many settlers' guides to Florida published during the 1820s and 1830s.[49] Yet to most twenty-first-century readers, "The Florida Pirate" seems to have nothing to do with Florida. The story involves Manuel—a runaway slave turned pirate captain—and a white British narrator who meets Manuel in the Bahamas and begs to serve as surgeon aboard the *Esperanza*, Manuel's pirate ship manned by a crew of escaped slaves seeking freedom on the seas. The plot follows the peregrinations of the pirates as they board and plunder ships in the Caribbean until a U.S. brig of war captures the *Esperanza* and takes the captain and crew to prison in Charleston, where Manuel dies by his own hand. No one in the story goes to Florida. The author never designates any character as "the Florida pirate." In fact, the word "Florida" does not appear in the tale.

Nonetheless, generations of North American readers have identified Manuel as "the Florida Pirate." An 1823 American reprint of the tale clearly designates him as such by placing a frontispiece image of Manuel labeled "MANUEL the PIRATE" across from the title page reading "The Florida Pirate" (Figure 17). And, perhaps building on the assumption of earlier

MANUEL, the PIRATE.

Pub.^d by Wm. Borradaile 130 Fulton St. N.Y.

Figure 17. John Howison, *The Florida Pirate; or, An Account of a Cruise in the Schooner Esperanza; with A Sketch of the Life of Her Commander* (1823), frontispiece. Jay I. Kislak Collection, Rare Book and Special Collections Division, Library of Congress (125).

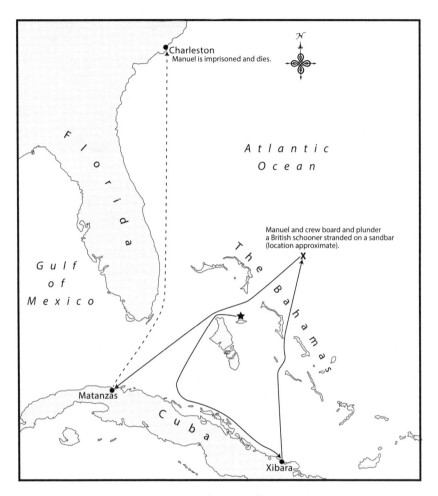

Figure 18. Approximate route of Manuel's ship in "The Florida Pirate" (1821).

audiences, a recent reader writes of "Manuel's 'Florida' nativity"—even though in the story Manuel declares, "I was born in South Carolina."[50]

If nothing in the tale's plot or Manuel's biography explicitly connects Manuel to Florida, then why did early American readers seemingly have no qualms about identifying Manuel as "the Florida Pirate"? A geographic consideration of the story offers a likely answer. Based on information the narrator provides, we can easily map the *Esperanza*'s route (Figure 18). Beginning near the Bahamas—where Manuel and the white narrator meet—Manuel sails southwest toward Cuba, then southeast along Cuba's northern shore to Xibara. Next, he sails far north into open sea where he and his crew board and plunder a British schooner stranded on a sandbar. Finally, Manuel returns to Cuba by sailing southwest to Matanzas, where a U.S. brig intercepts the *Esperanza* and transports the pirates north to Charleston, South Carolina, for sentencing. While Manuel never makes contact with the Florida today's readers know, he moves across an expansive seascape that early readers easily imagined as the space of Florida during a time when its boundaries had yet to be determined.

It turns out that Manuel is "the Florida Pirate" for a reason that only becomes clear when we read the story in light of a spatial understanding of Florida as ground in flux. To those who understood Florida as a "terraqueous region" of islands, keys, and sandbars that change shape, size, and location depending on which geography textbook or map one consults, "The Florida Pirate" easily takes place in Florida. Furthermore, Manuel is "the Florida Pirate"—not by birth, but by belonging to the fragmented, shifting ground he masters.

Recognizing that "The Florida Pirate" is about Florida by virtue of its geography enables us to interpret the tale as its early readers may have—that is, as a narrative of belonging on the elusive landscape of the nation's most recent territorial acquisition. In this way Howison's text belongs to an expansive archive of early American reflections on inhabiting Florida. It suggests that, while much of Florida could not foster the feelings and practices of solidarity that post-Revolutionary proponents of the continental ideal prized, the region generated models of habitation, community, and economy sustained by mobility.

This message is particularly clear in Howison's depiction of Manuel's occupation as a Florida wrecker. Wreckers flourished along the Florida Reef during the eighteenth and nineteenth centuries by mastering ground where cargo ships frequently foundered. Essentially, wreckers were salvagers who profited by rescuing stranded vessels and crews in exchange for a substantial portion of the cargo to sell to the highest bidder in the domestic and foreign ports they frequented.[51] Wreckers thrived, then, not only because of their intimate acquaintance with the intricacies of local terrain, but also because of their large network of associates, which often included escaped slaves, smugglers, Spanish fishermen, and independent adventurers—such as the white narrator of "The Florida Pirate" who supports himself by "forming a league with these outcasts of society."[52]

When Howison's fictional Manuel and his crew board a ship run aground on a sandbank and offer its captain assistance in exchange for "part of the cargo, which you of course have no means of preserving," they announce their identities as Florida wreckers, and thereby confirm their participation in the extensive, unsurveyable economic networks and alliances that Floridian geography sustained, frequently to the detriment of U.S. imperial mastery and expansion. Moreover, through Manuel's engagement with wrecking, "The Florida Pirate" underscores Florida's identity as a geographically dispersed region that, though part of the United States, produces economic and cultural networks that could not foster a nation celebrated in encomiums to continental wholeness. Rather, the region's expansive and indeterminate ground sustained those who profited from their capacity to move U.S. commodities into the hands of independent adventurers and imperial rivals.

"The Florida Pirate" is not Howison's only reflection on Florida. He had traveled through North America, the West Indies, and Cuba during 1820, and he published three nonfictional narratives of these experiences that offer additional information about those whom shifting North American ground sustains.[53] In these accounts Howison explains that geography determines the "character" of settlement, and that Florida, as a "southerly part" of the continent, boasts a more "interesting" history of "early settlement" than the rest of North America, where settlement was "tame, uninteresting, and deficient in variety."[54] Whereas north of the "Gulf of Florida"—which stretches along Florida's eastern coast—the British engaged in the "pacific and gentle occupations of agriculture," "cultivating the soil and forming themselves into an organized community," in Florida and parts south the Spanish disdained "to settle quietly in one place, and to pursue any regular occupation," preferring rather to set about "ransacking the earth and the waters for gold."[55] For in the South the temptations of the sea and the frequent "vicissitudes and disasters" of hurricanes and earthquakes discouraged fixed habitation, and thus "the agricultural and commercial settlements in these regions have never had much stability, and their population has always been liable to change and to fluctuation."[56] Put otherwise, while Northerners historically engaged in the kinds of pursuits that "attach men to the soil which they inhabit," men who went south "attached themselves by preference to expeditions."[57]

Florida pirates are just one version of those "outcasts," "vagabonds," and "adventurers," who have always called Florida home. According to three "anecdotes" of the "Florida pirate" that Howison "collected" from conversations he had in places across North America and the Caribbean, these persons live in the Florida Gulf among the "small rocky islands which are scattered over the Bahama banks," where "navigation is intricate and dangerous, the water being too shallow to admit the passage of any but small vessels, which are easily overpowered and plundered."[58] Although "little is known about these marauders," Howison learns that they "consist chiefly of negroes and people of color"; command stolen ships purchased from dealers in the West Indies; and are nonviolent, provided they receive the articles of cargo they demand.[59] And while Florida pirates live mostly at sea, they sometimes also belong to communities ashore. According to an anecdote told to Howison by one Captain Smychton, commander of a U.S. brig bound for Jamaica, a Florida pirate once led him to "a solitary part of the shore of Cuba," and thence down an "unmarked" path to a collection of "huts of the most simple construction and meanest appearance," essentially a maroon community of black men, women, and children.[60] To Smychton's surprise, the pirate explains, " 'I live here when not at sea,—I have merchandise and money in these huts; but this place is so secret, that were you now on the sea-shore, you could not find your way to it without a guide.' "[61] In another anecdote, related by a Frenchman from the U.S. South, Florida pirates nearly ruined his plantation in Cuba when they came ashore and made secret contact with his slaves, "induced" them to escape, plundered the estate, and plotted "revenge" for his "tyranny" as a master.[62] Howison's travels must have provided the material for his well-known story of Manuel the pirate, who also establishes himself by moving continually over a changing landscape and forming alliances with other populations who do the same.

The sources of Howison's 1820 anecdotes of the Florida pirate are far and wide, consisting of many persons he met on his travels, including the captain of a U.S. brig, a Frenchman from the U.S. South, and a fellow traveler staying at a Philadelphia boardinghouse. Collectively, the stories Howison hears suggest that, during the same years that U.S. officials worked toward ratifying the 1819 treaty by which Spain ceded Florida to the United States, many people living in and passing through early America shared an understanding of Florida as a place that would not promote the exclusive, individual proprietorship that could create federal revenue, nationalize settlement patterns, and sustain social order within the national domain.[63] Yet, while Florida would not foster an individual's "acquaintance" with and "attachment" to the shared "interests" of "their own country" (to borrow the language of Jedidiah Morse), community and belonging would not entirely dissolve along with the land. Rather, the nation's newest acquisition would encourage different attachments to others and to the ground than were possible on more solid parts of the continent, such as the prairies of the West. Florida would sustain Americans whose mobility and dispersal—in direct contrast to fixity and integration—granted them self-mastery and a place within the new borders of the republic.

Finally, Howison's reflections on Floridian geography offer a language of belonging unavailable in political and cultural works that celebrate the nation's destiny to become an ever-expanding polity of settlers cohering under a strong federal government. At the earliest moments of Florida's annexation, encounters with this indeterminately bounded part of the continent produced unconventional narratives of North American character. Such narratives would continue to proliferate throughout the middle decades of the nineteenth century, particularly as U.S. imperial pursuits into Florida and the Gulf of Mexico increasingly made Floridian land and populations the subjects of national scrutiny. The local features of the southeastern edges of North America even shaped the literature of the American Renaissance.

Chapter 3

Wrecker Empire: Harbor, Rock, Reef, Key, Gulf

In a pivotal scene in James Fenimore Cooper's *Jack Tier* (1848) the U.S. brig *Molly Swash* arrives in a harbor formed by a group of small islets in the Gulf of Mexico. As the brig drops anchor, geographic confusion descends on its first officer, Harry Mulford, an otherwise adept navigator: while he hears the sailors cry "land-ho!" he has trouble identifying what lies before him as land. "The land proved to be a cluster of low, small islands, part coral, part sand," he reflects, "the largest of which did not possess a surface of more than a very few acres." Altogether these "merest islets imaginable . . . would not probably have made one field of twenty acres," and that was "cut off from the rest of the world by a broad barrier of water. It was a spot of such singular situation and accessories that [Mulford] gazed at it with a burning desire to know where he was." He exclaims, "I cannot explain it . . . It is altogether an extraordinary place!" (499).[1] Yet readers soon discover that these isolated islets rising just above the surface of the sea, and forming land like none known to the New England-born Mulford, are the Dry Tortugas, the "western termination of the well-known, formidable, and extensive Florida Reef" (501).

It is unusual to associate James Fenimore Cooper with coastal Florida. When we think of Cooper's settings, we tend to think of the solid ground of the western frontier or the watery expanse of the sea.[2] Yet during the U.S.-Mexican War (1846–48) Cooper chose the outer edges of the Florida Reef as the primary setting for his novel about this conflict. Early readers embraced the novel, perhaps even more enthusiastically than some of the frontier fiction for which Cooper is better remembered today, as *Jack Tier*'s strong publication history suggests.[3] U.S. readers were particularly intrigued by the novel's Florida setting. Commenting on the full title of the American edition, *Jack Tier; Or, The Florida Reef*, an American reviewer observed that "the Florida Reef conjures up wrecks and adventures in all the vividness and graphic truthfulness for which Cooper stands unrivalled."[4] In truth, however, the "setting" of the novel can barely be called a setting, for the term implies a certain fixity that the Reef largely lacks, especially in the specific place where most of the novel's drama unfolds: the Dry Tortugas, islets located in the Gulf of Mexico seventy miles west of Key West, are among the most isolated, difficult to access, and elusive parts of the Reef, since they are continually reshaped and sometimes even drowned by the sea.

Why did Cooper set a novel of treason, smuggling, and maritime adventure during the U.S.-Mexican War on insubstantial grounds remote from the theater of conflict? The mystery of this choice seems only to deepen when we consider the central role the islets play in the plot: *Jack Tier* derives most of its suspense from the question whether the U.S. Navy will manage to master the Dry Tortugas, along with the secluded harbors and winding passages of coral constituting the Florida Reef more broadly. But while today's readers might justifiably wonder how the struggle to attain sovereignty over a place this remote, unfamiliar, and apparently irrelevant to U.S. history could make for a compelling literary drama, Cooper chose the setting because the region commanded tremendous geopolitical significance during the period in question.

For a number of reasons all but forgotten today, the Dry Tortugas were antebellum America's "key to empire" on and beyond the continent. This and other parts of the Reef offered ideal strategic military footholds from which to expand extra-continentally into the Caribbean and points south. Additionally, establishing a strong U.S. presence on the Reef was critical to protecting U.S. commerce: an increasing volume of goods flowing into and out of the Gulf of Mexico—on the way to and from the mouth of the Mississippi River—had to pass over the Reef, a site well known to pirates and wreckers who profited from intercepting cargo ships. And monitoring the Reef was also an important objective of the navy because the area was known to provide refuge for U.S. vessels smuggling slaves from Africa to plantations throughout the U.S. South long after the external slave trade became illegal in 1808.[5] As a southern site through which national, hemispheric, and even global flows of people and goods continually passed, the Reef sharply foregrounds what several scholars of the U.S. South have recently proposed: many southern sites that seem, upon first consideration, geographically and historically exceptional in their irrelevance to U.S. national and imperial identity were surprisingly central to it.[6]

Cooper's novel and a range of other antebellum reflections on the Reef—including military reports about fortifying the Florida Keys, Cooper's *History of the Navy of the United States of America* (1853), early images and travel narratives of the Dry Tortugas, and tales of shipwreck on the Reef in Audubon's *Ornithological Biography*—establish that the nation's path to national security, and to imperial expansion over and beyond the continent, lay through the labyrinthine terrain of the Reef.[7] They show that a country accustomed to a continental identity must manage alterations in that geography by finding a model of mastery suited to shifting, unstable, dispersed, and fragmented foundations.[8] And these texts also provide a sense of what that model might resemble. In the practice of Reef possession enacted by Florida wreckers—locals who monitor the Reef by hovering along it—Cooper, Audubon, and others identify a way to master the region and thereby secure both continental and saltwater empire. Antebellum writings on the Reef thus mark the limits of a land-based, continental model of U.S. expansion celebrated in popular novels of the West. They also suggest the need to preserve and emulate concepts of territory and sovereignty best known to Reef inhabitants whom imperial projects sought to erase.[9]

Reading the Reef: James Fenimore Cooper's Florida

Cooper's novel more than bears out the implication of the full title he gave it in 1848. In *Jack Tier; Or, the Florida Reef* the Reef vies for the leading role as its elusive islets, secluded harbors, and winding passages of coral become the substance of the story. Characters frequently pause to reflect on the Reef. They get their bearings in relation to it, as when antagonist Stephen Spike, captain of the *Molly Swash*, stops "to take a hasty survey of the reef" before proceeding. They consult charts of its "courses, distances, and general peculiarities." And they look upon its oddities with curiosity or desire, as when Mulford's paramour Rose "gazed at it with longing eyes," hoping that Mulford—as the brig's pilot—would manage to traverse "its channels and coral" (654, 540, 510). Whole paragraphs are devoted to reveries on the shape of the Reef, directions for navigating it, and considerations of its perilous "dangers, windings, and rocks," "intricacies," "mazes," and sheer vastness (580, 524 652, 510). We are reminded of its capacity for outright treachery to cargo and men, and of its unpredictable mutations, such as when the narrator observes that "places like those in which Mulford had waded on the reef, while it was calm, would now have proved fatal to the strongest frame" (657). Several characters sink beneath the "troubled waters of the reef," and the outcome of the novel's central conflict between the U.S. navy brig-of-war *Poughkeepsie* and Captain Spike—who is attempting to smuggle U.S. gunpowder to Mexico—turns on navigational mastery of the Reef, which ultimately swallows Spike whole: at the novel's conclusion his body is "washed away to leave its bones among the wrecks and relics of the Florida Reef" (658, 677).

Upon first consideration *Jack Tier* appears only to celebrate U.S. naval prowess.[10] After all, by the end of the novel the *Poughkeepsie* closes in on Spike's brig, which the navy had been monitoring since its departure from Manhattan at the start of the narrative. The smuggled gunpowder, concealed as barrels of flour until an accident proves otherwise, ends up with Spike at the bottom of the sea rather than in the hands of his accomplice, Mexican agent Don Juan Montefalderon of Cuba (491). Thus U.S. commercial interests are secured, treason is detected and prevented, and the traitor is effectively punished when consigned to the deep.

Yet *Jack Tier* is not just about the navy's ultimate triumph. Rather, it is also about a prolonged and nearly disastrous failure to master Florida's particular combination of geography and topography. A significant portion of the narrative concerns the navy's repeated difficulties in apprehending Spike, for despite the marines' early detection of his treachery the Reef continually prevents them from approaching near enough to intercept his nefarious transactions, until the novel's conclusion. And although Spike's plan is ultimately thwarted, the navy cannot be credited; his smuggling of ammunition to Mexico is prevented by an unexpected change in the weather that sinks the *Molly Swash*.

Visualizing the routes of the *Swash* and *Poughkeepsie* enables us to grasp at once the Reef's dual role as the marines' nemesis and Spike's accomplice. A map of the Florida seascape of *Jack Tier* shows that, long before the *Swash* reaches the Dry Tortugas, Caribbean grounds baffle the *Poughkeepsie*'s pursuit, blocking its approach and providing the smuggler with plenty of privacy and inaccessibility to exchange gunpowder for doubloons (Figure 19). The ships first meet southeast of Florida in Mona Passage, a strait between the islands of Hispaniola and Puerto Rico. The episode appears to establish the authority of "Uncle Sam" in foreign waters, for here the navy boards the *Swash* and demands to inspect its papers and hold, and Spike believes he is "now in the jaws of the lion, and his wisest course [is] to submit" (491). Yet

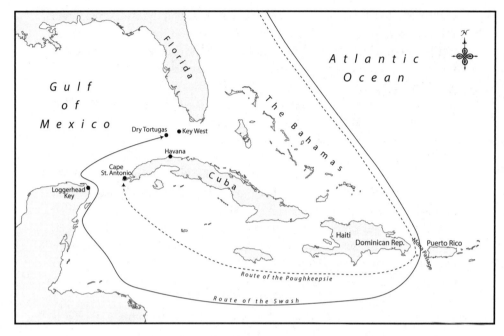

Figure 19. Map showing route of the Swash and narrator's suggested blockade points of Key West, the Havanna, Cape St. Antonio, and Loggerhead Key (marked from north to south).

the marines detect nothing amiss; they release Spike and determine to pursue him from afar, only to lose sight of him as the *Swash* sails west into the Gulf of Mexico.

Spike's entrance into the Gulf emphasizes the navy's lack of sovereignty over the region. While the marines correctly surmise that the Gulf is Spike's intended destination, they badly miscalculate his route, so their plan to station a naval ship near Cape St. Antonio, Cuba, to keep "a sharp look-out" for the *Swash* fails when Spike bypasses the area entirely.[11] Rather than entering the Gulf along Cuba's shore, where the marines are stationed, Spike enters along Yucatan's shore (see Figure 19). The narrator fashions this maneuver as a severe indictment of naval prowess. After declaring Spike's entry point a place "most easily blockaded, by a *superior* naval power," Cooper takes the liberty of advising the navy of a more effective strategy: "By maintaining a proper force between Key West and the Havanna, and another squadron between Cape St. Antonio and Loggerhead Key, the whole country [of Mexico] . . .

is shut up, as it might be in a band-box" (497; emphasis added).[12] In other words, the success of Cooper's smuggler instructively accentuates passages to the Gulf with which a navy of "superior" strength—especially one at war with nearby Mexico—should be most intimately acquainted.

And, as the *Swash* nears Florida, topography conspires with geography to confound the navy entirely, and thereby to aid the traitor's pursuit of criminal acts supporting Mexico. When Spike reaches his intended destination in a secluded harbor in the Dry Tortugas, Mulford's paramour observes that the spot seems ideally " 'suited to acts of villainy,' " and indeed the Reef assists the ensuing rendezvous of the *Swash* and Montefalderon's Cuban schooner by offering a "capacious and perfectly safe basin" and a "singular and solitary haven" surrounded by "narrow and crooked passages" that render the port all but inaccessible to the uninitiated (500, 499). A lighthouse at the harbor's mouth acts as a beacon not "to guide vessels into the haven," but rather "to warn mariners at a distance, of the position of the whole group" of islands, thereby enhancing the seclusion of the place and giving Spike time to transfer gunpowder from his ship to Montefalderon's and collect payment in doubloons before a tornado sinks the Mexican's schooner like a shot. And even after this unforeseen disaster prevents Montefalderon from departing with a hold full of American gunpowder, Spike and his crew still have time to raise the sunken schooner, recover part of the gunpowder from below decks, and sell the *Swash* itself to the Mexicans before the U.S. Navy even figures out where the smugglers are.

They who master the Reef win; its masters are not the U.S. Navy. When the *Poughkeepsie* finally locates the *Swash*, we learn the disappointing fact that "Spike felt little apprehension of the ship's getting very near to him," "Unless there was some one on board her who was acquainted with the channels of the Dry Tortugas" (520). Indeed, the Reef continues holding the *Poughkeepsie* at bay as Spike salvages more gunpowder from the sunken Mexican schooner and retrieves a good portion of the doubloons, all in plain sight of the marines, for "the distance between the vessels was so small, that a swift cruiser, like the ship of war, would soon have been alongside of [the *Swash*], but for the intervening islets and the intricacies of their channels" (524). And when the *Poughkeepsie* does approach closely enough to interfere, Spike and Montefalderon escape in a manner still further emphasizing the marines' topographic incompetence: the two villains unite aboard the *Swash* and force Mulford to maneuver it "through a most difficult part of the passage," and finally beyond the reach of the *Poughkeepsie*'s shot (530).[13]

An extended chase among treacherous coral passages drives home the message that Reef mastery matters. The *Poughkeepsie* eventually catches up with Spike, who is lured back to the wreck of Montefalderon's schooner by the prospect of more doubloons, but as the sloop-of-war approaches near enough to fire Spike realizes that his own damaged vessel will be unable to outrun its pursuer "unless some extraordinary external assistance was to be obtained" (651). Enter the Florida Reef. Just when Spike concludes that all is lost, his eye lights on a hitherto unnoticed "channel among the rocks" and, "To the surprise of all on board the man-of-war, the [*Swash*] continued on . . . finding her way deeper and deeper among the mazes of the reef without meeting with any impediment!" (651, 652). Spike's success proves an earlier claim that "The Florida Reef, with all its dangers, windings, and rocks, was as well known to him as the entrances to the port of New York . . . passages would be available to [the *Swash*], into which the *Poughkeepsie* would not dare to venture" (580). Even when Spike finally loses control of the *Swash* in the panic of the chase, he *still* outmatches the sloop-of-war by "running in the channels of the reef" in a small escape boat until forcing some of his hostages overboard to die by smashing against the Reef (655). Only after this gruesome spectacle does the *Poughkeepsie* actually come near enough to shoot. While Spike capitulates, the fact remains that he has engaged in smuggling, treason, theft, and murder before the marines' mastery of "the mazes of the reef" finally exceeds his own (652). In this labyrinthine terrain where safe harbors are reached by nearly unnavigable passageways, Reef knowledge— the ability to read and respond to the Florida Reef in all of its nearly unpredictable sinuosities and transformations—is the highest currency.

To the modern reader, Cooper's extreme Reef obsession can seem puzzling, especially given the Reef's initial obscurity for the novel's central characters. Upon the *Swash*'s arrival at the Dry Tortugas, even its first mate is unable to identify the place, for he has no idea where he is or whether to call it "land" (499). Yet several seemingly minor episodes register an awareness that these isolated islets are potentially the "key" to the Gulf of Mexico, and thereby to the Western Hemisphere at large. In a conversation that seems all but forgettable, one character asks another about the geography of Key West, inquiring, "Of what lock is this place the key?" "The key meant is an island," responds one interlocutor, but Mulford offers a different answer. Picking up on an earlier observation that "Gibraltar is the key of the Mediterranean," the first mate reflects that Key West "may turn out to be the key to the Gulf of Mexico, one of these days" (539).

This discussion identifies Key West as a "key" in two ways: as a low-lying island situated at the place where the Gulf meets the Atlantic, it is a topographic key *and* a metaphorical one that could open the door to U.S. command over the Gulf. The realization marks the development of Mulford's gradual understanding that the part of the Reef he is at first unable to call land is ground of great geopolitical significance. With the aid of a sextant and navigational charts he discovers that the "haven in which the *Swash* lay" is more than an abandoned coral outcropping; the Dry Tortugas is a site he already knows from books and "sea-gossip" as "the very spot in the contemplation of government for an outer man-of-war harbour, where fleets might rendezvous in the future wars of that portion of the world" (501). Such scenes tether the novel to a larger nineteenth-century political discussion of the Reef and announce Cooper's perception that the prospect of mastering "the merest islets imaginable" held high imperial stakes (499).

Gibraltar of the Gulf

In December 1846, just one month after the first installment of Cooper's novel in *Graham's Magazine* (Philadelphia) and *Bentley's Miscellany* (London), the U.S. Army began onsite planning of Fort Jefferson, a military fort that would stand on Florida's Dry Tortugas.[14] Though the fort's construction would not begin until 1847, plans for fortifying this part of the Reef had been under way since 1829, and Congress had recognized the strategic importance of the location as early as 1822—the year after Florida's official annexation to the United States—by appropriating funds for Garden Key lighthouse (303–4). Fort Jefferson would require several decades of slave labor. It was to be a massive six-sided structure three tiers high, a half mile in circumference, and large enough to house a garrison of 1,500 men in wartime (306). This expenditure of time, money, and resources on a gigantic fort set on tiny islets, today abandoned by all but the National Park Service, is difficult to understand without some historical context establishing the enormous global significance that the Florida Reef had achieved by the mid-nineteenth century.

The Reef's capacity to render its possessor sovereign of the seas had begun to emerge long before Florida became U.S. ground, as early modern reflections on the location illustrate. In *Report of the General Survey* (1772), the subject of Chapter 1, William Gerard De Brahm recognizes the geopolitical importance of the Reef by sincerely advising King George III to adorn it with a pair of beacons modeled partly on the ancient Pharos of Alexandria—a lighthouse considered one of the Seven Wonders of the World—and partly on the Pillars of Hercules, the name for the natural promontories at the entrance to the Strait of Gibraltar.[15] Accompanying De Brahm's sketch, titled *View and Profile of a Pharus* (Figure 20), is a set of instructions: the pharuses should be engraved "with the excellent appellations of George and Charlotte" so as to "eternalize the glory of those Royal Authors, who have stretched out parental hands to facilitate the hitherto dangerous, and inevitable, navigation of that dreadfull promontory [of Florida] and terminate your Majesty's conquest of that great Country, which sets the western bounds of the Atlantic Ocean."[16] This inscription suggests that Great Britain's conquest of the Reef would mark a hitherto impossible conquest of the Atlantic, much as the Pillars of Hercules sometimes signified Great Britain's capacity to sail beyond the *plus ultra* of knowledge itself. Perhaps De Brahm had even seen and borrowed from the frontispiece of Sir Francis Bacon's *Instauratio magna* (1620), for the pharuses strikingly resemble the Pillars of Hercules as Bacon portrays them (Figure 21).

By deeming the Reef a fitting site for these monuments to imperial mastery, De Brahm drew on and contributed to an understanding of the Reef that many other British persons voiced in response to public criticism of their government's acquisition of Florida from Spain in 1763. Such critiques stemmed from the fact that Great Britain's acquisition of Florida—widely considered an agricultural backwater—came at the cost of relinquishing claims to Cuba, a powerful foothold in the Caribbean. Defenders of the acquisition accordingly began to describe Florida as such a foothold. Despite its agricultural deficiencies, they averred, the place was so strategically positioned that it more than compensated for the loss of Cuba. For example, in an essay appearing in London's *Universal Museum*, the writer fashions Florida as a location that "will greatly facilitate our navigation to [the Gulf of Mexico]," and suggests that, by stationing a naval force on the Florida coast, it can become "as distressful" to the Spanish as Cuba.[17] The outer edges of Florida are thus interchangeable with an island of such importance to maritime dominion that European empires had long hailed it as the "key to the Gulf of Mexico."[18]

In fact, while Cuba continued to retain its status as Gulf "key," it was no longer singular in that regard after the early 1760s. As a direct result of Great Britain's struggle to maintain and expand control over the Gulf, the Florida Reef popularly gained an enormous strategic significance that it never quite lost. For, during the nineteenth century, Americans supporting the U.S.

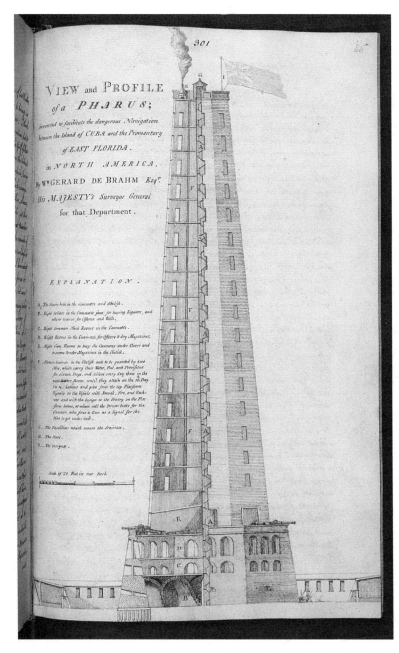

Figure 20. William Gerard De Brahm, *View and Profile of a Pharus* (1764). © The British Library Board. (Kings MS 211).

Figure 21. Francis Bacon, *The Pillars of Hercules* (1620), *Instauratio Magna*, title page. HM 601343, The Huntington Library, San Marino, California.

acquisition of Florida adopted the "key" metaphor as a particularly useful way to combat criticism of their nation's controversial annexation of the peninsula from Spain in 1821. A writer in the *National Advocate* declared in 1824 that "Thompson's Island"—the original name of Key West—"forms with the Havana the key to the Gulf of Mexico."[19] In 1829 naval strategists suggested that Cuba was unnecessary to the United States; for the Dry Tortugas are the "Key to the Mexican Gulf," and a "naval force, designed to control the navigation of the Gulf, could desire no better position."[20] And in 1845, as plans for Fort Jefferson neared completion, a Tallahassee newspaper proclaimed that the "Tortugas, properly fortified, would be as effectual a key to the Gulf of Mexico, as the Island of Cuba."[21]

Importantly, during this period, the phrase "key to the Gulf" designated a site enabling mastery over much more than the Gulf region. British and American observers alike frequently imagined the Gulf's "key" as a key to the Western Hemisphere. In 1824, Joel Roberts Poinsett, a U.S. statesmen best known for his interventions in Latin America, argued that "Cuba is not only the key of the Gulph of Mexico, but of all the maritime frontier south of Savannah, and some of our highest interests, political and commercial, are involved in its fate."[22] And in an 1849 essay, "Cuba: The Key of the Mexican Gulf," a prominent supporter of filibustering argues that Cuba, as "key," not only "locks up, in a closed ring, the whole sweep of the Mexican Gulf," but enables access to "all the other West India islands," "Central America," and "all the short routes to the Pacific—those routes through which a revolutionized commerce is preparing to pour a golden tide upon our shores."[23] Such statements attest that whoever held the "key to the Gulf" also mastered the Caribbean, South America, and even the Pacific.

As the Gulf's "key," then, the Florida Reef required nothing less than Fort Jefferson, an "American Gibraltar," as the fort was sometimes called.[24] The expensive and elaborate fortification of these tiny and remote islets even seems practical in comparison to the ornate "pharuses" that De Brahm had proposed. Yet the history of Fort Jefferson's construction during the nineteenth century is not, after all, a story of U.S. imperial prowess unfolding over new and uncharted ground.

Several infamous episodes in the fort's nearly forty-year construction history reveal that U.S. politicians, engineers, and architects proceeded in dangerous oblivion to the instability and impermanence of coral foundations, persistently failing to heed warnings that a site surrounded by the sea and rising only three feet above it could never sustain a fort of immense proportions. After construction began in 1847 it took almost nine years of slave labor for the fort's walls to begin showing above the waters of the Gulf. At the outbreak of the Civil War the fort was only half-finished, and the structure made an especially miserable confinement for prisoners of war, including Dr. Samuel A. Mudd, the physician who treated John Wilkes Booth. And then, during the 1870s, the partly built fort began to sink. As one historian observes, "the island was literally slipping from beneath the gigantic mass of masonry," and experiments on the subsoil revealed no bedrock within eighty feet of sea level. This discovery in no way deterred construction, however, which continued even after a hurricane ravaged the incomplete edifice in 1874. Only in the 1880s, as wharves rotted and walls sustained additional hurricane damage, was the fort's obvious impropriety acknowledged. After four decades of construction—impeded by tides, storms, and sinking sands—the project was terminated. Floridian topography, geography, and climate had won.[25]

Even in its most advanced stage of construction during the 1860s the fort conveyed a sense of its own obsolescence, as popular antebellum reflections suggest. An army surgeon stationed at the Dry Tortugas during the Civil War assures readers of *Harper's Magazine* that one day the fort "will be a work of extraordinary strength, and one of great importance to the country," yet many of his observations belie this claim. "How much this all looks like some fairy scene, some floating castle!" he marvels upon first sight (260, 261).[26] "The walls rise from the very sea and are only protected from it by a low wall which incloses a moat sixty feet in width." A print appearing in another volume of *Harper's* similarly conveys Fort Jefferson's vulnerability to the waves (Figure 22).[27] The structure appears afloat, as though it might easily come unmoored and drift away. Its external walls abut the ocean, and the right half of the edifice even slopes a little toward the water. Such descriptions and images of a fort slightly too susceptible to the sea could not exactly have inspired readers with confidence in the structure's durability and historical relevance.

Fort Jefferson's history indicates that, though Americans considered mastery of the Reef critical to the nation's security and expansion, they misunderstood the nature of Reef terrain. Popular metaphors of the Reef as "key" and "Gibraltar" promoted Florida's annexation and the fort's construction, yet falsely suggested that the Reef was solid rock, and thereby obscured the fact that coral foundations would not sustain a fort of massive proportions. In the end, the military could not pursue on the edges of Florida the princi-

Figure 22. "Fort Jefferson, Tortugas (Key West), Florida," *Harper's Weekly.* New York, February 23, 1861. HM 499752, The Huntington Library, San Marino, California.

ples of design and construction that might secure mastery of other land-scapes, and even other coasts and islands that shifted less continually. Yet not all antebellum observers used the same Reef metaphors.

During the same decades when many enthusiastic proponents of Fort Jefferson called the Reef America's "key," a different conception of the Reef also took shape, largely as a way of promoting another federal project in Florida that also failed to materialize: a trans-peninsular canal. Early proponents of the canal that would bisect Florida, connecting the Atlantic to the Gulf and allowing U.S. cargo ships to bypass the Reef altogether, asserted that Reef topography would compromise U.S. empire as long as a canal remained undredged. Arguing for the Florida canal, Senator Josiah Johnston of Louisiana characterized the Reef as "a narrow, crooked, and dangerous channel between Cuba and Florida," "bound by shoals, reefs, and keys, with a strong, irregular, and unequal current, exposed alike to the storms and calms that prevail there."[28] As the nation's "only outlet to the Atlantic," he continued, the Reef is "our vulnerable point" where "the loss of property and lives is incalculably great." Other canal boosters concurred, even pointing out that, without a canal, the "key" was still Cuba: the canal alone would remove the need to annex the island, for "Cuba [will cease] to be of any importance to us" once "the commerce of the Indies, and of the Southern continent" can "pass through our borders." Then "the various commercial, military, and political advantages of this great nation 'rising into destinies beyond the reach of mortal eye,' will be developed."[29]

Such descriptions betray that political acquisition of Florida had not secured the "key to empire." For despite the confidence of many politicians and naval strategists, possession remained nominal without the capacity to move deftly through shifting and intricate Reef terrain, a feat that no fort could accomplish. In truth, even supporters of Fort Jefferson sometimes implied as much when reflecting on the Reef. An especially illuminating example is "The Maritime Interests of the South and West" (1843), a series of essays that characterizes the Reef as America's "mouth." For the "welfare and safety of the whole country," the writer declares, the Dry Tortugas "must be fortified." This is because the true "*mouths*" of the Mississippi River are "not at the Balize [near New Orleans]; they are in the straits of Florida." "Key West and the Dry Tortugas are in a position for commanding these straits," he explains, and in fact "the Tortugas Islands occupy the most commanding position along the entire seaboard of this country. They are the *keys* to all the wealth which the Mississippi pours into the Gulf for commerce."[30] In other words, the Reef must be fortified because it is the inlet and outlet of the Mississippi.

The argument is persuasive, yet in making it the writer equivocates between two very different metaphors for locations along the Reef. While both "key" and "mouth" designate sites of strategic significance, a "key" differs vastly in character from a "mouth." Keys unlock and open a way that was before closed; the possessor of a key holds the power to block the path forward, to protect a coveted route, and to choose who passes through. But when it comes to mastery, a mouth is a less certain possession. As the entryway itself, a mouth is more than a portal to and from other places. It may also be a harbor or an inlet that contains, conceals, and even swallows, as the writer more explicitly suggests in another installment of the series. The Dry Tortugas, he explains, "afford shelter for vessels of every class, with the greatest facility of ingress and egress. And there can be no doubt that an adversary, in possession of large naval means, would, with great advantage, make these harbours his habitual resort, and his point of general rendezvous and concentration for all operations on this sea. With an enemy thus posted, the navigation of the Gulf by us would be imminently hazardous if not impossible."[31] As a "mouth" rather than "key," the Reef is much more difficult to master.

By equivocating between "key" and "mouth" the author of "Maritime Interests" concisely captures a familiar quandary for imperial expansion presented by places resistant to agrarian settlement. In the rhetoric of Manifest Destiny, passageways such as deserts, oceans, and rivers frequently figure as sites both critical to and potentially disruptive of expansionist projects.[32] For example, while the Mississippi River was the market road for western farmers, it did not just carry U.S. cargo to domestic and world markets; it also conducted foreign influences and bodies into U.S. space.[33] Like the Mississippi, the Reef had the power to both boost commerce and also compromise it because its fluid ground could enable illicit transactions and conceal populations resistant to the imperatives of empire. And, unlike a river's mouth, a reef's mouth has teeth: the physical nature of the Reef, with its sharp coral edges lining innumerable, sinuous passages, gave additional power to whoever could navigate it.

Antebellum Americans across the nation had reason to reflect on the difficulty of navigating the "mouths" of the Reef. First and foremost, ships laden with U.S. cargo almost always exited or entered the Gulf by passing between Florida and Cuba.[34] A great quantity of cotton and other commodities from the ports of New Orleans, Galveston, Apalachicola, and Mobile passed over the Reef on the way to ports along the Eastern Seaboard and in Europe, while merchants and planters of the Gulf region and the West relied on goods passing back in from the Atlantic.[35] By the 1850s, the estimated value of U.S. ships and cargo that passed annually over the Florida Reef was between $300 and $400 million. And because success required mastering a circuitous and narrow coral channel, which was made more impassable by a strong and irregular current, high winds, and poor charts, the insurance on vessels heading for the Florida Straits was equal to that of those passing around Cape Horn.[36] The illegal slave trade provided another reason for Americans to ponder the Reef's many mouths: it was not uncommon to take slaves from Africa to Cuba, and then smuggle them into the United States by way of Key West.[37] For these reasons, the developing commercial, political, and cultural potential of the United States largely belonged to those who accurately read the Reef.

Cooper's novel of a relatively small, onetime illicit exchange of U.S. gunpowder for Mexican doubloons in a secluded harbor at the Dry Tortugas thus registers a conceptual problem with large political stakes during the antebellum period: the navy's incapacity to read the Reef jeopardized U.S. empire. For the Reef of *Jack Tier* is the place of "narrow, crooked, and dangerous channel[s]" described by proponents of the Florida canal, and Cooper questions the propriety of fortification as an adequate military solution to the problems of surveillance that *Jack Tier* dramatizes. Reference to Fort Jefferson is conspicuously absent from the novel, given that construction of the structure began while Cooper was writing the work (1846–48) and on the very ground of the story's setting.[38] Furthermore, Cooper's Reef is entirely hostile to any permanent building. "To live at Key West is the next thing to being at sea," explains the narrator, who relates that the southern reaches of the peninsula boast "a climate in which hurricanes seem to be the natural offspring of the air," and where a storm once "converted into a raging sea" the lower part of Key West, and "washed away" most of the town, which had to be rebuilt once "the ocean retired and the island came into view again" (664).

It took the War Department several decades to discover the impropriety of fortifying a heap of sand and coral. Cooper seems more prescient. And the novel offers more than disenchantment with efforts to render the Reef an American Gibraltar. A key conceptual insight of *Jack Tier* is Cooper's proposal of a more effective model of surveillance in the form of Florida wreckers who appear at both the center and edges of the narrative, and master its setting by moving fluidly.

Reef Passages to Empire

An 1861 political cartoon by Currier & Ives titled "The Dis-United States. Or, The Southern Confederacy" features the leaders of several Confederate states seated atop objects that best represent their region's commercial interests (Figure 23). At the far left of the print governor of South Carolina Francis Pickens perches on the back of a slave and lamely attempts to proclaim himself the "file leader and general whipper in of the new Confederacy." "Obey and tremble!" he commands, while other opportunistic leaders disregard this call, demanding that the nation prioritize their particular state's economy: Louisiana declares, "A heavy duty must be levied on foreign sweetening," while Alabama proclaims, "Cotton is King!"

The cartoon explicitly satirizes dissension within the newly formed Confederacy, but it also registers a rather disturbing relationship between the Florida Reef and the nation's economy as a whole.[39] In contrast to the sharply

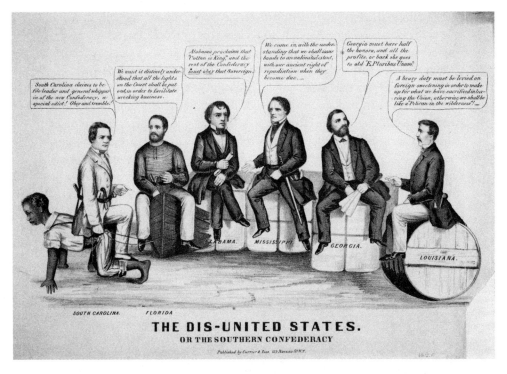

Figure 23. *The Dis-United States. Or The Southern Confederacy,* Currier & Ives (1861). The Library Company of Philadelphia.

dressed representatives resting on commodities such as slaves, cotton, and sugar, Florida's delegate, Senator Stephen R. Mallory, unceremoniously straddles the hull of a small boat and demands support for the Florida wrecker. Sporting a sloppy ensemble of slacks and tunic, the raffish Mallory states, "We want it distinctly understood that all the lights on the Coast shall be put out, in order to facilitate wrecking business." The unstated point of the cartoon is that Florida—via wreckers—thrives on the destruction of commodities that literally uphold other U.S. states.[40]

Florida wreckers, essentially salvagers of wrecked ships, were the true masters of the Florida Reef for much of the nineteenth century. Wreckers made the Reef their permanent home and source of income by spending most of their lives on small boats waiting for, and sometimes causing, shipwrecks so they could rescue distressed crews in return for a substantial portion of the cargo, sometimes as much as 75 percent. By the mid-nineteenth century, when hundreds of millions of dollars of U.S. goods passed annually over the Reef, the U.S. government sought to regulate the practice of wrecking by demanding that wreckers obtain licenses and bring goods to salvage courts where the nation's wrecked property could be legitimately adjudicated.

Arguments for the establishment of a salvage court at Key West emphasize the wide national stakes of the Florida wrecker's Reef knowledge. "You will at once admit that the interest of the United States is deeply involved" in the regulation of Florida wrecking, wrote Florida's first territorial governor, William P. DuVal, to the secretary of state in 1825. For, DuVal explains, "much of the property Wrecked is smuggled by [wreckers] under the pretence of taking it for adjudication to different ports."[41] While DuVal does not specify which ports, he probably has nearby Spanish and British ones in mind, since he notes the temptation wreckers find in "the Contiguity of Cuba and other Islands" (364). Later that year the Legislative Council of Florida urged Congress to establish a salvage court, without which "the planter is deprived in an hour of the product of his twelve months labour," "the capitalists of the Country become bankrupt and the energies and enterprise of the Citizen are enervated and destroyed" (379).

Antebellum calls for legal regulation of Florida wrecking reveal that it is not the peril of the Reef alone that "deprives" North American planters, capitalists, and citizens; for if the threat of shipwreck were the only problem, then a lighthouse or coastal survey would help. The real threat of the Reef is the wreckers. Whereas shipwreck renders U.S. goods valueless, salvage renders them valuable to someone other than their original owner. Through the hands of Florida wreckers who frequently sold their plunder to the highest bidder, the products of U.S. labor enriched local adventurers and "ports beyond the limits of the United States," including those belonging to empires rivaling for control over the Gulf.[42]

Popular antebellum representations of wreckers uneasily acknowledge the wrecker's Reef knowledge. This uncomfortable recognition drives the moral outrage of an 1807 essay in the *Natchez Gazette* wherein the writer asserts that, though wreckers could sometimes be "honest and serviceable," they were still *"men of prey"* who used their familiarity with the Reef to manipulate the weak.[43] As evidence, the writer offers a dialogue between one Mr. Kinen and a Florida wrecker "whom he fell in with in passing through the Bahamas." When Mr. Kinen learns that his interlocutor has just completed a four-month stint "along the Florida shore" with a company of "forty sail," he remarks that such a large group of wreckers "certainly . . . must have had many opportunities of being essentially serviceable to vessels passing the Gulf Stream," either "by directing them to keep off the danger, with which you made it your business to become acquainted," or by lighting beacons to give "timely notice" of the Reef. "No, no," the wrecker laughs, "we always put [the lights] out, for a better chance." In response to Kinen's closing question of whether there would not have been "more humanity" in showing the vessels their danger, the wrecker replies, "*I did not go there for humanity I went RACKING.*"[44] "So much for *Sea Wreckers*," concludes the writer.

The main subject of the writer's vitriol is the Florida wrecker's relationship to the Reef, which the writer calls "the danger, with which you made it your business to become acquainted." He emphasizes the exploitative nature of this relationship when, after the conversation between Kinen and the wrecker, the writer suggests that the label "wrecker" be applied to a variety of other beguilers who use their specialized knowledge to unscrupulous ends. These include such debased charmers as seducers of "the fair," ministers who "feed the flock with poisonous doctrines," corrupt politicians, and newspaper editors who abuse their privileges.

Charges of topographic treachery persisted as a mainstay of nineteenth-century depictions of the wrecker. In a newspaper article about the brig *Rising Sun*, which struck against the Florida Reef in May 1819, a passenger reports that the struggling ship was immediately beset by "harpies of wreckers," who, "basely taking advantage of our unarmed and dependent situation," "defrauded all the cargo" and "bore away with their spoil" before the crew managed to get the ship afloat again.[45] An 1823 settlers' guide to Florida warns prospective emigrants that wrecking along the Reef "has been reduced to a perfect system": the wreckers "know so well how much ships are exposed" along the Reef that they simply wait at a strategic location "for the sight of any ship, that is so unfortunate as to be driven ashore."[46] And in 1845, E. Z. C. Judson, who authored popular dime novels under the pen name Ned Buntline, repeated these sentiments in a periodical essay on John Jacob Housman, who lives on in local Florida lore as the "wrecker king" of Indian Key, an eleven-acre islet where he developed a thriving community of wreckers before his death at sea in 1841. Judson implies that Housman's success was due to a nefarious use of superior topographic knowledge: "I have heard loud whispers of 'false lights' and 'bribed captains' from those best acquainted with the man and his actions," records Judson, alluding to the frequent charge that wreckers used lanterns to confuse captains and pilots about the shape and location of the Reef, and thus lure them into perilous proximity.[47] And an 1859 *Harper's* essay recounts the tragic tale of the ship *America*, which smashed against the Reef near the Dry Tortugas. The writer, a passenger aboard the ship, explains that though many "speculations were indulged upon . . . how it was possible the ship could have been drawn so much out of our course," the captain believed the wreck was no accident, insisting that "the keeper of the light-house, in complicity with some wrecker, had willfully obscured the light, in the hope of luring the ship to her destruction on the reef." " 'We are,' he exclaims, 'victims of the piratical wreckers!' " The wrecker's characterization as arch-manipulator is complete with the assertion that the encounter of captain and wrecker is comparable to "Byron's description of the meeting of Gabriel and Satan."[48]

Given such vitriol, it is somewhat surprising to note that many antebellum Americans considered Florida wreckers to be saviors of cargo and men. Yet defenses of wreckers only confirm their superior aptitude on coral terrain, and thereby remind readers that the Gulf's "key" did not belong to the United States. A concise and widely circulating example of such a reminder is volume 3 of Audubon's *Ornithological Biography* (1835), which contains a defense of Florida wreckers that is haunted by the disturbing recognition of their true relation to U.S. commerce. When seeking waterfowl along the Keys during his trip to Florida (1831–32) Audubon recorded his experiences as "episodes" included in the *Biography* under short titles such as "The Wreckers of Florida," an installment that begins with a confession. Long before reaching "the lovely islets that border the southeastern shores of Florida, the accounts I had heard of 'The Wreckers' had deeply prejudiced me against them."[49] Having been told tales of the "cruel and cowardly methods . . . they employed to allure vessels of all nations to the dreaded reefs, that they might plunder their cargoes, and rob their crews and passengers of their effects," he associates "with the name of Wreckers . . . ideas of piratical depredations, barbarous usage, and even murder" (337–38). Yet Audubon is delighted to discover that the wreckers he meets are actually quite nice. They welcome him aboard their ship, supply him with natural specimens, serve dinner, admire his drawings, join him on a shooting and collecting expedition of "birds that were rare on the coast, and of which they knew the haunts," and even sing, "frolic," and collect seashells (339–40). In short, all were "extremely social and merry" and "we parted friends" (339). The episode concludes with an acquaintance's favorable account of these "honest-looking," "well-drest," "good-natured sons of Neptune, who manifested a disposition . . . to afford every facility to persons passing up and down the Reef," and the lyrics of a lively jig about Florida wreckers who "save de cargo and de people's lives" (342).[50]

While some of Audubon's experiences with wreckers contradict many popular perceptions, however, others confirm that wreckers are still "men of prey." Audubon's first encounter with a wrecking boat, for example, emphasizes the advantages that accrue to the wrecker by his absolute mastery over the difficult terrain of the Reef. "What a beautiful vessel!" Audubon exclaims. "[H]ow trim, how clean-rigged, and how well manned! She swims like a duck; and now with a broad sheer, off she makes for the reefs. . . . There, in that narrow passage, well known to her commander, she rolls, tumbles, dances, like a giddy thing. . . . Reader, it was a Florida Wrecker!" (338). The wrecker's ability to deftly maneuver the circuitous Reef is manifest in the very form of his vessel, "so well adapted to her occupation," and Audubon particularly marvels at its command of the Dry Tortugas, which are threaded with "deep channels" that, "although extremely intricate, are well known to those adventurers" (338, 349).[51]

And despite Audubon's enchantment, he is deeply aware of the wreckers' capacity to interfere with U.S. commerce. An episode entitled "The Florida Keys (II)" recounts the experience of a "hurricane, such as not unfrequently desolates the sultry climates of the South," and which "like the scythe of the destroying angel . . . [cut] everything by its roots, as it were, with the careless ease of the experienced mower." In its "wildness and fury" the storm demolishes mansions, crops, and flocks, forcing the planter to "clear his lands anew, covered and entangled as they are with the trunks and branches of trees that are everywhere strewn" (335). The storm even defeats sailors, their barks "cast on the lee-shore." Yet one class of men both survives and thrives on this ravaging of property: "if any are left to witness the fatal results, they are the 'wreckers' alone, who, with inward delight, gaze upon the melancholy spectacle" (335). When, "far off on the reefs," they begin salvaging "the last remains of a lost ship," Audubon "[turns] from the sight with a heavy heart" and counts himself fortunate in avoiding the gruesome spectacle of the crew's "floating or cast-ashore bodies" (337).

Yet he meets with other remains: in the wake of the storm there are "bales of cotton floating in all the coves" (337). Cotton wrecked, which is slave labor rendered valueless, is good cause for melancholy, but cotton salvaged is more so. These bales are likely to be collected by the wreckers gazing on the scene with "inward delight." And, by presiding over such remains, they in fact manage an economy intended to fuel U.S. empire. Audubon's reflections are thus haunted by a recognition of the wrecker's true potential that also troubles the Currier & Ives print, drove federal efforts to regulate wrecking, and caused many antebellum Americans to regard the wrecker with outrage and dread. For finally, whether viewed as savior or "Satan," the wrecker by his very existence signaled that the nation's path to empire in fact belonged to local drifters turning Reef knowledge into personal profit. In the wake of Florida's annexation to the United States, one writer put it this way: wreckers "have openly declared they will never leave the reef," and they "seem to consider themselves possessed of a right in the *wrecking ground* as their own individual property, independent of any change of government."[52]

Cooper, however, does not lament the wreckers' Reef mastery. In *Jack Tier*, he stands in awe of wreckers, largely because of the instructive possibilities they offer an expanding empire. Hundreds of pages into the novel, we learn that Florida wreckers had been there all along when Mulford remarks on how many of them are "hovering about the reef" (619). The narrator then relates that Key West is "the resort of few beside wreckers," who use the location as a temporary headquarters from which they are always ready to move quickly to any point along the Reef (664). Spike observes that a ship stranded anywhere near the Keys has a high chance of rescue, "when you consider how many of them devils of wreckers hang about these reefs." And, indeed, when Spike's brig finally sinks at the end of the novel, wreckers are the first responders, heading out to sea "the moment the news of the calamity of the *Swash* reached their ears" (632, 672). By using Key West as a "resort," and "hovering" and "hanging" about the Reef, the wreckers of *Jack Tier* enact a model of territorial possession that thrives on coral terrain.

Yet the novel's fullest endorsement of a wrecker's understanding of and adaptation to the Reef is the narrator's identification of Captain Spike and his crew as "wreckers." As the antagonists plunder Montefalderon's Mexican schooner in order to salvage more doubloons from its hold, the marines aboard the *Poughkeepsie* observe the action from a distance, and the narrator explains that "a swift cruiser, like the ship-of-war, would soon have been alongside of *the wreckers*, but for the intervening islets and the intricacies of their channels" (524; emphasis added). This identification encourages us to perceive the antagonists as more than traitors who thwart the U.S. Navy. As wreckers, they are successful practitioners of coral possession worthy of emulation. Viewed in this way, the novel's many scenes of Spike's near victory over the navy display and resoundingly recommend his superior acquaintance with the Reef's "singular and solitary" harbors, "mazes," and "crooked and narrow passages," and his use of small craft for "running in the channels of the reef" that a larger vessel could never manage (655, 500, 499, 520, 652).

Importantly, Cooper's description of how fictional wreckers master the Florida Reef of *Jack Tier* accords strikingly with an historical description of Commodore David Porter's mastery of the same region during the 1820s. In the 1853 edition of *History of the Navy of the United States of America*—a work published after Cooper's death, though partly authored by Cooper and based closely on his manuscripts and dictations—we learn that Porter secured Gulf commerce and diminished piracy in the West Indies by using a strategy of mobility and dispersal.[53] According to the *History*, Porter "divided his force into small detachments, and in this way thoroughly scoured the coasts of all the islands to the north of Porto Rico, including St. Domingo and Cuba" (25). Next, he established a naval depot at Key West, a "point he made the center of his operations, and the rendezvous of his vessels after their short cruises" (25). In other words, Porter ensured U.S. naval sovereignty over the region by using one location as a temporary "rendezvous" from which to continually send out "small detachments" over the reef- and island-studded seascape. The result is that "piracy as a system was effectually broken up" (25). Indeed, Porter's strategy was so effective that his "system of marine police . . . was still maintained by his successor" (30).

There are unmistakable resonances among Porter's effective mode of Reef surveillance and that of the Florida wreckers of *Jack Tier* and a wealth of other antebellum reflections on wrecking along the Reef. Just as Cooper's wreckers make Key West a "resort" from which to move out quickly over the Reef, Porter uses Key West as a central depot from which to send small boats on "short cruises." Just as the wreckers perpetually "hover" and "hang" about the Reef, Porter's forces move in "small detachments" among "the coasts of all the islands to the north of Porto Rico." The strategy succeeds because of continual motion: the message is that mobility enables ubiquity on terrain too treacherous for more stationary tactics, whether a fort or a massive naval ship. After all, had the navy of *Jack Tier* adopted a more mobile strategy, then the smugglers may never have entered the Gulf to disappear among the islets of the Florida Reef in the first place.

Finally, Cooper's examples of Reef mastery redefine "the key to empire" not as the Reef itself, but rather as the model of sovereignty, maintained by fluidity, that the Reef requires. In 1848, the year of *Jack Tier*'s publication in book form, the novel holds a valuable expansionist lesson for American readers. Scholars have considered 1848 a "watershed year" in the history of U.S. empire, for thereafter the United States would strive more ambitiously for commercial domination of the Americas.[54] Unlike continental expansion, the pursuit of an overseas commercial empire would not involve incorporating contiguous lands and large populations. Rather, the mid-nineteenth-century course of empire presented a new conceptual challenge because extending beyond the continent required assuming and managing an alternate geographic form altogether. This form is difficult to imagine within the terms of the more familiar, land-based, continental model of expansion. Yet the local terrain of the Florida Reef—both geographically dispersed and topographically shifting—provided a testing ground for sovereignty in the absence of stability, contiguity, and solidity. And, to a burgeoning empire, stories of those who mastered such terrain offered lessons—not only in territorial surveillance, but also in the resilience of local populations on ground that had eluded its grasp.

Chapter 4

Florida Marronage: Everglades, Swamp, Savannah, Hammock

Map of the Seat of War in Florida (1838) provided U.S. viewers with an unprecedented level of knowledge about the topography of the Florida peninsula (Figure 24).[1] It was quickly reproduced under the same title during the following year, and a publication notice appearing in the *Army and Navy Chronicle* hails the reproduction as a tremendous achievement: crediting the Army Corps of Topographical Engineers for their excellent work, the writer explains that the map would remove "the most serious obstacle" to winning the Second Seminole War (1835–42), "the want of an accurate knowledge of the topography of the country" (88).[2] Prior to the outbreak of the war few U.S. citizens had reason to venture very far south into Florida, and military actions during the Revolutionary War, the War of 1812, and the First Seminole War (1817–18)—which led to the annexation of Florida from Spain—were confined mostly to the northern part of the territory.[3] But the second war against Florida's communities of Seminoles and their African allies brought thousands of U.S. troops deep into the swampy southern half of the peninsula, where battles sometimes took their names from local features of the Everglades, such as Lake Okeechobee, Loxahatchee, and Big Cypress Swamp.[4]

Prior to their arrival most troops were acquainted with South Florida's topography only by name: "Everglades," a term that first appears in U.S. accounts of Florida in the 1820s, almost certainly means "everlasting glade" and captures the observer's sense of a seemingly interminable watery expanse without landmarks.[5] While today significant portions of the Everglades have been drained and filled by developers, during the nineteenth century the swamp spanned over 2.3 million acres that began at the south shore of Lake Okeechobee and stretched south in a slowly moving sheet of water that one antebellum observer described as a "vast lake" "extending in every direction, from shore to shore, beyond the reach of human vision . . . , studded with thousands of islands of various sizes," and pervaded by an eerie, "solemn silence."[6] But *Map of the Seat of War* was supposed to fill the many blanks in the army's understanding of the region. While a good map such as this one would have spared "much of the blood and treasure" already expended, reflects the author of the map's publication notice, troops would be "better prepared in the future" by having the upper hand on ground that had so far resisted their advances. For the mapmakers had gained a "thorough knowledge of the topography of the whole Territory," and "From the manner in which the map is dotted," he explains, "we should judge that no portion of the Territory had been unexplored." "Every hammock, swamp, lake and river is minutely traced," claims the writer of the publication notice.[7]

However, in truth this claim describes only some portions of the map, and especially the section depicting the northern part of the peninsula. Nearly all of Florida south of Lake Okeechobee remains vague. Instead of being "minutely traced," the Everglades are represented by a repeating pattern of broken horizontal lines and small tufts of grass, a stylized image for watery land that replaces a depiction of any particular swamp, lake, or hammock (see inset at lower right, Figure 24). While this representational choice signifies that the Everglades are terra incognita, another cartographic feature indicates that they are well known, just not to U.S. troops: the mapmakers designate the Everglades by their Seminole name, the label "Pay-hai-o-kee, or Grass Water" appearing in capital letters at the center of the swamp. And just below this label is a faint dotted line spanning the swamp from east to west that reads "Passage for small boats across the Everglades *as reported by the Indians*."[8] These labels acknowledge Indians as authorities on topographic knowledge of the region. One of the first U.S. maps of the Everglades thus portrays the region as territory that defies U.S. experience and understanding, while sustaining other populations.

In fact during much of Florida's Territorial period (1821–45), and well into the first decades of statehood, the Everglades sustained networks among a variety of populations invested in prolonging Florida's resistance to U.S. incorporation. While Indians native to the region had been almost entirely

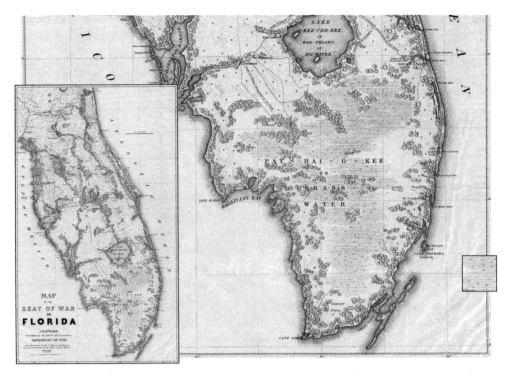

Figure 24. *Map of the Seat of War in Florida* (1838), Everglades detail; entire map pictured in left corner. David Rumsey Map Collection.

decimated by the end of Florida's first period of Spanish rule in 1763, Africans had begun escaping to Florida in the late seventeenth century, followed thereafter by migrating Creeks, today known as Seminole. Members of both groups, frequently united by their resistance to U.S. slavery and Indian removal, continued to live and associate on the peninsula long after the nation's annexation of Florida from Spain in 1821.[9] Additionally, Africans from Cuba, imported and armed by the British during the War of 1812, lived in antebellum Florida, as did white adventurers such as slave traders and filibusters. Florida's populations enlisted the sympathies—and sometimes assistance of—abolitionists in other parts of the country.[10] And the peninsula's geographic proximity to the British West Indies excited U.S. concern that free blacks, or even white emissaries of British empire, would collaborate with populations living on the peninsula to foment a large-scale slave rebellion throughout the South.[11] Thus, from the start of the Second Seminole War in 1835 through the end of the Third Seminole War in 1858—the time span of this chapter—South Florida's swamps, savannahs, and hammocks sustained multiple ethnic and cultural groups beyond U.S. surveillance.

Map of the Seat of War is only one of many published military documents—antebellum America's most plentiful source of information about the Florida interior—to tacitly acknowledge that the Everglades did not belong to the United States because it amply sustained other populations. This recognition infuses a broad range of military essays, letters, and reports that were disseminated widely as successive military invasions made the Everglades an increasing topic of national interest.[12] For example, a war correspondent records in 1836 that South Florida's "hammocks, cyprus swamps and marshes" are "almost impenetrable to the white man," yet "constitute the natural defense of the Indians" (234).[13] The next year a military court of inquiry pinned the failure of a recent campaign on "the impervious swamps and hammocks" that "[afford the enemy] cover and retreat at every step" (463).[14] And at the war's conclusion the nineteenth century's only comprehensive history of the conflict characterized "The swamps and hammocks of Florida" as enemy "strong-holds," a term conveying that these features are not impenetrable to everyone.[15] However, while these and other widely published firsthand accounts affirm that the Everglades resisted U.S. encroachment while harboring other populations, they rarely describe *how* the region's inhabitants established and sustained themselves. For descriptions of life in a place that U.S. troops deemed "impervious," we must turn to imaginative reflections on the antebellum Everglades.

The same swamps, savannahs, and hammocks that many Americans declared impenetrable provoked others to imagine what happened to people—Indian, black, and white—who chose or were forced to live on and among such landscape features. In *The Exiles of Florida: Or, the Crimes Committed by Our Government against the Maroons* (1858), Ohio congressman and radical abolitionist Joshua Reed Giddings uses the technique of literary bricolage to show that Africans in Florida are not escaped slaves, as popularly imagined, but rather settled and rightful claimants of Floridian land.[16] Giddings's account of African history and settlement in Florida exposes the pro-slavery, imperial motivations of popular claims that Africans in Florida are mere "runaways" or "rebels." It shows that the Everglades offers Africans roles other than slave, runaway, or rebel—the roles available to them within a plantocratic and imperial antebellum culture. Thereby Giddings explicitly identifies the central problem the Everglades poses for this culture: in this region, those whom empire sought to absorb were instead "salvaged." Like property wrecked along the Reef, people who retreated to Floridian swamps were both lost to the U.S. imperial project and potentially valuable to its opponents; put otherwise, they were as "impenetrable" as the landscape sometimes was, but only to an empire that could no longer recover them. Earlier Florida fictions similarly sought to narrate the lives of those whom empire could not recode: an anonymous captivity narrative, *Authentic Narrative of the Seminole War; and of the Miraculous Escape of Mary Godfrey* (1836); an anonymous female picaresque, *A Sketch of the Life of Elizabeth Emmons, or the Female Sailor, Who Was Brutally Murdered While at Sea, off the Coast of Florida* (1841); and a pair of frontier novels by Francis Robert Goulding, *The Young Marooners on the Florida Coast* (1852) and *Marooner's Island* (1867).

Collectively, these works use familiar conventions and genres of early U.S. fiction to demonstrate that the Everglades and adjacent swamps enabled Africans, Seminoles, and white adventurers to establish themselves, interact with allies on and beyond the continent, and pursue experiences, economic activities, and roles unavailable to them anywhere else in North America. While these narratives cannot offer access to the real experiences of the region's inhabitants, they affirm significant interest in alternatives to the "imperial construction of U.S. national space" promoted by military maps and other expansionist legal and political documents that sought to erase local populations or "recode" them as willing participants.[17] Local Florida populations, though targets of expansionist violence, could not be expunged from imaginative narratives of the country's incorporation, which they shaped by challenging concepts of subjectivity and space through which the nation was to be made manifest.

Joshua Reed Giddings's Maroon History of Florida

The Columbus, Ohio, printing firm of Follett, Foster, & Company is best remembered today for first publishing the Lincoln-Douglas Debates of 1858 in which Abraham Lincoln challenged the legitimacy of U.S. slavery, largely by emphasizing the dangers of a government that sanctioned the extension of slavery into the western territories. That same year, however, the firm also issued another popular text, Giddings's *The Exiles of Florida*, that challenged the legitimacy of slavery by focusing on another region.[18] A prominent endorsement of *Exiles* that appeared in an early edition of the Lincoln-Douglas debates hails Giddings's work as "The Great Exposé of the Crimes of our

Government against the Slaves."[19] The book is indeed an exposé, but the questions of what Giddings exposes, how he exposes it, and for what purpose, have remained largely unexamined.[20] While the publisher's advertisement describes the subject of exposure as the U.S. government's "crimes" against "slaves," this description is far too general because it could refer to any number of injustices legally carried out against Africans in any part of the nation. The specific crime Giddings exposes in *Exiles* is the government's attempt to sanction the Seminole Wars by concealing the history and ongoing story of African settlement in Florida.

Giddings claims that Florida has been an African homeland on the continent since the early eighteenth century, and that therefore the United States has no right to the land or the African populations living on it. He reasons that if the American public acknowledges this fact, then they must also acknowledge the illegitimacy of invading Florida. Accordingly, he aims to revise an existing perception: during a time when Africans in Florida were commonly considered escaped slaves, and therefore U.S. property, Giddings portrays them as a free, independent community whose sovereignty is grounded in an incontestable claim to the land. This revision depends almost entirely on exposing the imperialist, plantocratic underpinnings of a widely held perception of the relationship between Africans and Floridian ground. The "great Exposé" of *Exiles* is that Africans are *not* temporary occupants of Florida.

This revisionary project begins with Giddings's call for a new and more accurate language for describing Florida's African populations, whom many U.S. citizens have erroneously imagined as "runaways." As one origin of this long-standing misconception Giddings cites a September 1821 letter from Andrew Jackson to Secretary of War John C. Calhoun declaring that all Seminoles and Africans must be removed from Florida. Giddings considers Jackson's letter the first recorded argument for African removal, and he shows that Jackson draws significant support from the observations of the first subagent for Indian affairs in Florida, Jean-Augustin Pénières, who had written a detailed manuscript on the region's populations during July 1821. Giddings is particularly attentive to how Jackson uses, yet alters, Pénières's language: while the subagent occasionally refers to Africans in Florida as "maroons," such as when writing of "the maroon negroes, who live among the Indians," Jackson prefers the term "runaways." In the excerpt from Jackson's letter to Calhoun that Giddings includes in *Exiles*, Jackson declares, "These *runaway slaves, spoken of by Mr. Penieres*, MUST BE REMOVED from the Floridas, or scenes of murder and confusion will exist."[21] To this sentence Giddings appends the following footnote: "It will be observed that General Jackson discarded the term '*maroon*,' used by Penieres, as that in Jamaica, signifies '*free negroes* of the mountains,' who once fled from service, but have maintained their liberty so long that they cannot be identified, and are therefore admitted to be free."[22] According to Giddings, Jackson's revision of "maroons" into "runaways" is a claim that all Africans in Florida are escaped slaves who rightfully belong to masters on southern plantations.

As such a claim, this revision—which depends on Giddings's close reading of a single word—has enormous political implications, though fully comprehending them requires reflecting on some of the reasons why "runaways" was the term that the plantocracy, expansionists, and the political allies of both groups preferred for Florida's African populations. Imagined as "runaways," Africans seem temporarily absent from their proper place. By calling them "runaways" and by labeling maroon communities "camps" and "encampments"—terms suggesting temporary phenomena—the plantocracy and their allies could think of marronage as a brief, intolerable, and even irresponsible, deviation from the norm.[23] Additionally, "runaways" are perpetually unsettled and therefore vulnerable to recapture because they are in a state of continual flight from the plantation. By contrast, "A maroon does not run," but rather "absconds to the nearest and most familiar swamp," where he joins a community already engaged in cultural, economic, and familial networks that extend beyond the plantation.[24]

The observation that the term "maroon" signifies such networks is especially useful for understanding why, in the case of Florida in particular, many supporters of slavery were averse to calling Africans "maroons": Florida enabled networks not only among Africans who had already escaped and formed settlements in the swamp, but also between Africans and Seminole Indians who had inhabited the region since the eighteenth century and shared a hostility toward U.S. expansion and slavery. These Floridian affiliations and hostilities are emphasized by the term "maroon," while it also evokes associations with another group of Africans: the maroons of Jamaica, a population that Florida's Caribbean geography and topography already encouraged antebellum Americans to think of. In other words, it was already easy enough to envision Africans who escaped to Florida increasing the size and strength of a long-established community poised to become the U.S. version of the Jamaican maroons who resisted slavery for so long that, in Pénières's words, "they cannot be identified" by the British, and were consequently deemed legally free. This alarming prospect existed no matter what people chose to call Florida's Africans; yet the term "runaways" denies this prospect. The word implies fleeting and inappropriate occupation of the land and thus allows Jackson to fashion Florida, his most recent territorial annexation, an incipient extension of the U.S. South, rather than a node in a larger Caribbean network of maroon strongholds.

But Giddings's note punctures this fantasy. It exposes the large spatial and racial stakes of Jackson's seemingly minor revision of "maroons" into "runaways," and reveals the pressures that Floridian ground places on Jackson's effort to sustain an imperial perspective on recently annexed space. The geography and topography of Florida provided Africans with a range of experiences and affiliations that enabled them to take on roles other than those that were defined in relation to the plantation and its ideal of surveillance, yet the project of incorporating Florida partly depended on perceiving its Africans inhabitants in roles scripted by plantocratic culture, such as "runaway" or even "rebellious" slave; to do otherwise was to acknowledge Florida's status as maroon territory. When imagined as such, Florida attests that local versions of space and subjectivity persisted on U.S. ground during a time when their effacement was essential to the discourse of incorporation.[25] This version of Florida clearly appealed to Americans who opposed the intertwined projects of slavery and expansion, and many of them embraced the term "maroons" for the same reasons that Jackson opposed it. Giddings, however, preferred still another term.

Through *Exiles* Giddings seeks to forge a different language for Florida's African populations because he knew that he could not rely on the term "maroon" to encourage the perspective on Florida and its inhabitants that Jackson attempted to foreclose. For Giddings, one problem with "maroon" is that, while in some contexts it could signify African self-determination—as Jackson feared—in others it could be used interchangeably with "runaway," and thereby designate a temporary fugitive to be recaptured.[26] This is because, as Giddings recognizes, the English word "maroon" is a corruption of the Spanish *cimarron* or "runaway," a term first used in Hispaniola to refer to feral cattle, then to Amerindians who escaped slavery, and finally mainly to Africans escaping from slavery on Hispaniola.[27] However, in addition to a general concern that "maroon" could carry the connotation of its origin in *cimarron,* or "runaway," Giddings has a concern specific to Africans in Florida: because the English term "Seminole" also derives from the Spanish *cimarron* or "runaway," the word "maroon"—when applied to Africans in

Florida—could encourage people to collapse the distinction between this population and the Seminole, a distinction on which African sovereignty during this historical period sometimes depended.[28] Policies to enslave Florida's African population frequently relied on the claim that they were not distinct from the Seminole, but rather the same as, or slaves of, the Seminole. Both views supported an understanding of Africans in Florida as escaped slaves, and both tended to further their legal enslavement by denying them the prospect of negotiating their own treaties directly with the federal government.[29]

Because "runaway" and "maroon" could too easily suggest that Africans were merely absconding temporarily among the swamps of Florida, and thus sustain arguments for slavery and territorial expansion, Giddings finally rejects both words in favor of "exiles," a term he believes captures the way that members of this population perceived themselves and their relation to the land.[30] "Exiles of Florida" is a designation that anchors their identity not in the original, forced exile from Africa—as a common abolitionist phrase for slaves as "exiles of Africa" tended to do—but rather in their second, self-determined exile that began during the eighteenth century when the first generation, whom Giddings calls the "Frontier Exiles," chose to settle in Florida after escaping from plantations in the Carolinas.[31] Imagined as "exiles of Florida," Africans on the peninsula are not displaced from their native land abroad, but rather settled in a self-designated homeland within the borders of the United States.

Persuading readers to perceive Florida as an African homeland requires discrediting more official U.S. accounts of the region. To this end Giddings employs literary bricolage, an artistic technique that involves excerpting passages from texts that are already in circulation—such as the "official reports, orders, letters, or written evidences" that he mentions in the Introduction—and assembling these excerpts into a new narrative that reveals a message other than, and often counter to, the original intention of these texts.[32] This narrative method was not unfamiliar to antebellum readers. William Wells Brown's novel *Clotel* (1853) is a skillful example, and some observations on this work by Robert Levine are particularly useful for understanding Giddings's *Exiles*. Just as Brown does, Giddings juxtaposes his own original writing with passages imported from a range of existing texts from different discourses. Additionally, his "disruptive juxtapositions" of such texts urge readers to perceive "gaps and blindnesses" in official accounts, and thereby to question their validity.[33]

Giddings establishes this narrative method in the early chapters where he frequently interrupts a factual account, based on official documents, with his reflections on the daily routines, feelings, or thoughts of the Exiles as they cultivate the land, forge communal and economic ties among themselves and with others, and pursue homemaking in Florida. For example, when Giddings presents the history of U.S. attempts to claim Africans in Spanish Florida during the early 1790s, he cites and quotes from texts authored by a number of prominent officials, including the governor of Georgia, an Indian agent to the Creek (whom many in the United States misperceived as the "owners" of Africans in Florida), the U.S. secretary of war, members of the Circuit Court of the United States, officials of the Spanish Crown, and President Washington. But then he sharply breaks from this account, cutting to an imagined scene in the swamps: "While these incidents were transpiring, the Exiles were engaged in cultivating their lands, extending their plantations, and increasing their flocks and herds, and consolidating their friendships with the Indians around them."[34] He next moves the narrative forward to U.S. efforts to seize Florida's Africans during the administrations of Washington, Adams, and Jefferson respectively. But amid excerpts from official documents— a treaty binding the Creek to deliver Africans to the United States, the Fugitive Slave Law of 1793, and legislation holding slaveholders responsible when their slaves escape to Indian tribes—Giddings interjects, "During that period, the fugitives remained quietly in their homes, undisturbed by their former masters. Their numbers were often increased by new arrivals, as well as by the natural laws of population, and they began to assume the appearance of an established community" (26).[35] When the history next proceeds to the Madison administration, Giddings introduces it as follows: "When Mr. Madison assumed the duties of President (March 4, 1809), the Exiles were quietly enjoying their freedom; each sitting under his own vine and fig-tree, without molestation or fear. Many had been born in the Seminole country, and now saw around them children and grand-children, in the enjoyment of all the necessaries of life... feeling their right to liberty was 'self-evident,' they believed the United States to have tacitly admitted their claims to freedom. With these impressions, they dwelt in conscious security" (28–29).

Such juxtapositions prompt readers toward a number of realizations. First, Africans established themselves on Floridian ground long before the origin of the United States. Second, Africans in Florida are permanent landholders, even according to the terms of possession familiar to most U.S. readers: in Florida they own property, cultivate and improve the earth, and establish plantations that they sometimes bequeath to their children.[36] Third, until U.S. troops invaded Florida during the nineteenth century, African settlement of the region continued uninterrupted, and many families have occupied the land for several generations. Fourth, Africans enjoyed legal freedom under Spanish rule, and they have never belonged to anyone, least of all the Seminole, with whom their relationship is one of voluntary and communal "friendship." And finally, Africans in Florida did nothing to provoke U.S. aggression since they "were quietly enjoying their freedom [,]each sitting under his own vine and fig-tree" and considering themselves legally free while the plantocracy and other emissaries of empire drove the United States into the Seminole Wars.

Such realizations should, in turn, prompt antebellum readers to ask questions that erode the foundation of U.S. claims to Floridian land and its African inhabitants. For example, if one secures one's right to land by settling on and cultivating the earth, then why shouldn't Africans in Florida qualify as property owners? If the project of settler colonialism depends on the notion that land cannot rightfully belong to those who "wander" over it, then how is it justifiable to expel Africans from the ground they have remained on as settlers and cultivators, in some cases for successive generations?[37] If the U.S. right to North American land derives partly from an uninterrupted history of Anglo-American proprietorship, then how can the United States dispossess those whose record of settlement dates to a period long before the nation existed? And is it right or desirable to bind Africans in Florida by treaties made with a separate people (albeit Indians), or to enslave those who have already earned their freedom through military service (albeit to Spain)?

Ultimately the bricolage of *Exiles* provokes readers to perceive that military and other official histories of Florida and its populations obscure the fact that Africans rightfully possess Florida, even according to the nation's own nearly sacred definitions of property, possession, and personhood. As powerful as this formulation of Giddings's thesis is, however, it raises a consideration that could limit the potential of *Exiles* to disrupt imperial imaginaries: Giddings's argument for African sovereignty relies on collapsing perceived differences between Africans in Florida and whites in other parts of North America. While this strategy moves readers to sympathize with Africans on the basis of shared values and behaviors, it depends on a logic of sameness that disfranchised many populations in antebellum America by positing an ostensibly universal understanding of humanity. As we have seen,

Giddings insists repeatedly that Africans in Florida base their individual and collective identity on ideals of cultivation, settlement, permanent home-ownership, and domesticity that are familiar to readers of Anglo-American heritage: they "enjoy their plantations and property in peace" (38); bravely defend "their cultivated fields" (74); claim "permanent homes" (233); honor "all the relations of domestic life" (181); and feel deep "attachment to each other as parents and children, as husbands and wives, as members of the human family" (181, 208). These could be accurate assessments, and they would have evoked sympathy from many readers, but they risk missing or dismissing alternate understandings of human-ness that originate within African or African American cultures. Giddings did not observe or converse with Africans in Florida, so even though he purports to describe them in ways that they would endorse, his descriptions are largely products of his imagination, and they conform to certain liberal conventions of personhood that may or may not have structured the actual experiences, beliefs, and feelings of Africans in Florida.[38]

Yet even though *Exiles* may not provide the real history of Africans in Florida, Giddings's most important contribution may be that he provokes readers to recognize that this history has remained untold because of its power to undercut a culturally and politically significant narrative of the nation's incorporation. Early readers perceived the value of this provocation, as some early reviews of the work attest. A reviewer in the *Atlantic Monthly* claims that "Every American citizen should read" *Exiles* because until its appearance "The general impression has been, that [Africans in Florida] were mainly runaways of recent date, who had made their escape from contemporary masters." The reviewer proceeds: "How many of our readers know that for more than three quarters of a century before the purchase of Florida there had been a nation of negroes established there, enjoying the wild freedom they loved . . . ?"[39] A reviewer in *The Liberator* asserts that "The author has done in this work what none else could do. He has brought forth a long array of facts from a sleep that, but for his labors, might have been eternal in the archives of the nation."[40] Both reviewers perceive Giddings's central achievement as a successful exposure of more official histories of Florida as fictions serving slavery and expansion.

A third review best captures the method and stakes of Giddings's exposé. In an extended essay in the *Methodist Quarterly*, the writer praises Giddings because "his liberal quotations from official letters, reports, and state papers have enabled him so to fortify his statements as to put them beyond reasonable question."[41] The writer then zeroes in on Giddings's discussion of documents in which U.S. officials insist on calling Florida's African populations "stolen negroes" and "runaways," and identifies this language as the catalyst for "that long and bloody struggle, of which the world has heard so much, under the name of the Florida War."[42] This insight succinctly conveys the central claim of *Exiles*: many U.S. officials deliberately constructed an identity for Africans in Florida that sanctioned U.S. provocation of the Seminole Wars. And additionally, by recognizing this identity as a construction, the reviewer tacitly acknowledges the possibility that plantocratic and imperial accounts of Florida fail to capture the reality of African identity there. Considered in this way, it matters less that Giddings's reflections on the everyday lives, thoughts, and feelings of Africans are largely his own projections; their value derives from the effect they have of forcing the reader to pause, recognize that many official accounts largely eclipse the history and continuance of African settlement in Florida, and question why they exclude alternate possible versions of African identity.

Finally, then, by presenting the prospect that Floridian ground continues to enable Africans to take on roles that are unimaginable within imperial or plantocratic accounts of African identity, *Exiles* has the potential to dismantle the assumption that all newly acquired U.S. spaces and populations can be "recoded" as domestic. For a sense of what this potential dismantling meant to antebellum Americans invested in the intertwined projects of slavery and empire it is instructive to turn briefly to an official military account of Florida that Giddings knew well and cites frequently in *Exiles*, Lieutenant John T. Sprague's popular military history, *The Origin, Progress, and Conclusion of the Florida War*.[43] In a section of *Origin* called "Florida, Its Position and Destiny," Sprague reflects that the peninsula's geographic position, "in a national point of view, should be regarded," since it raises "a question upon which hangs the destiny of our country."[44] For Florida is uniquely positioned to be "the strong-hold of a powerful foe, who might increase his strength, by inducing" others to join him: blacks from "neighboring" southern states; "tribes of Indians in the interior, instigated by reckless whites of all nations"; and even extracontinental populations, for "Twenty-four hours' sail in a steamer, can transport from the island of New Providence, W. I., to the coast of Florida, a black force . . . backed by a powerful nation" of Britons who had recently freed West Indian slaves (the "black force" in question).[45] Here Sprague briefly envisions Africans using Floridian swamps to create and conceal networks among a variety of populations who combine to foment a large-scale revolt that would force the end of U.S. slavery. Even though in *Exiles* Giddings does not directly explore this possibility, Sprague's reflection hints at one of the terrifying prospects that emerges when, as *Exiles* encourages, antebellum Americans begin to think of Africans in Florida as something other than a brief deviation from the norm—that is, as something other than runaways in a state of continual flight from their proper place.

One way to think of the value of Giddings's text is that it interjects a much needed "what if" into a widely promoted narrative of U.S. expansion into Florida, dramatically extending a possibility only hinted at by military accounts like *Map of the Seat of War*, with which this chapter begins. By narrating the Everglades, and indeed all of Florida, as African space because of this population's relation to the land, Giddings asks whether it is right or possible for the United States to claim the region at all. His vignettes of Africans putting down local roots in Florida expose fictions of space and subjectivity necessary to sustain a broader narrative of imperial expansion. The "what if" of *Exiles*, then, could be phrased in the following way: what if, long after the moment of annexation, Florida draws people into affiliations, circulations, and activities that contribute to cultures and economies beyond and often detrimental to an expanding U.S. empire?

Exiles sharply foregrounds the question that implicitly shapes a broad range of fictional narratives of Territorial Florida that appeared during the two decades before the publication of *Exiles* in 1858, which was also the final year of the Third Seminole War. By the end of this final war in Florida, only small bands of Africans and Seminoles remained on the peninsula. Despite the ongoing violent erasure of these populations during most of the antebellum period, however, they shaped literary reflections on empire in and long after it. Each of the following stories of adventure and settlement on the peninsula emphasizes the difficulty of maintaining an imperial account of Florida and its inhabitants. Such tales are responses—ranging from dread to fascination—to Florida's power to expose the contingency of that account.

Swamp Salvage:
Mary Godfrey and Elizabeth Emmons in the Everglades

An Authentic Narrative of the Seminole War; and of the Miraculous Escape of Mary Godfrey and her Four Female Children is a sensationalized captivity narrative featuring a white woman and her daughters who survive in the wilds of war-torn Florida after being driven from their St. Augustine home by Seminole Indians. Published in the spring of 1836, the text was originally distributed in New York and Providence, Rhode Island, as a pamphlet of twenty-four pages. It likely appealed to antebellum Americans for the same reason that other captivity narratives did: the story provides glimpses of a world that most readers would never experience for themselves. Most of the pamphlet is a war correspondent's verifiable account of the origin and progress of the Second Seminole War, which had begun the previous year. Within this account Godfrey's tale appears as a third-person narrative followed by a first-person narrative purporting to be the words of Godfrey herself. However, like so many other captivity narratives, this one is likely fictional, for there is no evidence that Godfrey existed.[46]

The narrator characterizes Godfrey's story as one of "preservation and deliverance," and indeed the tale seems as "miraculous" as he claims (221). While at home in St. Augustine, "unprotected" by Mr. Godfrey, who had been drafted to fight in the war, Mary and her four daughters hear "the frightful yells of the approaching savages" setting fire to nearby houses (221). Thinking quickly, Mrs. Godfrey gathers the children—one a mere "infant at the breast"—and, as "the only alternative left her by which she could escape from her pursuers was obliged to penetrate into a thick and miry swamp!" (221). Thus the family avoids the "fatal tomahawk" only to find themselves in a desperate situation: concealed in the wilds of Florida with nothing to eat but roots and berries, they expect to be captured and subjected to unspeakable "tortures" at the hands of "savages" whose terrifying "yells" echo through the swamp (222). Days pass, and the family nearly perishes of "pinching hunger and burning thirst" when things turn from bad to worse: the baby's cries attract the attention of "a straggling black, who had enlisted in the cause of the enemy," and the family is stunned by the "sudden and unexpected appearance" of an African brandishing an axe (222). The women "[manifest] their terrors by a united shriek of horror and despair," the children clinging to their mother as she begs for mercy while "The negro, grinning a ghastly smile, as if elated with the discovery, [approaches] them with an uplifted axe, apparently intent on their destruction!" (222).

Until this point, the narrative of Mary Godfrey fully deserves the label of imperial propaganda that several scholars have bestowed upon it.[47] The account thus far resembles many other stories of white settlers in war-ravaged Florida whose plights were dramatized and circulated widely in print as a way of justifying the war.[48] The tableau of a white woman and her four

Massacre of the Whites by the Indians and Blacks in Florida.

The above is intended to represent the horrid Massacre of the Whites in Florida, in December 1835, and January, February, March and April 1836, when near Four Hundred (including women and children) fell victims to the barbarity of the Negroes and Indians.

Figure 25. "Massacre of the Whites by the Indians and Blacks in Florida" (1836). Foldout engraving accompanying the *Authentic Narrative*. Library of Congress, Prints & Photographs Division.

daughters cowering before an armed African would certainly elicit endorsement for ongoing military efforts at Indian removal. Indeed, the image accounts for part of the narrative's early appeal, for it is the subject of two promotional illustrations that accompanied the text. The first, a foldout panorama of Africans and Indians raising hatchets against their white victims, is captioned: "The above is intended to represent the horrid Massacre of the Whites in Florida in December 1835, and January and February 1836, when near four hundred (including women and children) fell victims to the barbarity of the Negroes and Indians" (Figure 25). The second image, a woodcut titled "Horrid Massacres," displays Godfrey and her daughters imploring mercy from an axe-wielding African, his "ghastly" grin sharply delineated by the artist, as if to underscore his malicious delight at discovering the group of helpless white females (Figure 26).

Yet no "horrid massacres" occur in the narrative of Mary Godfrey and her daughters. Here is what actually happens at the climactic moment when "The distracted mother" begs the hatchet-brandishing black to spare her children's lives: "the negro dropped his axe, and after contemplating the sad spectacle for a few moments, appeared much affected, and broke silence by assuring Mrs. G. that she had nothing to fear" (222). In sharp contrast to the terrors of slave revolt shamelessly stoked by the promotional images, the African not only spares the Godfrey family but also ensures their survival,

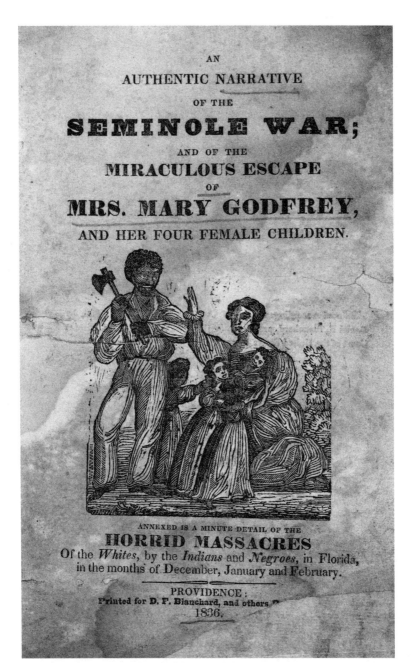

Figure 26. "Horrid Massacres" (1836). Title page of the *Authentic Narrative*. HM 23727, The Huntington Library, San Marino, California.

supplying water and blankets before guiding them to safety at a nearby plantation (223–25). Through the course of the denouement the militant escaped slave becomes "the relenting African," "the friendly negro," and even "the humane African (our deliverer)" (223, 224–25). The African character explains his mercy in the following way: while raising the axe, he was struck by the karmic thought that his own progeny remained enslaved and that, were he to murder the "innocent children" of whites, perhaps "God would be angry, and might doom his little ones to a similar fate" (222).

Yet despite the African's account of this unexpected turn of events, his decision to spare the Godfrey family requires further analysis because it appears radically inconsistent with the explicitly prowar agenda of the pamphlet containing the narrative. After all, the pamphlet's provocative cover image, which promises "horrid massacres" of whites by Africans leagued with Seminoles in Florida, validates the pamphlet's many descriptions of "brave" military actions against such populations (23). Why, then, would the author portray an African in Florida whose cross-racial sympathy on the basis of shared parental values prompts him to rescue a white family at the risk of his loyalties, liberty, and life? Seeking to answer this question, Kathryn Zabelle Derounian-Stodola, editor of this and other women's Indian captivity narratives, concludes that the slave's humane behavior implies that the author was probably an abolitionist: she reasons that the escaped slave's choice of "mercy" over "militance" signals the race's natural respect for and desire to join "a system of marriage and family," and that therefore the African's act, though surprising within the pamphlet's framework, constitutes an anti-slavery appeal (215). But this explanation would mean that the implicit politics of the narrative contradict the explicit politics of the pamphlet containing the narrative; why would an abolitionist portrayal of an African appear in the center of a pamphlet supporting a war waged to preserve the institution of slavery and ensure the southern expansion of a slaveholding empire? And this explanation falters for another reason: the portrayal of a benevolent African in Florida was not necessarily an abolitionist trope.

In fact, the representation of an African who lives in Florida and shows mercy toward a white family would probably be a powerful *pro-slavery* trope because it ultimately suggests that life in the wilds of Florida and the experience of marronage need not "damage" slave property beyond recovery. During the 1830s and 1840s abolitionists frequently insisted that Africans who had experienced Florida marronage had thereby lost the habit of servility toward whites, and thus were no longer fit to resume their roles as plantation slaves if captured. In "Troubles of Slaveholders," an essay appearing in *The Emancipator* in 1839, the writer asserts that "The best thing the slaveholders can do is to make no efforts to recover those runaway slaves among the Seminoles," for "Having once tasted the sweets of liberty, and learned the use of arms, they will, if again reduced to slavery, constitute a most explosive element in the South. Their machinations will result in something worse than a Seminole war."[49] This writer hopes to keep Florida's African populations away from the slave market and plantation by portraying them as property that is unsafe for slaveholders to "recover" because of the Floridian knowledge, allies, and skills that enable such Africans to rebel violently if they so choose. In other words, for explicitly anti-slavery objectives, the author of "Troubles of Slaveholders" evokes the figure of an African rendered irrecoverably rebellious by Florida marronage. Many other antebellum writers also did so, and this fact should inform our interpretation of the Godfrey narrative: by portraying an African who betrays his maroon community to serve a white family and guide them to safety at their friends' plantation, the writer appeals not to abolitionists, but rather to slaveholders.

Although the narrator of the Godfrey tale promises a story of Mary Godfrey's "preservation and deliverance," then, the text ultimately also seeks to preserve and deliver something else: an account of Florida and its populations that sustains plantocratic and imperial interests. The story initially terrorizes readers with the prospect of "horrid massacres," only to reassure them that the escaped slave's identity remains intact despite the experience of Florida marronage. Or, to describe the tale in terms previously discussed in relation to *The Exiles of Florida*, the Godfrey narrative appears to successfully revise "maroon" into "runaway" by acknowledging and capitalizing on the concern that Florida draws Africans into affiliations and experiences that make them permanently unfit for the plantation, only to assure readers that such a concern is groundless. And by confirming that Africans living in Florida can be restored to the plantation, the tale also denies Florida's status as maroon territory and portrays the peninsula as an incipient extension of the U.S. South.

Yet there is another way to read the Godfrey narrative. For even as the African's dramatic choice to drop the axe assures readers of his continued viability as slave property, this assurance is only momentary. The gesture in fact inaugurates a series of actions suggesting that the African can no longer be made to serve a scripted role in the U.S. imperial project—less because his Floridian skills, knowledge, and alliances enable him to rebel against the master, than because these skills enable him to avoid capture altogether and continue participating in a world that has little to do with the plantation.

This suggestion becomes apparent once we realize that the African's ability to serve the Godfrey family and simultaneously preserve his liberty depends entirely on the knowledge and deft navigation of local terrain and politics that signal his belonging to a community that thrives beyond plantation borders. The African knows how to find "wholesome provision" for the starving family in the Everglades. He can track the movements of both Indians and "mounted volunteers (whites)" so as to determine when it is safe for the family to escape the swamp undetected. He knows the ground well enough to locate a safe path to the family's refuge at "the plantation of some of their friends." And, perhaps most importantly, he manages to bring the family "within view" of the plantation's residents without himself being seen (223–24). Since the African last appears in the narrative when delivering the family to safety, we can assume that thereafter he slips back into the "thick and miry swamp" from which he originally emerged, there to rejoin the cultural, social, and economic networks that enabled him to preserve both the white family and himself in the first place.

Finally, then, although the narrative terrorizes readers with the specter of bloody insurrection, only to avoid the expected massacre, it ultimately foregrounds another and potentially more disturbing prospect: when the African drops the axe, he introduces the possibility that the unsurveyable space of Florida, beyond the plantation order and its ideal of surveillance, encourages Africans to assume roles unimaginable within a colonialist framework, roles such as Indian ally and politically savvy negotiator.[50] In other words, while the narrative sets out to revise "maroon" into "runaway," it ultimately emphasizes the difficulty of this revision, largely by suggesting that the Everglades draws Africans into locally specific social formations and spatial practices from which they may never be reclaimed. This is the true terror that the Godfrey narrative provokes, though most probably not on purpose. This is also the fear that the abolitionist writer of "Troubles of Slaveholders" deliberately evokes when asserting Africans are unsafe to "recover" from Florida. The assertion contests a plantocratic understanding of such Africans as recoverable property, yet it does so by implying that they are best perceived as wrecked goods: like cotton and other commodities frequently strewn along the Florida Reef, they become worse than valueless to their original owner because they are still valuable to others—and, in most cases, to those who thrive by weakening the plantation economy.[51] The conclusion of the pamphlet containing the Godfrey narrative emphasizes this prospect by warning that "The face of the country, interspersed with hammocks, cyprus swamps and marshes, almost impenetrable to the white man . . . constitute the natural defense of the Indians" (234).[52] This final reflection hints that Florida remains "impenetrable" to the United States because it sustains alternate communities, such as the ones that readers might imagine the African rejoining in the swamp.

When the Godfrey narrative appeared in New England in 1836, Seminole and African forces led by Osceola were powerfully resisting the U.S. military, and the Second Seminole War would continue for six additional years. For this reason most readers would not celebrate the prospect that Florida encourages people to pursue spatial, communal, and economic alternatives. Yet not all tales of Territorial Florida reflect on this prospect with dread.

A Sketch of the Life of Elizabeth Emmons, or the Female Sailor (1841) is about a woman who escapes the restrictions of New England society by disguising herself as a sailor and boarding a ship. Women seeking freedom on the seas were not uncommon in early national literature, and Emmons's tale is an instance of the subgenre Cathy Davidson calls the female picaresque, which centers on the exploits of a cross-dressing heroine whose travels bring her into contact with diverse populations and geographies of early America.[53] Printed in Boston, the narrative is presented as a true, first person account, edited by a publisher who has added footnotes, a preface, and a concluding letter purportedly written by a friend of Emmons residing in Key West. However, the thirty-six-page pamphlet containing the narrative is published under a false imprint, and the narrative is almost certainly fictional.[54]

Before her escape to sea, Emmons's life is a sad one. Orphaned by a drunkard father, bereft of a fiancé who dies of heartbreak after causing a carriage accident in which Emmons loses an eye, and abandoned by friends as a result of her disfigurement, she finds that she can sustain herself in her native city of Boston only by working "like a slave" in domestic servitude (14). Painfully aware that her straitened circumstances offer no avenue for social or economic advancement, she resolves "to bid farewell to the scenes of *terra firma*, and if possible to procure employment as a sailor—to go, I cared not where" (15).

In the three years following her departure from Boston in 1835 Emmons endures the vicissitudes of seafaring, changing ships and visiting a variety of ports, including New Orleans, Mobile, Galveston, Philadelphia, and

Charleston, before a tempest drives her vessel ashore at St. Augustine in 1838. Though the Everglades are far from her thoughts, Emmons is ready to exchange the hardships and tragedies of life at sea for one on land. Vowing never again to leave solid ground if she can help it, she seeks to enlist at a St. Augustine military headquarters that is recruiting soldiers to fight in the Second Seminole War, which had then been in progress for three years. Although partial blindness disqualifies Emmons from service, she enthusiastically joins a company of volunteers heading into the Everglades in pursuit of a band of Indians who have murdered a family of settlers from Massachusetts. After arriving at the scene of the massacre and helping to gather and bury the hacked, scattered remains of these emigrants from her home state, Emmons embarks on "the severest jaunt I ever experienced," a five-week march "through the swamps and everglades which abound in that territory." The march ends in a violent encounter with sixteen Seminoles who fight with "utmost desperation," killing one of Emmons's comrades before meeting their demise at the hands of Emmons and her fellow volunteers, who murder nine of the Indians and capture the rest. Here a publisher's note explains that altogether Emmons spent nearly four months in the swamps, "during which time she assisted in capturing and hanging forty-one Indians" (31).[55]

Until this point in the story Emmons's tale shares a number of features that have been characteristic of the picaresque since its Spanish origins, and that made the form particularly appealing to early American readers and writers. As Davidson shows, conventionally the picaresque involves a central character who moves across geographic, gender, and class boundaries; inhabits various and even conflicting political perspectives without endorsing any of them; and ultimately returns home unchanged by the experience. As she also explains, early Americans embraced the picaresque because its inveterate mobility underscores the complexity of the political and cultural world of the early republic, and thereby counters official attempts to downplay and restrict the "rambunctious heterogeneity" of the new nation. And they also favored the genre because it offered the possibility of critique with impunity: its narrative irresolution made it impossible for readers to pin down the political agenda of the author, and thereby the genre refrained from questioning the "governing assumptions" of a culture ultimately founded on gender, racial, and class hierarchies.[56] Building on this notion, Martin Brückner has recently suggested that the picaresque tends to "stabilize" the nation, for the central character's characteristic "lack of transformation" and eventual return "home" to the bonds of domesticity endorse an emergent sense of nationalism.[57] According to these scholars, the picaresque perfectly suited a new nation with imperial ambitions: unable to agree on a shared concept of national identity, and deeply ambivalent about the prospect of the United States as empire, Americans celebrated a literary form that exposed contradictions in national and imperial ideologies and enabled readers to consider a range of critiques without committing to any of them.

What should we make of the fact, then, that Emmons emerges from the Everglades a committed opponent of U.S. territorial expansion? Right after her violent encounter with a band of Indians, and immediately following the publisher's explanation that Emmons participated in the murder of no less than forty-one Seminoles during her four-month engagement in the imperial project of eradicating Florida's maroon communities, we come upon Emmons's impassioned plea for Seminole land rights:

> Fighting the poor, and, as I think, much abused Indians, I did not relish much. My sympathies were and now are decidedly with the red man. If there ever was a people wrongfully oppressed and persecuted, these have been the Indians of the United States. Driven by the white man from river to river, and from mountain to mountain, at the point of the bayonet, the breasts of ten thousand innocent beings have been made to heave with indescribable suffering. Humanity pleads with all her sympathies for the rights of the children of the forest, and the judgments of a righteous God will yet be visited upon those who have cruelly participated in driving them from their native and favorite hunting grounds. My blood boils within me when my memory recurs to the time when I, in company with others, employed my time in seeking the lives of those whom it is our duty to protect. Gladly would I blot the cruelties of that portion of my pilgrimage on earth from my recollection—but I cannot. (33)

Emmons's contributions to Indian removal in Florida, then, render her a decided supporter of Indian land rights. Her deepened opposition to settler colonialism is not fleeting, for the publisher notes that Emmons has written a separate account of her *Florida Travels* in which she offers "many gentle hints which it would be well for our government to take" on how to end Florida's wars of removal quickly and peacefully—presumably by ceasing to drive the Seminoles from Florida (33). And a subsequent plot development confirms Emmons's anti-imperialism: upon concluding her stint with the volunteers, she returns to St. Augustine, discovers a newspaper advertisement for Key West wreckers, and relocates south to begin this new position.

When Emmons moves from St. Augustine to Key West to become a Florida wrecker, the action suits her newfound antagonism to U.S. expansion, for Florida wreckers directly compromised the imperial project by salvaging U.S. goods.[58] Many of the commodities that fueled expansion—such as sugar, cotton, and slaves—passed along the Florida Reef aboard ships heading into and out of the Gulf of Mexico; when these ships foundered, their cargo frequently became salvage for wreckers who knew the Reef terrain and watched for ships in distress. Such goods did more damage to the North American economy as salvage than if they were sunk, for wreckers often made their living by selling salvage in the markets of foreign competitors for Gulf mastery. Thus, through the hands of wreckers, U.S. goods could enrich imperial rivals. By choosing to turn wrecker, then, Emmons compromises U.S. empire not by openly protesting or resisting settler colonialism, but rather by participating in an alternate economy that often supported the imperial projects of others.

Through Florida, Emmons herself is salvaged. Her wrecking career signals the story's engagement with the same set of concerns about Florida that fascinate Giddings and disrupt the Godfrey narrative: for the author of Emmons's tale, as for these other writers, Florida draws people into alternate affiliations and economic activities, and thereby enables them to contribute to cultures and economies beyond, and potentially damaging to, an expanding empire. This sense of Florida is reinforced by the unconventional conclusion of the story. Traditionally, at the end of a picaresque plot, the heroine sheds her male disguise and assumes the bonds of domesticity, an alteration that Davidson interprets as the genre's refusal to challenge governing assumptions about race, class, and gender that sustain the imperial project.[59] Yet we cannot similarly interpret Emmons's choice of female clothing, marriage, and motherhood. Although she eventually reveals her sex to a fellow wrecker from Boston, accepts his marriage proposal, and explains that "I put aside my sailor apparel, and assumed my rightful station in the community" as wife and mother (34), she ends up anything but "ensconced in domesticity" like the heroines who return home at the end of the stories that Davidson analyzes.[60]

For Emmons never exchanges a life of adventure for the roles of wife and mother, traditionally conceived. In fact, she uses the income that she earned by wrecking to purchase a schooner upon which she embarks with her family, and her first-person account concludes with the words, "I again went to sea under favorable circumstances" (34). The text containing Emmons's account closes with a letter from Key West recounting the heroine's tragic death at sea after being shot by a Spanish sailor employed by her husband; yet an editor's note assures us that Emmons's final years were happy, for "writing seemed to be her favorite employment," and she spent her days aboard ship composing poetry, travel narratives, and even an autobiography (34). The note confirms that, long after shedding her sailor's clothes, Emmons continued to pursue nontraditional gender roles made possible by her wrecking income and alliances.[61]

While *A Sketch of the Life of Elizabeth Emmons* begins as a picaresque, the picara's entrance into the Everglades derails some of the genre's primary conventions.[62] The mobility of the picaresque plot, which frequently avoids explicitly challenging the status quo, reinforces Emmons's anti-imperial sentiments and extra-imperial commitments, which grow as the plot propels her ever forward into new geographic locales and experiences. Her transformation in the wilds of Florida makes sense, however, if we consider that the story is about how Floridian swamps and reefs enable Emmons to achieve what New England ground cannot—namely, an alternative to the colonial restrictions of gender and class that leave her toiling "like a slave." Finally Florida unfits Emmons for her originally designated role in the U.S. imperial project by drawing her into local communities, activities, identifications, and alliances that bring adventure, lucrative employment, relative independence, and unconventional political views. Emmons's tale announces the cultural, political, and economic pressures Florida places on an unfolding narrative of nation and empire, and embraces these pressures as a path to new opportunities for the nonelite, and particularly for lower-class women, to experience adventure and independence. The narratives I turn to next explore these pressures at a later historical moment, when statehood and settlement depended more than ever before on the region's potential to resemble other parts of the U.S. South.

Florida Maroon(er)s

When the story of Elizabeth Emmons appeared in print in 1841 the Second Seminole War was still in progress, although by that time thousands of Seminoles and Africans had been killed or forcibly relocated to Oklahoma. The estimated six hundred who remained in Florida at the conclusion of the war in 1842 lived mostly in the South, in the Everglades and other swamps.[63]

Though they occupied places most American citizens considered unfit for living, their presence was a deterrent to U.S. settlement of South Florida, and Congress passed the Armed Occupation Act of 1842 to incentivize homesteaders with arms and land in return for their promise to build a "fit habitation" and remain for at least five years. The act and other legislative and political documents indicate that U.S. officials planned the region's incorporation according to a familiar model for incorporating other frontier spaces: settler colonialism would peacefully expel preexisting populations and efface all traces of their presence. Yet this model would not resemble reality on the ground in more than a handful of places on the peninsula until well after Florida became the nation's twenty-seventh state in 1845.[64] Meanwhile, the remnants of African and Seminole populations continued to develop their own settlements on hammocks and other natural rises of land elevated just inches above the surface of the swamp.

While many historical and military accounts of settler colonialism in Territorial Florida obscure the continued presence of African and Seminole communities, this presence shapes two widely circulating fictions of white settlement in frontier Florida on the cusp of statehood, Francis Robert Goulding's *The Young Marooners on the Florida Coast* (1852) and *Marooner's Island* (1867). These works have not received the attention they deserve, likely because of their status as juvenile fiction.[65] Yet both novels were international bestsellers for several decades during the second half of the nineteenth century.[66] *Young Marooners* sold 13,000 copies at home and as many abroad, and it was printed and reissued in major cities (such as Philadelphia, London, and New York), translated into several languages (including Dutch and Russian), and hailed by Joel Chandler Harris (of *Uncle Remus* fame) as a book "known in many lands and languages" that "has survived its own success . . . entered into literature[, and] . . . become a classic."[67]

The novels were clearly important to early readers, and for this reason they deserve consideration, even though we might conclude upon first analysis that they differ little from other frontier novels of the period that imaginatively "transformed conquered foreign lands into the domestic sphere of the family and the nation."[68] An assessment of the texts as imperial propaganda would be supported by Goulding's biography: a Southerner by birth and supporter of the Confederacy, he likely would have endorsed the project of Indian removal in Florida.[69] Yet instead of assuring readers of Florida's incipient transformation into an extension of the United States, Goulding's work foregrounds the near impossibility of this transformation. Albeit unintentionally, the novels confirm the difficulty of pursuing a familiar ideal of settler colonialism on ground that continues to provoke imagined, and sometimes actual, associations with maroon communities. Particularly when read alongside one another, the two novels attest that Florida's identity as maroon territory inevitably intrudes on a traditional narrative of incorporation that might transpire on other frontiers, for these stories ultimately propose that settling Florida will "maroon" U.S. Americans.

Young Marooners and *Marooner's Island* are not sequential. Rather, both novels concern the same story that unfolds in Florida over seven months during the early 1830s when the fictional Gordon family leaves their Georgia home and starts a new life in Florida. The story begins as a familiar tale of frontier settlement that could take place in any recently incorporated part of the United States during the mid-nineteenth century. The family patriarch, Dr. Gordon, purchases land, sight unseen, near Tampa Bay, and upon arriving in Florida the family undertakes the challenges of domesticity, renovating an abandoned, dilapidated structure that they hope to call home. Yet after some generic scenes of pioneer life the plot quickly takes a Crusoic turn when Dr. Gordon decides to occupy the children by accompanying them on an extended excursion to a nearby island in the Gulf of Mexico. Just as the four children board a boat loaded with a few days' camping gear and provisions, a "hideous monster known in our waters as a Devil Fish" trips the anchor, entangles itself in the cable, and carries the children out to sea.[70] The accident separates the children from their father, and most of the narrative focuses on the children's survival during three months on a desert island near the west coast of Florida while their parents scour the region with a search party. Eventually the family reunites at a makeshift campsite beneath a canopy of orange trees, and the story ends with their decision to return to Georgia for good.

Marooner's Island, the latter of the two novels, almost fully erases Florida marronage from the family's experience. Indeed, several episodes seem intended to allay prospective settlers' fears of continuing African-Seminole alliances in Florida. For example, when a band of Seminoles approaches the Gordon family's loyal slave Sam and offers him freedom, marriage, and even his own slaves, Sam responds with "strong disgust," states his preference for life as the Gordons' slave, and returns to his white owners (420). And a subsequent episode forcefully conveys the message that any remaining communities of Africans and Seminoles are so weak as to naturally recede as the United States advances into the region anyway.

In one of the most memorable scenes in *Marooner's Island*, the Gordon family battles and easily conquers a remnant of armed maroons, despite the family's near total lack of training and preparation. The battle occurs when "a gaudily dressed negro, fantastically painted," and leading a band of Seminoles brandishing guns, ambushes the family and their Indian allies. Importantly, Goulding identifies the African in command as "Yobly," which is also the name of a historical figure, an infamous escaped slave frequently called Abraham who awed U.S. soldiers as a formidable leader of the Seminole.[71] While many readers would have known of Yobly's ferocity, Goulding renders him and his crew anodyne when one of the Gordon children, known for his lack of experience with guns, instantly and fatally shoots the African, whose death "seemed to greatly disconcert" the entire band of maroons, who are then quickly captured (466).[72] This event propels the narrative toward a conclusion in which the Gordon family becomes the rightful possessors of most of Florida. The battle fatally injures the family's Indian ally Mahinlo whose veins run with "the last blood of the Caloosas," natives of Florida's southwest coast who occupied the region long before the Seminole arrived during the eighteenth century (478). In a deathbed scene that serves as the trope of the "vanishing Indian," Mahinlo resigns himself with the words "My time come," transfers his vast coastal landholdings to his son, and proclaims Dr. Gordon the child's "future guardian," thereby making way for the Gordon family's claim to the land (480).

While these and other scenes in *Marooner's Island* effectively efface Africans and Seminoles, along with most troubling traces of the activities, identifications, and associations that Florida enabled them to pursue, no such scenes appear in the earlier novel, *Young Marooners*. Even though Goulding composed this work between 1847 and 1850, a period of aggressive U.S. empire-building and the heyday of popular "imperial adventure fiction," the novel tells the story of the Gordon family's settlement without the "scenes of empire-building" that were already a staple of the genre, and that propel the plot of *Marooner's Island*.[73] And *Young Marooners* not only lacks scenes that overtly sustain the imperial logic of *Marooner's Island*; it also includes scenes that prompt readers to question this logic by confronting the history and persistence of marronage in Florida.

A scene that Goulding deleted from *Marooner's Island* attests that, long after maroon communities have largely been expelled, Florida's status as maroon territory persists in white settlers' conceptions of space and personal identity. Just before the accident that sends Robert, Mary, Frank, and Harold to sea unaccompanied, the four children stand ashore at Bellevue, their Tampa home, and Dr. Gordon asks them, "Who can tell me what 'maroon-ing' means?" His question prompts the following conversation:

> [Robert answered,] "I should say, [marooning is] living pretty much in the way we have lived most of the time since we came to Bel-levue. A person maroons when he lives in an unsettled state."
>
> [Dr. Gordon replied,] "You are nearly right; but to be more criti-cal. The word 'maroon' is of West Indian origin—coming I think from the island of Jamaica. It meant at first a free negro. But as those who ran away from their masters became virtually free for the time, it came afterwards to mean a runaway negro. To maroon therefore means to go from home, and live like a runaway negro. I wish to ask if any one present is in favor of marooning?" All were silent, and Dr. Gordon continued, "To maroon means also to go to some wild place, where there is plenty of game or fish, and to live upon what we can obtain by our own skill. Are there any persons now in favour of marooning?"
>
> "I am—and I—and I!" was the universal response. (58–59)

In this conversation several definitions of "maroon" vie for space. The initial conception of marooning as "living . . . in an unsettled state," as the Gordon family has done since arriving in Tampa, conveys an understanding of the term that was popular in some parts of North America when *Young Marooners* appeared in print during 1848. That year's edition of John Russell Bartlett's widely read *Dictionary of Americanisms* defines "marooning" as "an expression used in the Southern States [that] means to make up a party and have a picnic" for several days "on the shore or in the country."[74] This definition appears twice in the conversation: Robert evokes it at the start, and Dr. Gordon returns to it at the end by defining "marooning" as living "in some wild place . . . upon what we can obtain by our own skill." However, sandwiched rather uncomfortably between these lighthearted connotations are others that stun the children to silence: as Dr. Gordon explains, the term also "meant at first a free negro" and later a "runaway negro" once "those who ran away from their masters became virtually free."

According to Dr. Gordon, then, "maroon" now means "runaway negro," but only *because* those Africans originally called "maroons" were so suc-cessful at avoiding capture and reenslavement that they forced the British

Empire to consider them free. This explanation evokes associations between Florida and the Caribbean and also indicates that in 1848 calling runaway slaves "maroons" suggests that they, too, may remain away for so long that eventually they will be called free. As such, the scene participates in the same debate about African identity in Florida that provoked Andrew Jackson to reject the term "maroon" and inspired many abolitionists to embrace it: the term punctures plantocratic and imperial accounts of Floridian ground. It suggests that Africans in Florida are not running from the plantation, but settled in communities beyond U.S. surveillance. No wonder Dr. Gordon's definition of "marooning" confounds the children; essentially, he proposes that the family live like Africans who have left the plantation and cannot be reclaimed.

Importantly, this meaning of "maroon" endures in the novel, even though the conversation about marooning concludes by repeating that a "maroon" is an extended picnic in the South. For when Dr. Gordon explains that "To maroon *means also* to go to some wild place . . . and to live upon what we can obtain by our own skill," he suggests that both meanings apply to the family's incipient Florida maroon.[75] By tethering the family's marooning adventure to Florida's history of marronage, the scene proposes that the young marooners do not inhabit Florida *instead of* irreclaimable Africans, but rather *like* them—a proposal subtly borne out by other events in *Young Marooners*, and most forcefully by an episode titled "Evading Bloodhounds."

"Evading Bloodhounds" places two of the Gordon children in a situation that many Africans who had left the plantation faced in Florida and other parts of the Caribbean. The episode begins when a white man on horseback approaches Harold and Frank and asks whether they have seen a "villainous Indian-negro, who has been skulking here this morning" (49). The man explains that the "Indian-negro"—a common antebellum term for Africans allied with the Seminoles—"has been detected in stealing, and several persons will soon come with blood-hounds to hunt him" (50). Once convinced that the children have not encountered the African, the man rides on and Harold expresses his wish to avoid becoming "the spectator of the scene" of chase and violent capture, only to realize that he and Frank could become the scene's victims. As "the thought flashed into his mind that possibly the dogs might fall on his own trail," Harold reflects that "The dogs were probably fierce, and it would be exceedingly difficult, in case of an attack, to defend himself and Frank too" (50). Hearing "afar off the deep bay of the blood-hounds," Harold doubles back on his tracks as the only way to avoid capture and almost certain death (50). Hurrying ahead "into the wet low ground," he retraces his footprints toward the younger Frank, takes the boy in his arms, and then "[springs] with all his might, at right angles, to his former course" (51). From a safe vantage point Harold confirms that "the hounds were actually upon his track" as they come "roaring along the road" by his trail (51). Thankful for "having made so narrow an escape," the boys rejoin the rest of the family (52).

By placing the young marooners in the position of an African fleeing from bloodhounds, "Evading Bloodhounds" suggests that "marooning" in Florida can never quite be the extended "party" and "picnic" that it is in other southern spaces. The bloodhound chase scene directly alludes to the Second Seminole War, often called the "Bloodhound War" after 1839, when the U.S. military imported Cuban bloodhounds to track down Africans.[76] This decision was controversial, but not unprecedented. Because the British had used bloodhounds to hunt maroons in eighteenth-century Jamaica, many in the United States endorsed the military's plan by reasoning that the peninsula was topographically similar to Jamaica.[77] Thus "Evading Bloodhounds" also emphasizes Florida's Caribbean history and topography, and thereby attests that the Florida setting of *Young Marooners* is less an incipient extension of the United States than a node in a larger network in which maroons continue to circulate. And Florida's persistence as maroon territory could account for the novel's ultimate failure to produce a traditional scene of domesticity, despite its original promise to do so.

As a number of scholars have shown, scenes of domesticity on the U.S. frontier were intricately intertwined with, and often sanctioned, the violence of empire.[78] In Amy Kaplan's influential formulation, a "generic picture of pioneer domesticity" that "could happen anywhere" on the continent enabled readers to imagine imperial expansion as a benevolent process of regulation and improvement through which recently conquered lands and populations became part of an expanding "domestic sphere."[79] The Gordon family's Florida story begins with homemaking in an abandoned structure at Tampa Bay called "Bellevue."[80] Yet this home never fully materializes, and the closest thing to a recognizable domestic space in either novel is a makeshift campsite called "Marooners' Home" where the family gathers near the end of the narrative before returning to Georgia for good.[81] Unlike the generic sounding "Bellevue," "Marooners' Home" evokes the specificity of Florida, particularly because it appears in *Young Marooners* after earlier scenes that tell us what "marooning" in Florida means. When Goulding wrote *Marooner's Island* over a decade later, did he uncomfortably sense its lack of a domestic scene that could shore up the narrative's imperial logic?

Whatever the reason, Goulding adds to the latter novel an episode that imagines domesticity in Florida, if only momentarily. On their final evening the family gathers at a renovated "Marooners' Home" for dinner. The makeshift tent of *Young Marooners* has developed many "apartments," "several sheds or wings" including a poultry house, a kitchen "furnished with a stove and pipe," and even slave quarters (324–25). There is also "a dining-table of mahogany" with "handsome chairs," and the children eagerly assume the roles of "hostess" and "host" while the slave "Sam, acting as waiter, [stands] behind the chair of his young mistress" awaiting "calls upon his service" (324).[82] The message is clear: roughing it on the Florida frontier need not involve abandoning familiar race, class, and gender roles. Except for the scene's rustic setting beneath "the canopy" of an orange-tree, its "pure white blossoms . . . filling the air with their delicious odors," this is an episode of domestic bliss rivaling any that, according to Kaplan, "made the nation into home."[83]

The domestic scene of *Marooner's Island* is part of a larger pattern of revision through which Goulding renders Florida a U.S. southern space by affirming that Anglo-American identity remains intact there. Yet the original story explores what happens when Anglo-Americans try to pursue a familiar narrative of settlement on the same land that sustains the history and remnants of African and Seminole populations developing their own settlements on hammocks in the swamp. The message of this earlier novel is that Florida "maroons" Anglo-Americans by drawing them into contact with the region's history and persistence of marronage, which alters their experience of settlement, shapes their understanding of Florida's geographic identity, and forces them to contend with the military violence used to expel most of the region's inhabitants. Put otherwise, *Young Marooners* foregrounds Florida's pressures on imperial ideals of space and subjectivity, the two coordinates through which the U.S. nation was supposed to appear.[84] Goulding's earlier work vividly captures a provocative prospect that would be increasingly foreclosed as more of Florida began to resemble other parts of North America.

*   *   *

Upon first consideration the frontier adventure narrative of Francis Robert Goulding, Georgia slaveholder, makes an odd pairing with reflections on Florida by Joshua Reed Giddings, Ohio abolitionist. Yet the pairing is instructive because it suggests that antebellum Americans who lived in many places beyond the borders of Florida, and held different cultural and political affiliations, shared a similar difficulty imagining a familiar expansionist narrative unfolding on Floridian ground. A turn to the brief appearance of the Everglades in the work of two other antebellum writers provides a useful coda to this claim.

In *Army Life in a Black Regiment* (1870), the Civil War memoir that Thomas Wentworth Higginson based on his diaries as colonel in the First South Carolina Volunteers, a regiment of refugee freedmen, Higginson records his longing to be a maroon in the Florida Everglades during 1863. Lamenting that most of the North American landscape hinders marronage, lacking features such as the mountain passes and "impenetrable swamps" that harbored maroon communities in eighteenth-century Jamaica and Surinam, he finds an exception "in the everglades of Florida," where U.S. slaves once "united with the Indians, and would stand fire" against the U.S. military during the Seminole Wars.[85] This exception makes the deployment of Higginson and his regiment to northern Florida so "attractive to them and even to me": the region "was so much nearer the everglades. I used seriously to ponder, during the darker periods of the war, whether I might not end my days as an outlaw,—a leader of Maroons."[86] When a Union victory seemed uncertain the Everglades were an especially enticing prospect because they offered his troops an alternate life to that which awaited them should the Confederacy prevail. Higginson's attraction to the Everglades in 1863, then, is grounded in a perception of the region that also structures the range of Florida fictions that this chapter comprises, and as such it suggests the longevity of the region's identity as a space that cannot be recoded.

This understanding of Florida explains many antebellum narratives about the region, but it may also help us make sense of Florida's appearances in antebellum writing about other places as well. For example, when we think of Harriet Beecher Stowe's second anti-slavery novel, *Dred: A Tale of the Great Dismal Swamp* (1856), we rarely think of Florida. Yet the Florida Everglades appear suddenly and unexpectedly near the conclusion of *Dred*. Long after Stowe has thoroughly established that Dred's mastery over the Great Dismal constitutes "a considerable check on the otherwise absolute power of the overseer," in the twenty-ninth chapter we learn that Dred "had been a great traveller . . . through regions generally held inaccessible to human foot and eye. He had explored not only the vast swamp-girdle of the Atlantic, but the everglades of Florida, with all their strange and tropical luxuriance of growth."[87] Upon first consideration, Dred's familiarity with the nation's southernmost swamp seems only to reinforce Stowe's warning about slave rebellion: though Dred's particular plans are, by the novel's end, "All Over"—the title of chapter 29—the insurrectionary threat he figures is also "all over" geographically because the entire Eastern Seaboard is a vast "swamp-girdle" where slaves gather and plot against masters, from Virginia all the way down to the tip of Florida.

Yet might Stowe's mention of Dred's time in the Everglades signal something in addition to the concern that slaves who have left the plantation are busy plotting against masters? Perhaps this particular swamp provoked readers to reflect on a prospect other than the novel's primary focus on slave rebellion. The Everglades may have prompted them to consider that some places enabled Africans, Indians, and their allies on and beyond the continent to engage in a range of activities and roles that had little to do with the plantation, although they could challenge the economic basis of both slavery and empire. After all, long after the United States officially claimed Florida, a range of imaginative reflections attested to the region's irreclaimability. It is not hard to imagine, then, that the names of features that harbored Seminoles, Africans, and their allies—Everglades, swamp, savannah, hammock—remained code for the message that some U.S. spaces belong to others.

Florida Roots: Scrub-Palmetto and Orange

"For three hundred years has Florida been open to settlement," wrote William Cullen Bryant in a letter from Florida to the *New York Evening Post* in 1873; "how does it happen that East Florida is still for the most part a wilderness?"[1] In the spring of that year Bryant visited "East Florida"—as the peninsular part of the state was still sometimes called—and found that very little had improved since he first journeyed to the region three decades earlier. In a series of letters to the *Post*, where Bryant served as editor, he observed that in the past thirty years "several of our western states, which [once] lay in wilderness, have become populous and boast their large cities and intersecting railways," while "East Florida still remains for the most part a forest."[2] Bryant blames the soil for the state's underdevelopment. "The long peninsula of sand," he explains, has been rightly called "'the despair of the cultivator'" (106). True, there are some "fertile" spots where "the settler makes his openings, and builds his dwelling, and plants his orchard of orange trees," but such places "are merely stations in the great forest, which for the most part, where it is not swamp, is a sandy plain covered with the trees of the long-leaved pine" and the "growth of the dwarf palmetto" (106).

Bryant rehearses a familiar perspective on postbellum Florida also espoused by many of his Northern peers: for a place that had been "open to settlement" for centuries, and a U.S. state since 1845, Florida remained remarkably resistant to growth and development. While a plantation culture had in fact flourished briefly in some places in the Panhandle and in the Northeast near Jacksonville and the St. Johns River, postbellum Florida was the least populated and poorest state in the South.[3] It had been ravaged repeatedly during three Seminole Wars, it lacked a basic infrastructure of roads and railroads, and it contained millions of acres of unsurveyed land at a time when no other state on the Eastern Seaboard contained any. Travel narratives and settlers' guides to Florida penned after the Civil War repeatedly echo Bryant's impression that Florida's foundations of swamp and sand sustained not the familiar markers of belonging—such as fixed dwellings, sturdy fences, and cultivated fields—but rather tangled roots of the kind that notoriously thwarted settlement, such as "the dwarf palmetto," a plant more commonly called "scrub-palmetto" and lamented by settlers because it clings tightly to the ground, overspreading the surface of the earth and disrupting the foundations of houses and gardens.[4]

But many visitors found a notable exception in the home and grounds of Harriet Beecher Stowe at Mandarin. When Bryant visited Stowe's home in northeastern Florida in 1873 he described Mandarin as a civilized "station" in the wilderness "where Mrs. Stowe has her winter mansion, in the shadow of some enormous live oaks, and here she has planted an orange grove" surrounded by a green "lawn."[5] Each winter from 1868 to 1884 Stowe lived and wrote at Mandarin along the St. Johns River—the same river that Bartram explored a century earlier—and Bryant's description of Stowe's cottage as a "mansion" with "orange grove" and "lawn" conveys his sense of the site as a bastion of domesticity and cultivation that Stowe and her family had laboriously wrested from an otherwise forlorn landscape of swamp and wild palmetto roots. Bryant perceived Stowe as part of a group of people that one historian has called the postbellum South's "new masters," Northerners on a "civilizing mission" to manage and uplift land and populations in the wake of the Civil War. This perception of Stowe in Florida continues to inform the small number of scholarly assessments of her Florida writings, which include a collection of letters published as *Palmetto-Leaves* (1873), additional Florida letters published in U.S. periodicals, and a short story in the *Atlantic Monthly* called "Our Florida Plantation" (1879).[6] Based on these works, a twentieth-century biographer declares Stowe's mission at Mandarin an imperial foray that "depended on founding a New England colony," and several literary scholars demonstrate that Stowe conceived of the South as the nation's "internal other," "a realm of unenlightened tyranny and bondage" that accentuated the North's devotion to enlightened ideals.[7] Yet whatever ideals of progress Stowe originally carried south from Connecticut to Florida, her perspective on the region became more complicated as the direct result of living in Mandarin each winter for nearly two decades.

Stowe's experience of domesticating postbellum Florida challenged her own imperial ideology at times by prompting her to value locally specific forms of root-taking, even when they thwarted the "forms of civilized life" she elsewhere idealized in classic expressions of "manifest domesticity" such as *The New Housekeeper's Manual* (1874) and other guides to homemaking.[8] During a time when Florida's comparative underdevelopment frequently confirmed a modernizing narrative—according to which southern spaces and people required reformation and reconstruction by those from more "enlightened" parts of the country—Stowe perceived in postbellum Florida another conceptual possibility. The features of Florida that others deemed evidence of its resistance to domestication—such as Florida's lack of a traditional plantation past, the labor practices of its recently freed black population, and the tangled roots of its ubiquitous orange tree and scrub-palmetto—provoked Stowe to rethink the logic of growth and development underpinning the "civilizing mission" of Reconstruction more broadly. While Stowe supported this mission, pursuing in Florida a range of domestic, cultural, and social projects aimed at the state's improvement, her direct experience of the region's past, populations, and local landscape also led her toward new conceptions of roots, belonging, and even settlement.

Attention to Stowe's underexamined postbellum Florida writings revises literary scholars' chronological and geographic designation of Stowe as an antebellum Northern writer.[9] It also provides further evidence that, as scholars have begun to show, Stowe's views on race are more complex than they appear when we focus exclusively on her most canonical work, *Uncle Tom's Cabin* (1852).[10] Finally, such attention encourages us to continue rethinking the South's conceptual role in U.S. narratives of national incorporation.[11] For while Stowe found Florida resistant to the reproduction of neatly ordered households and grounds, she also embraced a specifically Floridian logic of growth and development, valued the knowledge and practices of local black and white laborers, and perceived that Florida could sustain poor, mobile, and landless populations who were unable or unwilling to take root in more traditional ways. Her reflections provide a way to imagine Florida's attachment to the nation by unconventional roots; more broadly, they offer the postbellum United States a different model for managing the disintegration of plantations and the displacement of populations, both white and black. This is not to say that Stowe was more subversive, progressive, or ahead of her time than scholars have so far imagined. Rather, it is a claim that concepts of founding during this period were more variegated and more dependent on the material specificities of Florida than we have imagined.

Serenoa repens

In the later and less well-remembered stages of her literary career, Stowe sometimes became a theorist of Florida roots.[12] For the cover image of *Palmetto-Leaves* (1873), her published collection of letters about settling at Mandarin, she chose the scrub-palmetto, or *Serenoa repens*, the plant maligned by Bryant and many Florida settlers for its grasping and seemingly ubiquitous roots (Figure 27).[13] Interestingly, Stowe did not select an image of the *Sabal palmetto*, which for several reasons seems like a more fitting choice upon first consideration. The *Sabal palmetto*, a tall, upright, and iconic feature of Florida, would have been readily identifiable for readers across the country, including those in Boston, where *Palmetto-Leaves* first appeared in print. In fact, since the lowly scrub-palmetto grows only on the Florida peninsula, any reader unfamiliar with local Florida flora can be forgiven for assuming that the volume's title refers to the much better-known *Sabal palmetto*. And, after all, the *Sabal palmetto* would be an apt choice for a book of letters about settling Florida anew because of the tree's popular associations with territorial claiming and founding: the *Sabal palmetto* had become the symbol of South Carolina during the Revolutionary War when white, proindependence Carolinians began to associate themselves with the distinctive palm after building a fort of palmetto logs that withstood bombardment by British forces in 1776. The *Sabal palmetto*'s appearance on the state's Revolutionary seal signified U.S. identity founded on a claim to the soil.[14]

Stowe admired the *Sabal palmetto*, and in *Palmetto-Leaves* she lovingly describes the beauty of its broad leaves and the "perfect shape" of the tree when full grown. She even expresses regret that she never had time to explore any of Florida's "perfectly magical" palmetto-groves.[15] Yet she encountered plenty of the scrub-palmetto, for she observes that clearing the earth of the "wild embrace of the snaky scrub-palmetto"—a task involving indescribable "toil"—was frequently the necessary first step toward building a home or cultivating fields in Florida (272). Reflecting on the difference between the two species of palm, Stowe explains that "the palmetto-shrub is essentially a different variety from the [*Sabal palmetto*] tree. In moist, rich land, the shrub rears a high head, and looks as if it were trying to become a tree; but it never does it" (79). The contrast is displayed in a frontispiece engraving that features the shrub in the lower left foreground, where it appears to crouch before the majestic grove of *Sabal palmettos* filling most of the print (Figure 28). To Stowe, then, the columnar tree is "perfect" and "magical," while the shrub signifies thwarted growth and impedes settlement. Why, then, choose the ignoble shrub, instead of the stately palm, as the eponymous tree that graces the cover of the book?

A careful reading of *Palmetto-Leaves* and other letters by Stowe reveals that *Serenoa repens* suits a book of reflections and advice on settling in Florida because the plant offers a crucial lesson: establishing oneself in Florida requires the abandonment of what constitutes "settlement" in other parts of the United States, and the adoption of a different understanding of the term. Even as Stowe continued to disparage Florida's prospects for development, she also perceived a problem with the concept of development that required Florida to resemble other parts of the nation. The roots of scrub-palmetto and orange trees prompt her to imagine a version of growth more fitting for postbellum Florida.

Sailing along Julington Creek, a tributary of the St. Johns River, Stowe indulges in "speculations on Nature" amounting to a recognition that the same characteristics of the scrub-palmetto that signify thwarted growth may just as certainly signify endurance and resilience. Observing the unique nature of plant roots in "these regions," she records that in Florida "Roots of plants become scaly, contorted, and lie in convolutions like the coils of a serpent. Such are the palmetto-shrubs, whose roots lie in scaly folds along the ground, catching into the earth by strong rootlets, and then rising up here and there" (73–74). Elsewhere she compares the shrub's roots to "great scaly serpents, which, after knotting and convoluting a while, suddenly raise their crests high in air, and burst forth into a graceful crest of waving green fans" (109).

The convoluted and contorted coils of a plant that spreads "along the ground," then, need not signify stunted growth; rather, they are necessary adaptations that enable the scrub-palmetto to send numerous "strong rootlets" into the earth, and thereby cling to ground that might not support deeper and less expansive roots. While admittedly the shrub will never "become a tree" that resembles the *Sabal palmetto*, it will nonetheless establish itself, "burst forth," grow, and expand in a way that is specifically adapted to "these regions." After all, the same qualities that render the scrub-palmetto an impediment to traditional houses and farms also make it a model for how to maintain steadfast hold on Floridian ground.

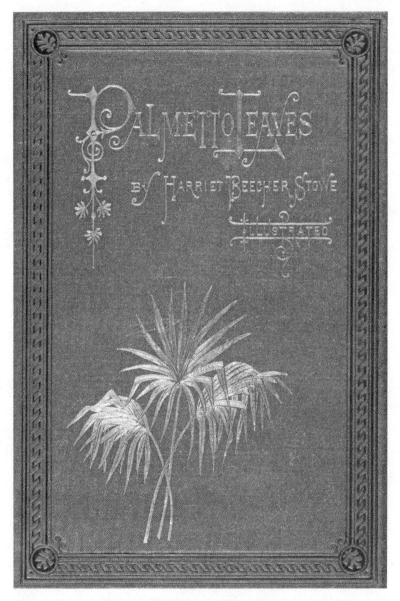

Figure 27. Harriet Beecher Stowe, *Palmetto Leaves* (1873), cover featuring scrub-palmetto. HM 5468, The Huntington Library, San Marino, California. See scrub-palmetto in lower left foreground of Figure 28.

Figure 28. Harriet Beecher Stowe, *Palmetto-Leaves* (1873), frontispiece featuring upright *Sabal palmettos* and scrub-palmetto growing along the ground at lower left. HM 5468, The Huntington Library, San Marino, California.

The scrub-palmetto is not the region's only tree displaying a logic of growth ideally adapted to the landscape of Florida: Stowe's reflections on local orange-tree culture are also illuminating in this regard. To Stowe, the iconic orange trees of Northeast Florida grow in unusual ways that provide much-needed metaphors for imagining Florida's progress. In "Swamps and Orange-Trees," the tenth letter of *Palmetto-Leaves*, Stowe addresses orange cultivation, which she decides to pursue at her Mandarin home after learning from "old, experienced cultivators, and from those who have collected the traditions of orange-growing," that "the orange-crop is the most steady and certain of any known fruit" (142). Daily observation of her orange grove reveals to Stowe that the orange tree's resilience is due largely to its remarkable roots. "The wonderful vital and productive power of the orange-tree would not be marvelled at could one examine its roots," she reflects, for "[t]he ground all through our grove is a dense mat or sponge of fine yellow roots, which appear like a network on the least displacing of the sand. Every ramification has its feeder, and sucks up food for the tree with avidity. The consequence is, that people who have an orange-grove must be contented with that, and not try to raise flowers. . . . Every fertilizer that we put on our roses is immediately rushed after by these hungry yellow orange-roots" (143–44). In Stowe's estimation, then, orange roots impede the growth of other and more familiar garden plants, such as roses, by spreading forth and rushing after all available nutrients. Yet they also enable the tree to thrive by way of a vast, shallow "network" of "fine, embracing fibres" that assure "steady" and "certain" growth on Floridian ground. Thus, like the horizontal, expansive roots of the scrub-palmetto, those of the orange tree thwart more familiar forms of possession and cultivation, while pursuing and displaying a more durable way to embrace local grounds.

And the orange tree also has an additional advantage in its apparent capacity to regenerate itself. From conversations with locals Stowe learns of the unforgettable frost of 1835 when almost every orange tree in Mandarin was "killed even with the ground" (18). Yet remarkably, a large number of the trees soon "started up with the genuine pluck of a true-born orange tree, which never says die, and began to grow again." They did so of their own accord: "Nobody pruned them, or helped them, or cared much about them any way," for many of their owners had abandoned the apparently lifeless trees and moved away (18–19). Yet the owners severely misjudged their crops, for "the fine groves of Mandarin sprang up again from the root, and have been vigorous bearers for years since" (243). In a letter from Florida published in the *Christian Union* several years after *Palmetto-Leaves*, Stowe reflects that the orange tree is "almost impossible to kill. . . . It will grow and flourish and bear golden fruit even in the most slovenly, neglected orchards."[16]

The roots most likely to establish themselves successfully in Florida, then, are those that impede conventional forms of cultivation; grow where more familiar, vertical roots cannot; spring up when seemingly dead; and revive and thrive almost entirely unaided.[17] The metaphorical dimension of Stowe's discussion of roots is not lost on Stowe. In one of several encomiums to the tree, she reflects that it is "the best worthy to represent the tree of life of any that grows on earth" (18). And the local application of this metaphor is also clear: these trees are "full of the lessons of perseverance," and thus "It is certainly quite necessary to have some such example before our eyes in struggling to found a colony here" (19–20). The specific history and growth of local trees, then—rather than notions about roots and foundations imported from other areas of the country—structure Stowe's vision of founding a Florida colony.[18]

After all, then, *Serenoa repens*, which grows in strikingly similar ways to the orange tree, is an ideal choice for the title and cover image of *Palmetto-Leaves* because the plant alerts us to a complexity in Stowe's response to Florida that we might otherwise miss. In particular, two tacit acknowledgments emerge from her reflections on scrub-palmetto and orange roots. First, founding must take forms adapted to local material realities, a realization also infusing Stowe's description of the commercial value of scrub-palmettos and oranges to Florida's poor whites and recently freed blacks, as I will discuss below. Second, however, the roots also reveal that first impressions are deceptive: characteristics that many people initially perceive as signs of underdevelopment, devitalization, and resistance to progress turn out to signify—or actually be—an alternate form of growth.

Stowe's fascination with Floridian flora of all varieties did not escape the notice of one reviewer of *Palmetto-Leaves*, who remarked in an essay in *Literary World* (Boston) that "while flowers hold the place of honor" in the book, "humbler representatives of the Floridian flora receive due recognition." For "side by side with the more romantic orange-tree" are more "vulgar" and low-growing plants.[19] Indeed, both the stately orange tree and the lowly scrub-palmetto prompt Stowe to perceive that Floridian forms of development can be unexpectedly "fine" and "vigorous," even when they differ from and disrupt traditional "forms of civilized life" that she also promotes. Stowe's personal experience of homemaking at Mandarin would ultimately confirm that domestication sometimes requires the abandonment and reconstitution of what it means to take root.

Harriet Beecher Stowe at Home in Mandarin

During the year after *Palmetto-Leaves* first appeared in print, Stowe and her sister published *The New Housekeeper's Manual* (1874), a revised and enlarged edition of the popular guide to housekeeping, *The American Woman's Home* (1869). The *Manual* contains several illustrations, among which is "a sketch of what may be properly called a Christian house; that is, a house contrived for the express purpose of enabling every member of a family to labor with the hands for the common good, and by modes at once healthful, economical, and tasteful" (Figure 29).[20] Accompanying the sketch is a blueprint titled "Plan of a Model Cottage" (Figure 30) and a chapter on "principles of house-building and house-keeping." These principles are "of necessity universal in their application" and, by ensuring the development of proper domestic economy in all places, they preserve "every social, civil, and political institution" (24). Put otherwise, Stowe's ideal home is a classic expression of "manifest domesticity": endlessly reproducible, it would standardize practices of domestic labor across the variegated spaces and populations of an ever-enlarging nation, and thus achieve national incorporation.

It is important to note the specific characteristics of the household form that would incorporate the nation. For one thing, the home is symmetrical. In particular, it is forty-three feet long and twenty-five feet wide, and each of the four outer walls contains a projection that exactly mirrors the one directly across from it. Rooms are either square or rectangular, sectioned into smaller squares or rectangles; some of these smaller spaces are closets, cabinets, or pantries containing the yet smaller symmetrical structures of shelves, which in turn hold boxes with lids.

There is no room for improvisation in the cottage's construction, for it is supposed to be built anew and all at once, and its design anticipates all present and future requirements of its occupants. Every conceivable personal possession has a designated space, for "time, labor, and expense are saved not only in the building [of the home] but in furniture and its arrangement" (25). Accordingly the plan specifies where to place ironing table, cistern, sofa, piano, and beds, and assembly instructions are provided in the accompanying text. For example, beds are to be placed at the far ends of rectangular bed-

II

A CHRISTIAN HOUSE.

In the Divine Word it is written, "The wise woman buildeth her house." To be "wise," is "to choose the best means for accomplishing the best end." It has been shown that the best end for a woman to seek is the training of God's children for their eternal home, by guiding them to intelligence, virtue, and true happiness. When, therefore, the wise woman seeks a home in which to exercise this

Figure 29. Catherine E. Beecher and Harriet Beecher Stowe, *The New Housekeeper's Manual* (1874), exterior of a model cottage. HM 253589, The Huntington Library, San Marino, California.

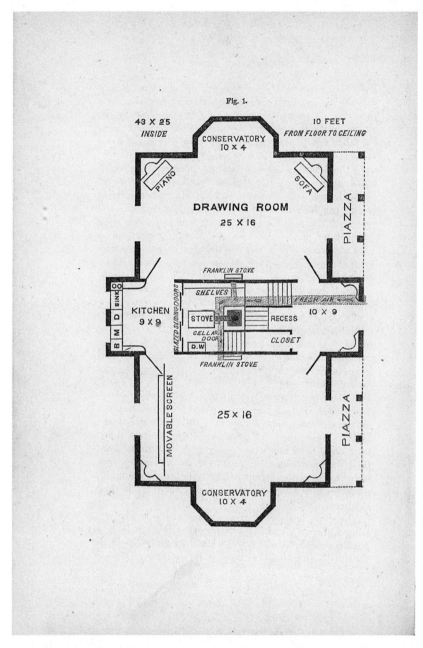

Figure 30. Catherine E. Beecher and Harriet Beecher Stowe, *The New Housekeeper's Manual* (1874), plan for ground floor of a model cottage. HM 253589, The Huntington Library, San Marino, California.

rooms, and should consist of mattresses of oat straw resting on frames with one-inch wooden slats of ash or oak set on two-inch casters; nearby ottomans should double as boxes with hinged lids. Each piece of clothing has its place as well: overclothes should hang on hooks mounted in arched recesses behind doors; flannels, calico, and cottons (both "old white" and "new white") should be stored in dedicated shelves and pockets within closets. And instructions for kitchen arrangement are exhaustive (and exhausting): wood and coal, vegetables, dishcloths, the rye, the corn meal, the flour, the salt, the molasses jug, the knife, and the spoon are arranged to maximum efficiency. Outside the cottage, a garden, vineyard, and orchard stand in neat array. Like a modern tract home, the cottage is fully serializable: down to every shelf, hook, and bracket, it "can be adapted to a warm or cold climate with little change," so that those inside each cottage can maintain standard "modes of economizing," regardless of geographic location.

I belabor Stowe's insistence on principles of symmetry and seriality as the signs and security of domesticity—and, by extension, civilization—so as to emphasize how sharply she departs from these principles at home in Mandarin. During the same years that Stowe saw *The New Housekeeper's Manual* through to press, she built and furnished a Florida home in near total disregard of the construction that universally enables civilized life.

In a letter from Florida to George Eliot in May of 1872, Stowe offers a brief "history of the cottage" that records her abandonment of the domestic ideals she simultaneously endorsed:

> The history of the cottage is this. I found a hut built close to a great live-oak twenty-five feet in girth, and with overarching boughs eighty feet up in the air, spreading like a firmament, and all swaying with mossy festoons. We began to live here, and gradually we improved the hut by lath, plaster, and paper. Then we threw out a wide veranda all round, for in these regions the veranda is the living-room of the house. Ours had to be built around the trunk of the tree, so that our cottage has a peculiar and original air, and seems as if it were half tree, or something that had grown out of the tree. We added on parts, and have thrown out gables and chambers, as a tree throws out new branches, till our cottage is like nobody else's, and yet we settle into it with real enjoyment. There are all sorts of queer little rooms.[21]

Figure 31. Oil of the Mandarin, Florida winter home of the Stowe Family painted by Harriet Beecher Stowe. Harriet Beecher Stowe Center, Hartford.

Whereas the "Christian house" of the *Manual* must be built at once and anew, Stowe's Florida home is adapted from a "hut" upon which she slowly improvised, "[making] up our home as we went along." Whereas the *Manual* stresses the use of a blueprint, the Stowe family models their Florida home after and around a tree: the house grows as a tree does—organically and asymmetrically, with oddly shaped rooms "thrown out" like "new branches"—and is "half tree" itself, accommodating "a great live-oak." Thus, while the Christian home is endlessly reproducible, the Mandarin home is "peculiar and original," growing as and with the oak tree that partly constitutes it.

Yet even though "our cottage is like nobody else's," records Stowe, "we settle into it with real enjoyment." Stowe embraced her Florida home, to which she returned for nearly twenty winters and made the subject of many letters and even an oil painting (Figure 31). In this painting, and many photographs and drawings by nineteenth-century visitors to the home, the oak features prominently (Figure 32).[22] Whereas a large tree grows beside the model home in the *Manual*, the oak pushes through the cottage's veranda and roof, all but declaring the inhabitants' blatant disregard of symmetry, system, and seriality.

Figure 32. Photograph of Calvin and Harriet Stowe, Stowe twin, unidentified girl and woman on Florida home porch, c. 1870. Harriet Beecher Stowe Center, Hartford.

Stowe's embrace of the pressures Florida placed on traditional models of domesticity is especially evident when she describes the cottage's surroundings, delighting in precisely those characteristics that differentiate this space from the orderly garden and vineyard of the *Manual*. After ten years at Mandarin Stowe reported in a letter to her son Charles and his wife that her garden "is grown into such a jungle that I could hardly get about in it." The lawn is "littered with fallen oranges," and roots "range and run rampant over the ground." Altogether, "the place looks shockingly untidy," yet Stowe finds it "so beautiful that I am quite willing to forgive its disorder."[23]

Such wistful musings on the irregularities of Florida appear, upon first consideration, to conform to the conventions of "picturesque" writing and "local color" fiction, modes of description that many postbellum U.S. writers used to portray parts of the United States that they considered hopelessly, yet delightfully, out of step with a rapidly developing nation.[24] For example, Stowe's remarks on her Mandarin garden share certain features with a travel essay on Northeast Florida, "The St. John's and Ocklawaha Rivers," which opens *Picturesque America* (1872–74), a series of views of various North American landscapes. The essay's author, Thomas Bangs Thorpe, had traveled to the region and witnessed foliage in an array of "grotesque and weird forms," moss-covered trees, and "decayed vegetation"—phrases that could easily appear in *Palmetto-Leaves* or any number of Stowe's letters from Florida.[25] And Stowe's emphasis on her home's and garden's irregularity and disorder could imply that Florida was doomed to remain a "cultural backwater" of the kind that featured in many tales in the local color genre, which Stowe herself sometimes wrote, as I will discuss.[26]

Yet Stowe's descriptions lack a defining feature of picturesque and local color modes. By nature these modes perform "cultural elegy," memorializing a place and its people as belonging to the past.[27] Stowe's Florida, however, is not a last vestige of quaint folkways. For her, Floridian nature is a dynamic force that adapts to present circumstances and shows a way forward. The surroundings of Stowe's Mandarin home evince Florida's progress, differently conceived. "In New England," she writes, "Nature is an up-and-down, smart, decisive house-mother, that has her times and seasons, and brings up her ends of life with a positive jerk," while Florida Nature is an "easy, demoralized, indulgent old grandmother, who has no particular time for any thing, and does every thing when she happens to feel like it" (28, 29). If Florida's way of doing things appears an unfavorable and antiquated contrast to that of the North, Stowe cautions against appearances: for while Florida has "a great deal that *looks* rough and desolate, and coarse," she explains, these qualities are signs of energetic development (36). "If we painted [Florida]" Stowe relates, "she would be a brunette, dark but comely, with gorgeous tissues, a general disarray and dazzle, and with a sort of jolly untidiness, free, easy, and joyous" (36). This type of woman is embodied in the swamp fronting Stowe's Mandarin home, where, for all to see, "Nature has raptures and frenzies of growth, and conducts herself like a crazy, drunken but beautiful *bacchante*" (138).

The bacchante is certainly more appealing than the "up-and-down, smart, decisive house-mother," but how does one live with her? The question "occasions a never-ceasing conflict of spirit," Stowe claims, for the swamp is alluring precisely because it resists cultivation, a fact that makes it an "impropriety" at once both "glorious" and "bewildering" (138). Yet Stowe so luxuriates in the swamp's productivity that it is impossible to believe she feels conflicted about nature bacchanalized. The swamp is "a perpetual flower-garden" of lilies, irises, and roses that, "together with strange flowers of names unspoken, make a goodly fellowship"; a place where "jays babble and jargon . . . in green labyrinths made by the tangling vines," "red-birds glance like gems through the boughs," "elms feather out into graceful plumes," and the "cypress . . . puts forth its fairy foliage" (139). The "glorious, bewildering impropriety" is to her more glorious than bewildering: "Verily it is the most gorgeous of improprieties, this swamp," she concludes (138, 139). Ultimately, she even mocks "suggestions of ditching and draining . . . that shall convert the wild *bacchante* into a steady, orderly member of society," dismissing such proposals with a dubious "We shall see" (140). Stowe's intoxication with the swamp on the grounds of her home betrays an attraction to Florida Nature's resistance to all that is "finished," "neat," and "inviting," and suggests that, for all of her charges of "impropriety," she is drawn irresistibly toward the "wild freedom" of tangled roots and foliage that to others signify—and sometimes are—impediments to domesticity (171).

Finally, Stowe's reflections on the Mandarin cottage and surroundings function much like her response to the roots of the scrub-palmetto. Just as the scrub-palmetto can never achieve the "grace" of the "stately" *Sabal palmetto*, with its nearly neoclassical trunk forming a "regular and exact pillar," the "Florida cottage" and grounds cannot attain the order and symmetry of the "Model Cottage" and grounds idealized in the *Manual*. The disorder may have perturbed Stowe at times, for a well-known detail of the Stowe family's seasonal relocation to Florida suggests that Stowe had tried to replicate her actual New England home: the chairs that stood in her Hartford living room were yearly broken down, shipped to her house in Mandarin, and reassembled upon arrival.[28] Yet Stowe's frequent embrace of Florida's "rough" and "coarse" homes and gardens suggests that she also adopted another perspective. For she settled in Florida by departing radically from certain principles of a domestic ideology that she considered the safeguard of civilization.

If the most intimate act of putting down roots—that of building and arranging one's own domestic space—compelled Stowe to embrace Floridian forms of growth and development, then why have scholars insisted that Stowe regarded her Florida venture exclusively as a doomed civilizing mission among "underdeveloped lands" and "barbaric peoples"? One reason is that most readers of Stowe's Florida writings focus less on her portrayals of homemaking in *Palmetto-Leaves* and other letters than on her more popular and widely circulating portrayal of another Florida home, "Our Florida Plantation" (1879). Scholars have yet to consider all of these portrayals in dialogue, and within the context of the local landscape features, history, populations, and geography that Stowe came to know so intimately in Florida, and that sometimes prompted her to see the limits of approaching Reconstruction as a colonizing project.

Floridian Domesticity

The year before Stowe began making a home at Mandarin, she lived directly west across the St. Johns River at a former cotton plantation in present-day Orange Park (Figure 33).[29] Stowe had leased this plantation for her son Frederick in 1866 upon his return from the Civil War, and it was to help settle Frederick and his family there that she first wintered in Florida the following year. By then the plantation—known mostly by the name "Laurel Grove" since its establishment after the American Revolution—was largely in ruins, having been abandoned during the Civil War when raided by Union troops, who imprisoned its owner. Renovating the home and grounds was an arduous task, and ultimately Frederick remained at Laurel Grove for less than a year (winter through summer of 1867). But sometime during her family's 1867 stay at Laurel Grove, Stowe purchased her own plot of land to the east at Mandarin, which she had seen when rowing there to send and collect the mail.

The Stowe family's short-lived attempt to restore Laurel Grove as a functioning cotton plantation employing newly freed black persons is the substance of "Our Florida Plantation," which scholars have rightly called evidence that Stowe fashioned herself as one of the South's "new masters."[30] Published in the *Atlantic Monthly* in 1879—over a decade after the Stowe plantation failed, and six years after the publication of *Palmetto-Leaves*—the story recounts the "history of 'our plantation'" as a glorious project of civilizing land, home, and laborers.[31] The story begins with Stowe's first visit to the neglected Laurel Grove, where her task is to restore the "forlorn, ruinous" main house that initially resembles "a lair of banditti rather than a home

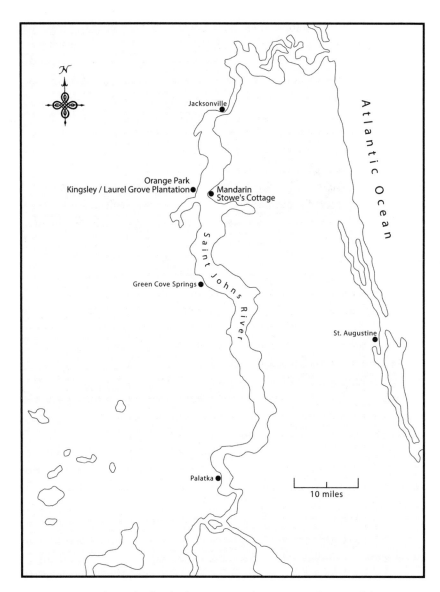

Figure 33. Map of Stowe's Florida showing Laurel Grove, Mandarin, and the geography of peninsular Florida's plantation culture.

for settled Christian people" (643). She takes a "housekeeper's survey," begins improvements, and, "after a few days," Stowe, her daughter-in-law, and
the black cook Winnah "succeeded in giving what we fancied was a tolerable
air of comfort to our house." While the home's "primitive coarseness and
roughness" persist in its design, the place is rendered "presentable" after a
thorough cleaning and the introduction of domestic goods and furniture
brought from the North, such as curtains, carpet, kitchen utensils, ottomans,
and flower vases (643–65).

Winnah's own progress is intimately linked to her participation in that
of the home. Upon the family's arrival she appears "a tall, gaunt, black
shadow" that "cackled . . . like some uncanny gnome laughing at our per-
plexities," yet under proper management she instantly becomes "the most
active, versatile, ingenious, and energetic of negro mammies": the next
morning sees her washing dishes "with scrubbing-brush and pail," milking
the cows, and delivering a "cheerful chorus" of praise for Northern ladies
and housewares (642–43, 644, 647). While Winnah retains her gnome-like
"cackle," she takes to the Northerners' expectations with alacrity, as do the
outdoor laborers: once "the old plantation regime was adopted," they proved
to be "a sober, steady set of people" (648–49).[32]

Although the house and grounds soon flourish, the plantation quickly
fails because of a terrible cotton-worm infestation, yet Stowe finds "consol-
ing reflection" in her family's successful employment of former slaves. Her
sense that the recently freed require white-supervised labor is underscored
by sketches of two employees: Tom, whose vain attempts to read announce
his suitability to physical work; and Mose, who shines as "our head man" by
calling his fellow laborers to the fields each morning by blowing a shell (648).
Thus, while the plantation fails, the Stowe family succeeds in temporarily
improving house, land, and people that would otherwise have remained
primitive and forlorn.

Yet "Our Florida Plantation" does not tell the full story of Stowe's brief
experience at Laurel Grove, which she also described six years earlier in the
final letter of *Palmetto-Leaves*. The appearance of Laurel Grove in *Palmetto-
Leaves* has been overlooked because there Stowe refers to the plantation as
the "Mackintosh Plantation" after John H. McIntosh, one of its many previous owners. It is also easy to miss Laurel Grove in *Palmetto-Leaves* because
Stowe omits her personal involvement with the property; while by the publication date of 1873 Stowe had long since leased, lived on, and abandoned
Laurel Grove, she suggests she is barely acquainted with it. "One of these

days we are projecting to spend a day picnicking on this old plantation, now deserted and decaying," she writes, "and then we can tell you many curious things in its history" (56).[33] Nonetheless, Stowe's own Laurel Grove of "Our Florida Plantation" is the "Mackintosh Plantation" she described earlier in *Palmetto-Leaves*, where her plantation experience challenges the idea that the postbellum South requires Northern intervention and improvement.

The account of Laurel Grove in *Palmetto-Leaves* almost ironizes the civilizing mission endorsed by "Our Florida Plantation." At the beginning of the letter Stowe briefly adopts the imperial stance sustained throughout the short story: "As the first white ladies upon the ground," she says of herself and daughter-in-law, we "had the task of organizing this barbaric household, and of bringing it into the forms of civilized life" (306). Yet she quickly abandons and even ridicules this stance by relishing the plantation's resistance to such "forms." The first day's effort to impose domestic order on the house and servants does not conclude with the black cook dutifully milking cows and scrubbing dishes. Rather, Stowe awakes the next morning to find "the table standing just as we had left it the night before,—not a dish washed, not a thing done in the way of clearing" (302). Then follows a humorous episode of domestic ineptitude as Stowe and her daughter-in-law try to teach the proper ways of dish washing—despite a lack of dishcloths—and cooking—despite a badly neglected stove (304). Unsurprisingly, things progress less smoothly than in "our Northern home," yet there is joy in this haphazard kitchen: the morning is a "picnic excursion" and an "experience . . . so weirdly original, that . . . we rather enjoyed it" (304).

Delight in domestic disorder emerges more fully in descriptions of the black cook, whom Stowe calls "Minnah" rather than "Winnah." She of the gnomish cackle in "Our Florida Plantation" appears in *Palmetto-Leaves* as Minnah the "Libyan sibyl" with a "laugh of barbaric exultation" (301, 309). Whereas the short story depicts the cook's sudden transformation into an industrious domestic worker, the cook of *Palmetto-Leaves* remains intractable, yet admirable for her contrariness. In passages Stowe would exclude from "Our Florida Plantation" she praises Minnah for her "tongue that never hesitated to speak her mind to high or low"; her back that bears the marks of the "free speech" she exercised as a slave; and her boldness as a recently freed woman who "still asserted her rights as a human being to talk to any other human being as seemed to her good and proper" (298–99). Minnah makes plain that "anything like a regular domestic routine was simply disgusting" (313): she is "'kinky' and argumentative" from start to finish, beginning tasks without finishing them, and doing everything when, in her own words, she "felt just like it" (308, 312). Even though Stowe laments the difficulty of rendering this "picturesque specimen of a human being . . . useful in the traces of domestic life," Minnah fully conquers Stowe's affections and thereby succeeds in working in her own way: though "exhausted with the strain of getting [domestic] work out of Minnah, we could not help laughing," and then acceding to Minnah's wish to labor in the fields (306, 313–14). "'I don't want none o'your housework,'" Minnah declares, and with that the cook—who would become the most "energetic of negro mammies" in "Our Florida Plantation"—heads out of the house for good (314).

While in both accounts the black cook remains on the plantation, her determination to work as she chooses in *Palmetto-Leaves* underscores an important departure from the civilizing mission endorsed by "Our Florida Plantation": in both works labor at Laurel Grove runs according to a familiar plantation regime, but in *Palmetto-Leaves* Stowe and her family are not responsible for this regimen. Rather, the laborers themselves "clung to the old ways of working—to the gang, the driver, and the old field arrangements— even where one would have thought another course easier and wiser" (290). And when Stowe and her family suggest improvements to the "old ways," the workers explicitly reject a "New-England manner" of labor arrangements, and the Northerners find themselves "met by the difficulty, nay, almost impossibility, of making the negroes work in any but the routine to which they had been accustomed" (290). Tom, the dependent illiterate of "Our Florida Plantation," has no place on the Laurel Grove of *Palmetto-Leaves*, from which he is conspicuously absent, while Mose appears not as "our head man," responsible solely for calling workers to the field, but rather as "foreman of the plantation," who also manages the laborers, dividing them into gangs, appointing places in the field, and resolving internal disputes (289).

What could have compelled Stowe to describe life and labor at Laurel Grove so differently than this six years later in "Our Florida Plantation"? The answer is probably not that Stowe experienced a dramatic change in her perspective on Florida during the intervening years, since during this period (ca. 1873–79) she steadily continued writing letters and essays that express a continued interest in the region's unique forms of growth, which she began to explore in *Palmetto-Leaves*.[34] A more likely answer is that the publication context of "Our Florida Plantation" in the *Atlantic Monthly* accounts for Stowe's 1879 revision of her 1873 portrait of Laurel Grove. Under the editorship of William Dean Howells (1871–81) the *Atlantic Monthly* became a major venue for postbellum local color fiction portraying places beyond New England as "quaint" or "barbaric" deviations from the norm.[35] During a time when such portrayals sold well, Stowe would have employed literary formulas and conventions that appealed to the journal's readership, some of whom probably embraced a "geographic fantasy" that the postbellum South lay in barbarous neglect awaiting improvement by enlightened Northerners. Certainly Stowe, like other writers, adopted different stances toward her subject matter for different audiences; and a specific historical fact about antebellum Florida renders it especially likely that the stance she takes in "Our Florida Plantation" does not convey the full scope of her perspective on the postbellum South.

When we consider that Laurel Grove—and Florida more broadly—largely lacked a traditional antebellum plantation culture of the kind that flourished in other parts of the South, it becomes difficult to uphold the claim that Stowe's central mission throughout her time in Florida was to civilize the region by resurrecting the plantation order.[36] Facts that could not have escaped Stowe's notice reveal that Laurel Grove's specific history is one of repeated disruption, desertion, and destruction punctuated by just two brief periods of prosperity. British Loyalists established Laurel Grove in Spanish Florida in 1787, and it first flourished on a large scale after 1803, when purchased by the slave trader Zephaniah Kingsley. With the labor of one hundred slaves imported from the Caribbean Kingsley developed Laurel Grove into 1,800 acres extending along the St. Johns River and boasting two major crops—citrus and cotton—as well as dwelling houses for owners and managers, thirty-six houses for laborers and families, a shipyard, and a number of wells, waterwheels, barns, blacksmith shops, and retail stores. Yet the plantation was entirely destroyed during and after the Patriot War of 1812 when Seminoles raided it and Kingsley's wife deliberately burned all remaining buildings to the ground. For four decades thereafter the plantation lay mostly fallow until the early 1850s, when a new owner, John H. McIntosh, revived Laurel Grove, and it flourished for the second time. The plantation remained productive under the subsequent owner, Confederate colonel Stephen Bryan, who purchased Laurel Grove in 1853 and lived there, according to Stowe's neighbors, in "grandeur," "abundance and comfort in a highly cultivated place."[37] Yet the plantation fell to ruin again with Bryan's capture by mostly black Union troops who raided the grounds in 1863. By 1866, then, when the Stowe family leased Laurel Grove, the plantation had been abandoned for the past three years, and had prospered in earnest for only two periods of about ten years each (ca. 1803–13 and 1853–63) during its nearly eighty-year history.[38]

Stowe's awareness of Laurel Grove's history of destruction and desertion is evident in her reflection that local "tales of former grandeur" are incommensurate with her own experience of "the primitive coarseness and ugliness of the construction of the house we lived in."[39] Laurel Grove was located in a part of Florida that had been ravaged by the Seminole Wars, and where plantation culture on any large scale had last flourished during the eighteenth century under British rule, save for a few estates revived by wealthy planters during the antebellum period. So while Stowe's neighbors fondly recalled Laurel Grove's "splendor" during the 1850s and early 1860s, it seems unlikely that this brief period of prosperity saw the property's achievement of anything like the grandeur of many plantations in other parts of the South's vast plantation belt that thrived continuously for half a century or more before the Civil War. Put otherwise, when the Stowe family arrived at Laurel Grove, they must have perceived that there was comparatively little "plantation order" to "resurrect."

In this environment it seems more likely that Stowe would consider possibilities for developing Laurel Grove, and Florida more broadly, that were less firmly anchored in and adapted from a traditional plantation past that most of the region never sustained.[40] In fact, there is much in *Palmetto-Leaves* and other letters to indicate that Stowe perceived the outmodedness of the plantation order altogether. In addition to the scenes of self-determined labor on the plantation that we have already explored, *Palmetto-Leaves* features black laborers who achieve economic independence off of the plantation. For example, one of the male cooks at Laurel Grove—a character notably absent from "Our Florida Plantation"—discovers that he is "worth more than we could give" and goes to work at a hotel (314). Like many former slaves who now "command their own price," the cook takes advantage of new opportunities "to make contracts, choose locations, and pursue their own course like other men" (315). Stowe praises many black cooks, farmers, and even a steamboat stewardess, and the final image of *Palmetto-Leaves* may even capture her respect for the self-determination of black persons (314–15, 249; Figure 34).

The illustrations in *Palmetto-Leaves* are untitled, but this one appears to be a drawing of Mose, the "efficient and intelligent" foreman of Laurel Grove who blows a horn to call laborers to the field. On the other hand, however, when read within the context of other letters, the image also signals possi-

Figure 34. Harriet Beecher Stowe, *Palmetto-Leaves* (1873), untitled illustration of Mose/Cudjo. HM 5468, The Huntington Library, San Marino, California.

bilities available beyond the plantation: in the penultimate letter, "Old Cudjo and the Angel," horn blowing announces progress toward enfranchisement. The story of Cudjo is at first disparaging. When Stowe and her husband first meet him on the Mandarin wharf standing forlornly next to a bale of cotton, Cudjo unfolds the tale of his recent dispossession by a white foreigner who "robbed and cheated" him of his homestead by claiming the land as part of a recently purchased tract (273). Cudjo imagines that his only justice will be in heaven, where "de angel Gabriel" will "blow de trumpet" for him, an action he pantomimes by raising his cane "trumpetwise to his mouth" just as the figure in the final drawing raises a trumpet (273–75). Yet a happy addendum to the story reveals that Cudjo's "redress was nearer than we imagined": white neighbors come to his defense, and he is legally "re-instated in his rights" to the land (276–77). "Well, Cudjo, 'de angel' blew for you quicker than you expected," remarks Stowe's husband, and Cudjo heartily assents

(277). Stowe's inclusion and potential visual commemoration of Cudjo's legal guarantee of a path to property ownership thus complicate the logic of white mastery she elsewhere upholds.[41]

There is no question that Stowe held and endorsed racist sentiments that betrayed the promise of emancipation, not least by portraying Northern, elite whites such as herself as the South's new masters.[42] After all, white supremacy was alive and well in Reconstruction Florida, as the history of black struggles for political and social justice in the state attests.[43] Yet so many scenes in *Palmetto-Leaves* and other letters record Stowe's interest in forms of development that could emerge only from an attenuation of white mastery that these writings finally display Stowe's negotiation of competing possibilities for the South's future.

The letter that opens *Palmetto-Leaves*, titled "Nobody's Dog," seems at first the most unlikely piece of evidence for this interpretation of Stowe in Florida. It begins with her encounter with a lost dog aboard a steamboat to Florida: "Yes, here he comes again! Look at him! Whose dog is he?" she asks, after which she relates the dog's progression from mourning his "lost master" to selecting a new master among the passengers (4–5). Scholars have puzzled over this odd beginning. Since *Palmetto-Leaves* mostly features letters that Stowe had already written and published in the *Christian Union*, why not begin with one more explicitly suited to an audience of prospective settlers, such as "Who Ought to Come to Florida?"[44] And what does the lost dog episode really mean? One reader concludes that the dog's plight is a "tidy metaphor" for Stowe's "civilizing mission."[45] In the letter Stowe imagines only two possible futures for the dog, who is last seen following the carriage of his self-selected mistress: either he is "now blessed in being somebody's dog" or he "roves the world desolate-hearted as 'nobody's dog,' with no rights to life, liberty, or pursuit of happiness" (9–10). These two options, concludes the reader, are the only ones Stowe imagines for Florida's population of recently freed slaves: they will either find new masters or forfeit even this circumscribed civic identity.

While this interpretation ideologically aligns *Palmetto-Leaves* with "Our Florida Plantation," it cannot account for many of Stowe's discussions of black labor and laborers as the letters proceed. An alternate reading of "Nobody's Dog," then, is that the futures Stowe imagines there convey an imperialist perspective challenged by the experience of Florida that follows. This interpretation of the letter would align it with the theme I have been tracing in this chapter, that of Stowe's interest in the unexpected prospects of self-determination that she experiences at Laurel Grove and continues to explore once she moves across the river to Mandarin.[46] For just as the groves of Mandarin are remarkable for an appearance of underdevelopment that conceals surprising capacities for self-propagation, so too are many of the laborers Stowe describes.[47] And these same capacities feature importantly in Stowe's explicit answer to the question of "Who Ought to Come to Florida?," her first published letter from Florida.

In this letter Stowe declares that "Florida is a raw, unsettled State," and thus it is "not the place for "Conventional people who are wedded to the forms and usages of settled and uniform society." Rather, those who will thrive are those "willing to begin small, to encounter difficulties and work their way up" to "a handsome independence." Here as elsewhere Stowe declares Florida's "rawness" desirable: precisely because it remains undeveloped in a more traditional sense, it can sustain those who establish themselves via unconventional "forms and usages." And, as an ideal form of economic sustenance for prospective settlers willing to "work their way up" from nothing, Stowe suggests orange culture. All one needs is a few seeds, for oranges "raised from the seed" can flourish into a grove in just ten years' time, and "when an orange grove once begins to bear it is a fixed and stable fact, and continues pouring forth year after year with a wonderful generosity."[48] Thus the trees not only start from seed and thrive via the shallow network of widespreading roots that Stowe elsewhere describes, but they also enable persons without deep roots to establish themselves by way of shallow ones.[49]

Stowe was not the only writer for whom orange trees provided new metaphors and practices of development. Orange culture plays a central role in *Letters from Florida* (1879), a work by Stowe's sister-in-law and fellow emigrant to Florida, Eunice White Bullard Beecher. Drawing on the orange tree as a model of self-sustenance, regeneration, and new growth, Beecher presents Florida's primary value to the nation as its continued resistance to traditional forms of settlement, which offers unmatched opportunities for those seeking "to establish their future from the foundations" during the last quarter of the nineteenth century.[50] Beecher shares Stowe's fundamental recognition that local Floridian sources and models of growth, attachment, and belonging can appear uncultivated and even uncivilized. Yet, while she praises "Northern enterprise and activity," she warns that Northerners are too prone to miss signs of growth, such as those that the orange tree exhibits even when seemingly dead. Beecher imagines a fictitious Northern interlocutor exclaiming that "an effort to reclaim such old, half-dead trees . . . seems

preposterous. I should prefer to grub up such unsightly objects" and plant a
new grove. She replies by declaring the speaker's "ignorance as regards orange-
culture." In this culture, that which has been "long-neglected" and appears
"gnarled," "unsightly," and "unpromising," only awaits "the first touch of
kindness and proper care" to be "rejuvenated" and become profitable: "Scrape
off the moss, remove the lichens, cut away all dead branches, wash and scrub
the bark . . . and in a year or two an old half-decayed grove will amply repay
the owner by a crop of bright and healthy fruit" (34–35).[51]

Just as for Stowe, for Beecher the orange tree exemplifies a logic of growth
that enables Florida's progress toward incorporation. Writing nearly thirty-
five years after Florida had officially become a state in 1845, she declares
Florida "most truly a 'new State,' because, after incredible rebuffs and disasters, she is once again struggling to rise above the many obstacles that have
so often well-nigh destroyed her . . . here, as elsewhere, *first steps* are always
surrounded with hardships . . . one rises for a moment, but to fall again"
(69). Florida's prolonged and continuing resistance to settlement positions
it to solve one of the expanding nation's most vexing problems: the accom-
modation of the poor and landless. Indeed Beecher envisions Florida's resistance to conventional cultivation as the condition that enables these
populations to take "the first fair start toward independent, useful citizenship!" (33). Considering the kinds of people Florida could best accommodate, she writes that "There are some who by marriage step at once into
elegant homes, and without exertion on their part are provided with ample
income. . . . These are not likely to find any great attractions in Florida" (42–43).
Yet Florida is ideal for those who are unable "to build up their own future on
the old foundations which their fathers laid," and for whom "it is ruinous to
remain in familiar localities, hampered by old methods, endeavoring to
force their way, till all they possess is wasted in the useless struggle to find a
firm and permanent foothold" (44): "for all those who are ready thus to begin
an independent life, and establish their future from the foundations, there
is no place within my knowledge where this can be so easily, rapidly, and
successfully accomplished as in this State" (44–45). The state itself is "once
again struggling to rise above the many obstacles that have so often well-
nigh destroyed her," and thus it can accommodate those willing to do the
same (69).[52]

Finally, then, by drawing on alternate metaphors of growth and development, Stowe and Beecher convert the region's reputation for impeding
traditional forms of founding into a valuable resource. Like many other

frontiers, Florida during the latter part of the nineteenth century became a major destination for those who lacked or abandoned "old foundations" and sought to experiment with new ones. During this time ground frequently disparaged as unfounded sometimes became the ideal foundation for a nation and empire in which incorporation must take a variety of forms.

Coda

For all the bright ideals Stowe sometimes imagined at Mandarin, we must remember that the realities of root-taking on Florida's shifting ground in the late nineteenth and early twentieth centuries were frequently grim. The attempt to live and establish a community in a place historically, geologically, and geographically resistant to long-term settlement sometimes had catastrophic results. Few U.S. writers have been more keenly aware of this fact than Zora Neale Hurston, particularly when reflecting on African American root-taking in Florida.

In *Their Eyes Were Watching God* (1937), Janie and Tea Cake find a home near central Florida's Lake Okeechobee among workers who come seasonally "from east, west, north and south," and even the Bahamas, to plant and harvest sugarcane and beans in the Everglades.[1] A rich, multinational culture forms around farming "the muck": when not at work in the fields, laborers join to tell stories, gamble, fish, sing, and even dance to "the compelling rhythms of the Bahaman drummers" (139). The home of Janie and Tea Cake fills nightly with friends, and although "the 'job'" is difficult, there is relative economic stability. Yet the laborers live at the mercy of wealthy white landowners and under significant racial oppression.

These realities come to the fore in the event and aftermath of a devastating hurricane that drives Lake Okeechobee over its dike and across the land.[2] The flood sweeps away the laborers' shanties, forcing families to flee for their lives by running or swimming through "raging waters and screaming when they couldn't" (161). Hundreds drown, and in the wake of the storm white men with guns force black survivors to collect and bury bodies, separating the dead into white and black, and dumping the latter into mass graves (170–71). The storm sharply underscores the fact that life on unstable ground is more deadly for some than for others.[3]

Yet Hurston's Florida writings also reveal that the same instability that rendered life particularly precarious for poor and black persons also made it possible for these persons to establish themselves. Late nineteenth- and early twentieth-century Florida drew black workers from across and beyond the nation because the state had more open land than other areas of the South.[4] And it had more open land, in part, because of the region's long history of intertwined political and physical instability.

At the start of her autobiography, *Dust Tracks on a Road* (1942), Hurston attributes the 1886 founding of Eatonville, Florida—her childhood home and "the first attempt at organized self-government on the part of Negroes in America"—to the fact that post-Reconstruction Florida remained relatively unsettled by a white, landholding populace.[5] "This had been dark and bloody country since the mid-seventeen hundreds," she explains, a place where "Spanish, French, English, Indian, and American blood had been bountifully shed" (2). This history of violent contestation, combined with more recent struggles between "resentful Indians" and "white planters" of the South attempting to enslave Africans in Florida, had thwarted U.S. plans to settle the region (2). According to Hurston, it is because South Florida is still an "unsettled country" that it attracts the notice of three Union veterans of the Civil War seeking to establish a new town where persons white and black could live on more equal footing (2). This town—Maitland, just north of Orlando—drew a large black population, some of whom went on to found nearby Eatonville, the first incorporated town in America entirely governed by black persons.

Although Hurston focuses on the political instability that enabled Eatonville's founding, environmental factors also contributed significantly to the relative unsettlement of the peninsula. On a number of occasions during the last quarter of the nineteenth century U.S. plans to build a transportation infrastructure and retain a white populace in Florida were delayed or derailed by strong hurricanes.[6] Flooding was a severe problem both before and after large-scale reclamation of the Everglades began in the early 1920s. Federally funded canals and dikes opened new farmland to populations both black and white. Yet, as Hurston well knew, the dikes did not always hold.[7]

To this landscape come people such as Hurston's father "to put down roots."[8] Like many black workers hailing from other parts of the South, he chose Florida to escape "the ordeal of sharecropping" on the grounds of a former plantation and to seek more self-determination (7). With its two churches, school, and a store that is "the heart and spring of the town,"

Eatonville sustains a rich community of black people from many parts of the South. This is why Hurston returns to the town in 1927 as a recent college graduate seeking to collect "Negro folklore" under the direction of Franz Boas. Research takes Hurston to several black communities in Florida. She goes to Polk County, where men and women work on saw-mill, turpentine, and railroad "jobs" by day and gather at "jooks" after dark, and "down into the Everglades where people worked and sweated and loved and died violently."[9] In the Everglades, along the banks of Lake Okeechobee, black laborers lived at the mercy of a changing landscape. Because farming was seasonal most could not afford to remain year-round. Rather, as in Janie and Tea Cake's community, they migrate continually as "Permanent transients with no attachments," save temporary and provisional ones that form each year at houses, fields, and jooks along the muck. But these are attachments nonetheless, and they would be unavailable on more solid ground. And these contingent attachments gave rise to one of the most important novels of twentieth-century U.S. literature.[10]

Importantly, Hurston does not confine her reflections on root-taking in Florida to Africans and African Americans. In *Mules and Men* (1935) she explains that "Florida is a place that draws people—white people from all over the world, and Negroes from every Southern state surely and some from the North and West."[11] And in her contribution to *Florida: A Guide to the Southernmost State* (1939) Hurston describes Florida as a place of several enclaves of persons from on and beyond the continent. The Seminole form communities in the Everglades, "Negro bean pickers from the Bahamas and the West Indies" live near Lake Okeechobee, people from "Cuba, Spain and Italy" settle at Ybor City and Tampa, "Greek sponge fishermen" reside at Tarpon Springs, "Conchs" from the Bahamas dwell in Key West, and there is an "Austro-Hungarian farm colony," a "Swedish settlement in Dade County," and "Polish families" near Daytona Beach (131, 133–35).[12]

Hurston's reflections on Florida support and extend several claims of *Liquid Landscape*. They bear out the argument that Florida's local land and populations are more than local in meaning because Florida is continually constituted by and influencing many places and people on and beyond the continent. And, much like the Florida of De Brahm, Bartram, Audubon, Cooper, Giddings, Stowe, and many others, Hurston's Florida is a place where land and water change places with little warning, dissolving homes and communities along with concepts of land, boundaries, and foundations— yet thereby encouraging modes of root-taking that would not elsewhere emerge. Most importantly for the purposes of this book, however, Hurston shows us that Florida's combination of topographic instability, geographic indeterminacy, and demographic fluidity sustains *histories* and *stories* that could not elsewhere emerge.

In this way, Hurston's work accentuates an environmental implication of this book: encounters with dramatically shifting ground produce a crucial language of place and attachment. This fact urges us to think about climate change not only as the severe ecological loss that scientists have begun to document, but also as an intellectual loss of important ways to conceptualize roots, community, and belonging. As rising seas continue to encroach on the Florida peninsula, we are steadily losing a vibrant language through which to imagine our relation to others and the natural world.

Notes

Introduction

1. For more on European pursuit and dissemination of these practices in the Americas, see Patricia Seed's landmark study, *Ceremonies of Possession in Europe's Conquest of the New World, 1492–1640* (New York: Cambridge University Press, 1995).

2. For studies of this "problem" perspective on the U.S. South in a broad range of U.S. writing (a perspective that *Liquid Landscape* complicates), see Natalie J. Ring, *The Problem South: Region, Empire, and the New Liberal State, 1880–1930* (Athens: University of Georgia Press, 2012); and Jennifer Rae Greeson, *Our South: Geographic Fantasy and the Rise of National Literature* (Cambridge, Mass.: Harvard University Press, 2010), 256–59. As John T. Matthews explains, Greeson, Ring, and others have traced how the early South served as "the new nation's internal Other," "a realm of unenlightened tyranny and bondage that sharpened the rest of the new republic's revolutionary devotion to enlightenment ideals" and "served the conceptual needs of a modernizing nation." Matthews, "Southern Literary Studies" in *Companion to American Literary Studies*, ed. Caroline Field Levander and Robert S. Levine (Malden, Mass.: Wiley, 2011). However, scholars including Matthews, Matthew Pratt Guterl, and Michael P. Bibler have begun calling for new approaches that unearth other conceptual roles and influences of southern spaces, challenge the notion that there ever was a totalizing concept of "the South" in U.S. culture and letters, and even bring an end to "southern studies" on the grounds that a North/South divide ultimately risks reproducing an "abjection of the South as the nation's internal Other." Matthews, "Southern Literary Studies"; Guterl, "South," in *Keywords for American Cultural Studies*, ed. Bruce Burgett and Glenn Hendler (New York: New York University Press, 2007); Bibler, "Introduction: Smash the Mason-Dixon! Or, Manifesting the Southern United States," *PMLA* 131, 1 (2016): 153–56.

3. See Edward E. Baptist, *Creating an Old South: Middle Florida's Plantation Frontier Before the Civil War* (Chapel Hill: University of North Carolina Press 2002). A notable antebellum writer living in Florida's antebellum plantation frontier is Caroline Lee Hentz, who resided in the area around Tallahassee and wrote traditional plantation novels that, Baptist speculates, borrow their settings from this part of Florida.

4. Because many of the works that figure importantly in *Liquid Landscape* will be unfamiliar to today's readers, endnotes for each work offer publication and reception history wherever possible.

5. The marginalization of scholarship focused on early Florida was the topic of spirited inquiry among the literary scholars and historians gathered for a conference roundtable, "Florida at the Margins," which was organized by Thomas Hallock at the Society of Early Americanists in July 2015 and included Anna Brickhouse, Amy Turner Bushnell, Jonathan DeCoster, Alejandra Dubcovsky, Michele Navakas, Tom Shields, and Lisa Voight. The panel began with a consideration of the relative absence of Florida in major academic journals publishing scholarship on early American literature and culture, such as *American Literature, William and Mary Quarterly, Early American Literature,* and *Early American Studies.* I join my fellow panelists and other scholars in seeking to change this marginalization. An important contribution to this change is Dubcovsky's recent book, *Informed Power: Communication in the Early American South* (Cambridge, Mass.: Harvard University Press, 2016).

6. The following history of Florida's fluidity relies on historical studies of early Florida that may seem marginal to many Americanists focusing on the early United States. My objective in this section, and in this book as a whole, is to suggest some ways of placing these studies of Florida in conversation with one another and with existing studies of eighteenth- and nineteenth-century U.S. literature and culture more broadly.

7. William P. Cumming, *The Southeast in Early Maps,* rev. Louis De Vorsey (Chapel Hill: University of North Carolina Press, 1998), 2–3.

8. Amy Turner Bushnell, "The Sacramental Imperative: Catholic Ritual and Indian Sedentism in the Provinces of Florida," in *Columbian Consequences,* vol. 2, *Archaeological and Historical Perspectives on the Spanish Borderlands East,* ed. David H. Thomas (Washington, D.C.: Smithsonian Institution Press, 1989), 475–90.

9. For a discussion of the significant assistance that Florida's Indians sometimes provided the Spanish, see Bushnell, "Ruling 'The Republic of Indians' in Seventeenth-Century Florida," in *American Encounters: Natives and Newcomers from European Contact to Indian Removal, 1500–1850,* ed. Peter C. Mancall and James H. Merrell (New York: Routledge, 2000).

10. Most of these pirates were French and British, as Bushnell explains in *Situado and Sabana: Spain's Support System for the Presidio and Mission Provinces of Florida* (New York: American Museum of Natural History, 1994), 161–69.

11. Bushnell, *Situado and Sabana;* also see James Axtell, *The Indians' New South: Cultural Change in the Colonial Southeast* (Baton Rouge: Louisiana State University Press, 1997), 25–44.

12. Axtell, *The Indians' New South,* 37. Also see Alan Gallay, *The Indian Slave Trade: The Rise of the English Empire in the American South, 1670–1717* (New Haven, Conn.: Yale University Press, 2002).

13. A royal proclamation of 1693 granted sanctuary to Africans escaping to Spanish Florida. Though this sanctuary policy would be discontinued during the eighteenth

century, Africans continued running south to freedom until the Civil War, as Christina Snyder explains in *Slavery in Indian Country: The Changing Face of Captivity in Early America* (Cambridge, Mass.: Harvard University Press, 2010), 213–48. Snyder's chapter "Seminoles and African Americans" is my primary source for the historical information in this paragraph. Also see Jane G. Landers, *Black Society in Spanish Florida* (Urbana: University of Illinois Press, 1999).

14. Snyder, *Slavery in Indian Country*, 213–17. It is important to note that the Seminole also held some Africans as slaves, a fact that demonstrates the complexity of Seminole-African relations. The term "Spanish Indians" refers to the Calusa, Tequesta, Timucua, and Guale, among other Indian groups.

15. For a more thorough discussion of these maps, see Chapter 2.

16. S. Max Edelson offers the most comprehensive study to date of British Florida, 1763–83. Edelson, *The New Map of Empire: How Britain Imagined America Before Independence* (Cambridge, Mass.: Harvard University Press, 2017).

17. For a discussion of "Florida fever," see Kathryn E. Holland Braund's Introduction to Bernard Romans's *A Concise Natural History of East and West Florida* (Tuscaloosa: University of Alabama Press, 1999), 23. Also see Charles L. Mowat, "The First Campaign of Publicity for Florida," *Mississippi Valley Historical Review* 30, 3 (1943): 359–76. For more information on the specific publication and wide circulation of Romans's *Natural History* (New York: 1775), see my discussion of this text in Chapter 2.

18. Florida's major plantation crops during this period were rice, cotton, indigo, oranges, and sugarcane. For more on Florida's colonial plantations, see Jane G. Landers, *Colonial Plantations and Economy in Florida* (Gainesville: University Press of Florida, 2000), 1–8.

19. At the start of the Revolutionary War, many American political figures imagined the United States as a "successor state" to Great Britain on the continent, and thus imagined that the new nation would consist of all British holdings to date, including the Floridas, as J. C. A. Stagg explains in *Borderlines in Borderlands: James Madison and the Spanish-American Frontier, 1776–1821* (New Haven, Conn.: Yale University Press, 2009).

20. Snyder, *Slavery in Indian Country*, 216.

21. For accounts of the "multiculturalism" of Florida during this period, see Jane G. Landers, *Atlantic Creoles in the Age of Revolutions* (Cambridge, Mass: Harvard University Press, 2010), 35 ff. Also see Deborah A. Rosen, *Border Law: The First Seminole War and American Nationhood* (Cambridge, Mass.: Harvard University Press, 2015).

22. Daniel L. Schafer, "Zephaniah Kingsley's Laurel Grove Plantation," in Landers, *Colonial Plantations*, 101.

23. Snyder, *Slavery in Indian Country*, 216; also see Rosen, *Border Law*.

24. The Patriot War was one of many attempts on the Spanish borderlands by filibusters acting independently of—though with varying degrees of support from—the U.S. government, as James G. Cusick explains in *The Other War of 1812: The Patriot War and the American Invasion of Spanish East Florida* (Gainesville: University Press

of Florida, 2003). See also Frank L. Owsley, Jr., and Gene A. Smith, *Filibusters and Expansionists: Jeffersonian Manifest Destiny, 1800–1821* (Tuscaloosa: University of Alabama Press, 1997); Landers, *Atlantic Creoles*; and Stagg, *Borderlines in Borderlands*.

25. Snyder, *Slavery in Indian Country*, 222–23. See also Gerald Horne, *Negro Comrades of the Crown: African Americans and the British Empire Fight the U.S. Before Emancipation* (New York: New York University Press, 2012).

26. Owsley and Smith, *Filibusters and Expansionists*, 141 ff.

27. See Chapter 4 for a discussion of the difficulties that U.S. troops faced when mapping this region during the nineteenth century.

28. Albert C. Manucy provides a construction history of this fort, Fort Jefferson, which I discuss at greater length in Chapter 3. Manucy, "The Gibraltar of the Gulf of Mexico," *Florida Historical Quarterly* 21, 4 (1943): 303–31. See also Dorothy Dodd, "The Wrecking Business on the Florida Reef, 1822–1860," *Florida Historical Quarterly* 22, 4 (1944): 171–99.

29. Although today much of the Everglades has been drained and filled, a large part of the region is now legally protected. For the fascinating story of repeatedly thwarted Everglades drainage plans, from the mid-nineteenth to the mid-twentieth century, see Michael Grunwald, *The Swamp: The Everglades, Florida, and the Politics of Paradise* (New York: Simon & Schuster, 2006).

30. John K. Mahon, *History of the Second Seminole War, 1835–1842* (Gainesville: University Press of Florida, 1985), 313–14. See also John Campbell, "The Seminoles, the 'Bloodhound War,' and Abolitionism, 1796–1865," *Journal of Southern History* 72, 2 (2006): 259–302.

31. In the wake of the Second Seminole War, the Armed Occupation Act of 1842 drew white settlers onto the peninsula by granting 160 acres of land to any head of family in return for a pledge to reside on and develop it for five years.

32. As late as 1880 Florida still contained well over seven million acres of unsurveyed land, while no other state in the East had any; it was the South's poorest and emptiest state (Grunwald, *The Swamp*, 117). Yet some isolated areas had once supported a traditional plantation culture. As Baptist (*Creating an Old South*, 7) explains, around Tallahassee in the middle decades of the nineteenth century, planters, slaves, and nonplanter whites migrated from other parts of the South and struggled to transform the region into a part of the cotton frontier. Earlier, in the area around Jacksonville, plantations thrived under British rule during the eighteenth century and again under the second period of Spanish rule, particularly before the War of 1812. Wealthy planters revived some of these plantations later in the antebellum period. See Daniel Schafer, *William Bartram and the Ghost Plantations of British East Florida* (Gainesville: University Press of Florida, 2010); and Schafer, "Zephaniah Kingsley's Laurel Grove Plantation."

33. It is also worth noting that Florida ports served as strategic sites in the coastal blockade during the Civil War. My source for many of these facts about Reconstruction-

era Florida is Jerrell H. Shofner, *Nor Is It Over Yet: Florida in the Era of Reconstruction, 1863–1877* (Gainesville: University Press of Florida, 1974).

34. Eric Foner explains that Florida and Texas were the only states funding black education during Reconstruction, but that this funding came from special taxes levied on blacks. Foner, *Reconstruction: America's Unfinished Revolution, 1863–1877* (New York: Harper and Row, 1988), 207. See also Lawrence N. Powell, *New Masters: Northern Planters During the Civil War and Reconstruction* (New York: Fordham University Press, 1998).

35. There have been many recent studies of the unexpected "roots and routes" of U.S. writing, particularly as a result of increased attention to spatial, transnational, hemispheric, and oceanic turns in Americanist scholarship. Those studies that have especially influenced *Liquid Landscape* include Martin Brückner, *The Geographic Revolution in Early America: Maps, Literacy, and National Identity* (Chapel Hill: Omohundro Institute for University of North Carolina Press, 2006); Sean X. Goudie, *Creole America: The West Indies and the Formation of Literature and Culture in the New Republic* (Philadelphia: University of Pennsylvania Press, 2006); Christopher P. Iannini, *Fatal Revolutions: Natural History, West Indian Slavery, and the Routes of American Literature* (Chapel Hill: University of North Carolina Press, 2012); Stephanie LeMenager, *Manifest and Other Destinies: Territorial Fictions of the Nineteenth-Century United States* (Lincoln: University of Nebraska Press, 2004); Robert S. Levine, *Dislocating Race & Nation: Episodes in Nineteenth-Century American Literary Nationalism* (Chapel Hill: University of North Carolina Press, 2008); and Susan Scott Parrish, *American Curiosity: Cultures of Natural History in the Colonial British Atlantic World* (Chapel Hill: University of North Carolina Press for Omohundro Institute, 2006).

36. William Bartram, *Travels Through North & South Carolina, Georgia, East & West Florida, the Cherokee Country, the Extensive Territories of the Muscogulges, or Creek Confederacy, and the Country of the Chactaws; Containing an Account of the Soil and Natural Productions of those Regions, Together with Observations on the Manners of the Indians: Embellished with Copper-Plates* (Philadelphia: Printed by James & Johnson, 1791), 226. Subsequent references cited in text.

37. Though Bartram's own attempt at an indigo and rice plantation in Florida in 1766 came to naught, recent scholarship documents Florida's early plantation culture, and even suggests that Bartram saw many flourishing plantations during his visit to Florida in the 1770s. See Landers, *Colonial Plantations*; Schafer, *William Bartram and the Ghost Plantations*; and Baptist, *Creating an Old South*.

38. Ed White explains that while some portions of *Letters* celebrate British North America as a polity of yeomen, each cultivator pursuing freedom and independence on his own plot of ground, other portions critique and revise this ideal in favor of a more communal existence modeled on the narrator's perception of Indian life on the frontier. See White's fascinating interpretation of Crèvecoeur as a "theorist of seriality par excellence" in *The Backcountry and the City: Colonization and Conflict in Early*

America (Minneapolis: University of Minnesota Press, 2005), 35. Also see White, "Crèvecoeur in Wyoming," *Early American Literature* 43, 2 (2008): 379–407; and J. Hector St. John de Crèvecoeur, *Letters from an American Farmer and Other Essays*, ed. Dennis D. Moore (Cambridge, Mass: Belknap Press of Harvard University Press, 2013),

39. In 1791 James & Johnson of Philadelphia published the first edition of Bartram's *Travels*; in 1793 Matthew Carey of Philadelphia issued an edition of Crèvecoeur's *Letters*. Upon publication *Travels* was reviewed in several major U.S. and British journals, including *Universal Asylum and Columbian Magazine* (Philadelphia), the *Massachusetts Magazine*, and *Monthly Review; or Literary Journal* (London). Francis Harper, introduction to William Bartram, *The Travels of William Bartram: Naturalist's Edition*, ed. Harper (New Haven, Conn.: Yale University Press, 1958), xiii–xxv. Within ten years eight European editions appeared, though another U.S. edition was not issued during Bartram's lifetime (Harper, Introduction, xviii). For more, see Charlotte Porter, "Bartram's Legacy: Nature Advocacy," in *Fields of Vision: Essays on the Travels of William Bartram*, ed. Kathryn E. Holland Braund and and Charlotte M. Porter (Tuscaloosa: University of Alabama Press, 2010), 221–38.

40. The influence of *Travels* on eighteenth- and nineteenth-century U.S. and European literature, natural history, and art was enormous. In addition to its influence on Chateaubriand (see below), the work was embraced by Coleridge, Wordsworth, Emerson, and Thoreau. Nathan B. Fagin, *William Bartram: Interpreter of the American Landscape* (Baltimore: Johns Hopkins University Press, 1933); pored over by Titian Ramsay Peale in Florida during an 1817 expedition for the Academy of Natural Sciences. Charlotte M. Porter, "Following Bartram's 'Track': Titian Ramsay Peale's Florida Journey" (Tampa: Florida Historical Society, 1983), 433); examined and critiqued by Audubon. John James Audubon, *Audubon in Florida: With Selections from the Writings of John James Audubon*, ed. Kathryn Hall Proby (Coral Gables, Fla.: University of Miami Press, 1974); consulted and cited by authors of several published guidebooks to Territorial Florida (see Chapter 2); probably used as a source for Martin Johnson Heade's images of animals and plants (Porter, 229–30); and, as I discuss in Chapter 1, valued by ethnographer Frank Hamilton Cushing in *Exploration of Ancient Key-Dweller Remains on the Gulf Coast of Florida*, ed. Randolph J. Widmer (Gainesville: University Press of Florida, 2000).

41. François-René Chateaubriand, *Atala; René* (Berkeley: University of California Press, 1980), 18. *Atala*, a fragment of Chateaubriand's later work *Les Natchez* (1829), is sometimes popularly called the first Florida novel. The work was extremely well received in the early United States, particularly after its translation into English by Caleb Bingham. However, as John Seelye explains, "Chateaubriand's own travels did not take him farther south than the mouth of the Ohio River," and many of the landscape scenes in *Atala* are indebted to Bartram's *Travels*. Seelye, *Beautiful Machine: Rivers and the Republican Plan* (New York: Oxford University Press, 1991), 174. Chateaubriand credits Bartram as a significant inspiration in the preface to *Travels in America and Italy*, vol. 1 (London: Henry Colburn, 1828), writing that he had translated Bartram's

Travels and drew on it so extensively in his own travel narrative that "it is almost impossible for me to separate what is mine from what is Bartram's, or indeed frequently even recognize it" (177). For more on Chateaubriand's extensive use of *Travels*, see E. P. Panagopoulos, "Chateaubriand's Florida and His Journey to America," *Florida Historical Quarterly* 49, 2 (1970): 140–52; and Fagin, *William Bartram*.

42. In other words, why not excerpt Bartram in American literature anthologies, right alongside excerpts from Crèvecoeur? Fortunately, recent studies demonstrate that *Travels* is valuable for more than its historical information about the plants and peoples of Florida; two studies especially attentive to Bartram's metaphors, tropes, and literary form are Iannini, *Fatal Revolutions*; and Monique Allewaert, *Ariel's Ecology: Plantations, Personhood, and Colonialism in the American Tropics* (Minneapolis: University of Minnesota Press, 2013).

43. For more on this topic, see Mark Rifkin, *Manifesting America: The Imperial Construction of U.S. National Space* (Oxford: Oxford University Press, 2009); and Rifkin, *Settler Common Sense: Queerness and Everyday Colonialism in the American Renaissance* (Minneapolis: University of Minnesota Press, 2014).

44. As Myra Jehlen concisely observes, "the solid reality, the *terra firma*" of the continent was "the decisive factor shaping the founding conceptions of 'America' and 'the American'" from the early national period until the mid-nineteenth century. Jehlen, *American Incarnation: The Individual, the Nation, and the Continent* (Cambridge, Mass.: Harvard University Press, 1986), 3, 5. For more recent literary studies examining how the ideal of the United States as a stable, solid, contiguous reality served such ends during the eighteenth and nineteenth centuries, see Brückner, *The Geographic Revolution*; James D. Drake, *The Nation's Nature: How Continental Presumptions Gave Rise to the United States of America* (Charlottesville: University of Virginia Press, 2011); and Anne Baker, *Heartless Immensity: Literature, Culture, and Geography in Antebellum America* (Ann Arbor: University of Michigan Press, 2006). Also see the following historical studies of private property, westward expansion, and settler colonialism: Edward T. Price, *Dividing the Land: Early American Beginnings of Our Private Property Mosaic* (Chicago: University of Chicago Press, 1995); Peter S. Onuf, *Jefferson's Empire: The Language of American Nationhood* (Charlottesville: University of Virginia Press, 2000); and Onuf, *Statehood and Union: A History of the Northwest Ordinance* (Bloomington: Indiana University Press, 1987).

45. Several recent scholarly works examine this topic. For example, Rifkin focuses on nineteenth-century writing by American Indians and Mexican Americans who did not seek "to belong to, or to be superintended by, the United States," and concludes that many populations living in the antebellum United States challenged the "imagined map of the republic" by asserting sovereignty over some of the same land that proponents of U.S. expansion designated as "domestic space" (*Manifesting America*, 3–7). Rifkin's work resonates with that of legal historian Lauren Benton, who encourages us to think of the spaces of empire before 1900 as "politically fragmented," "legally differentiated," and "encased in irregular, porous, and sometimes undefined borders"—

both because peoples or polities demanded (or negotiated) spaces of autonomy, and because the irregularities of the ground itself resisted an even expansion of sovereignty. Benton, *A Search for Sovereignty: Law and Geography in European Empires, 1400–1900* (New York: Cambridge University Press, 2010), 2. Also see Laura Dassow Walls, "Literature, Geography, and the Spaces of Interdisciplinarity," *American Literary History* 23, 4 (2011): 860–72, and particularly her discussion of the spatial turn in humanities scholarship.

46. Benton, *A Search for Sovereignty*, 3.

47. Many scholars have already shown how places seemingly peripheral to the early nation in fact constituted it politically and territorially, often by putting pressure on or generating alternatives to a more familiar nationalist narrative. *Liquid Landscape* particularly draws from and builds on the work of scholars who have pursued these approaches and grounded their studies of the early United States in places beyond New England. Looking west, for example, LeMenager shows that the continent's "apparently landless places"—such as desert environments and riverine zones—challenged Manifest Destiny and produced narratives of a "maritime" America sustained by oceanic commerce, populations, and spaces far beyond the continent (*Manifest and Other Destinies*). Looking south, Matthews, Greeson, and Guterl uncover the centrality of southern plantations to U.S. national identity. Matthews, "Southern Literary Studies," 294; Greeson, *Our South*; Guterl, *American Mediterranean: Southern Slaveholders in the Age of Emancipation* (Cambridge, Mass.: Harvard University Press, 2008). And looking just beyond the continent's edges, Iannini, Parrish, and Goudie describe a North America sustained by Caribbean economies, geographies, and cultures (Iannini, *Fatal Revolutions*; Parrish, *American Curiosity*; Goudie, *Creole America*). See also Caroline F. Levander and Robert S. Levine, *Hemispheric American Studies* (New Brunswick, N.J.: Rutgers University Press, 2008); and Shelley Streeby, *American Sensations: Class, Empire, and the Production of Popular Culture* (Berkeley: University of California Press, 2002).

48. I borrow the phrase "changes in the land" from William Cronon's study of interactions between land and people in early New England, *Changes in the Land: Indians, Colonists, and the Ecology of New England* (New York: Hill and Wang, 1983).

Chapter 1

1. John James Audubon, *Ornithological Biography; or, An Account of the Habits of the Birds of the United States of America* (Edinburgh: Adam & Charles Black, 1835), 3:383. Subsequent references cited in text. Audubon visited the Florida Keys during his trip to Florida (1831–32) and wrote about the experience in short sketches in volumes 2 and 3 of *Ornithological Biography*, a five-volume text published in Edinburgh between 1831 and 1839, as a narrative companion to *The Birds of America* (London: 1827–38). While volume 3 of *Biography*, containing Audubon's reflections on the Mangrove, was not published in the United States, volumes 1 and 2 were, and all volumes were heavily marketed there in conjunction with U.S. editions of *The Birds* (Philadelphia

and Boston). *Biography* received enthusiastic reviews abroad and in the United States, where readers praised Audubon's lively, engaging, and almost novelistic prose. Margaret Curzon Welch, "John James Audubon and His American Audience: Art, Science, and Nature, 1830–1860" (PhD diss., University of Pennsylvania, 1988); Duff Hart-Davis, *Audubon's Elephant: America's Greatest Naturalist and the Making of the "Birds of America"* (New York: Holt, 2004). Thoreau's "winter reading" in 1842 must have included volume 2 and/or 3: in an essay in *The Dial* he records, "I read in Audubon with a thrill of delight, when the snow covers the ground, of the magnolia, and the Florida keys, and their warm sea breezes" ("Natural History of Massachusetts," quoted in Welch). The *Biography*'s appeal to early North Americans calls for more attention by early Americanists.

2. Nelson Manfred Blake, *Land into Water—Water into Land: A History of Water Management in Florida* (Tallahassee: University Press of Florida, 1980), 301.

3. Greeson, *Our South*, Part 1; Ring, *The Problem South*. For more discussion of this view of the "problem" South, which *Liquid Landscape* challenges, see my Introduction.

4. Although "the Floridas" is the historically accurate name of the region I describe during the period of British rule, I use "Florida" for simplicity and consistency.

5. For more on this imperial ideology, see Ralph Bauer and José Antonio Mazzotti, *Creole Subjects in the Colonial Americas: Empires, Texts, Identities* (Chapel Hill: Published for Omohundro Institute of Early American History and Culture by University of North Carolina Press, 2009).

6. For more on the cartographic uncertainty surrounding East Florida during the eighteenth century, and on British colonial mapping of the region during the 1760s and 1770s, see Edelson, *New Map of Empire*, Chapter 6: "Defining East Florida," 249–87. See also William John Gerard De Brahm, *De Brahm's Report of the General Survey in the Southern District of North America*, ed. Louis De Vorsey (Columbia: University of South Carolina Press, 1971), 33–59.

7. Edelson (*New Map of Empire*, 249–54) shows that these two maps by Emanuel Bowen are part of a larger cartographic trend on British maps of East Florida during this period.

8. Mowat, "First Campaign of Publicity."

9. Harry J. Carman et al., eds., *American Husbandry* (New York: Columbia University Press, 1939). Subsequent references cited in text. As Carman explains, the authorship of *American Husbandry* remains undetermined. The text was published anonymously with a subtitle followed by a single line reading "By An American." While an anonymous reviewer in a London periodical seems to attribute the work to Arthur Young, scholars have more recently concluded that the author was probably John Mitchell, who emigrated from England to Virginia in about 1700.

10. By the Treaty of Paris of 1763, Spain ceded Florida to Great Britain in exchange for British claims to Cuba. While some British subjects expressed boundless enthusiasm for the new territory in a flurry of promotional tracts, others found the trade ques-

tionable. The vitriol expressed by the author of *American Husbandry* is probably motivated by frustration at what he perceives as a bad bargain. For more on the enthusiastic response to Florida, see Mowat, "First Campaign of Publicity."

11. John Locke, *The Second Treatise of Civil Government*, ed. C. B. MacPherson (Indianapolis: Hackett, 1980), 5.27.

12. Ibid., 5.32, 5.30.

13. David L. Hume, *A Treatise of Human Nature*, ed. A. Selby-Bigge and P. H. Nidditch (Oxford: Clarendon, 1978), 3.2.2.

14. Crèvecoeur, *Letters*, 54. Although Crèvecoeur considers whaling an acceptable alternative to farming, his discussions of landed possession leave little room to imagine *how* ground such as that of Florida could produce an acceptable civic identity. For more analysis of *Letters*, see my Introduction.

15. Jefferson imagined the inhabitants of the United States becoming enterprising "settler-developers" who synthesized farming and commerce and would advance the nation's westward frontier by maintaining commercial networks with distant markets for their agricultural goods. Peter Onuf explains this idea in the following terms: "Jefferson's agrarianism juxtaposed virtuous farmers to avaricious merchants, but the territorial expansion that would create a great 'empire of liberty' depended on a synthesis of his antithetical terms. In Jefferson's paradoxical vision, enterprising Americans would come together by moving apart. Americans would therefore have to develop a transportation and communication infrastructure across their vast continental domain. Providentially, nature showed the way, in the great system of rivers that would link farmers to distant markets, transforming inland trading centers into bustling 'seaports.'" Onuf, *Statehood and Union*, 111. For a detailed study of a pro-manufacturing version of Jeffersonianism that developed in the urban North, see Andrew Shankman, *Crucible of American Democracy: The Struggle to Fuse Egalitarianism & Capitalism in Jeffersonian Pennsylvania* (Lawrence: University Press of Kansas, 2004).

16. For more on the legal and cultural importance of landed possession in North America from the colonial period onward, see James W. Ely, *The Guardian of Every Other Right: A Constitutional History of Property Rights* (New York: Oxford University Press, 1992), 51. For a thorough account of the way that North American land was divided and distributed, see Price, *Dividing the Land*. For a discussion of the power of property to determine political personhood during the late eighteenth century, see John Phillip Reid, *The Concept of Representation in the Age of the American Revolution* (Chicago: University of Chicago Press, 1989), 35–39. On how the "propertyless" were frequently deemed threatening because of their ostensible lack of attachment to the nation, see Willi Paul Adams, *The First American Constitutions: Republican Ideology and the Making of the State Constitutions in the Revolutionary Era* (New York: Rowman & Littlefield, 2001), 210. Also see Drew R. McCoy, *The Elusive Republic: Political Economy in Jeffersonian Amer-*

ica (Chapel Hill: Published for Omohundro Institute of Early American History and Culture by University of North Carolina Press 1980), 131, 197. However, the work of Joyce Appleby, and more recently that of Onuf and Shankman, provide important correctives to McCoy's tendency to overstate Jefferson's anxiety about commerce.

17. Ann Vileisis, *Discovering the Unknown Landscape: A History of America's Wetlands* (Washington, D.C.: Island Press, 1997), 17.

18. Ibid., 38.

19. William Byrd, *The Westover Manuscripts: Containing the History of the Dividing Line Betwixt Virginia and North Carolina* . . . , ed. Edmund Ruffin (Petersburg: Printed by E. and J.C. Ruffin, 1841), 19, 92. Given Byrd's many and conflicting alliances, there is a strong possibility that his bold declaration is satirical; see Susan Scott Parrish, "William Byrd II and the Crossed Languages of Science, Satire, and Empire in British America," in Bauer and Mazzotti, *Creole Subjects*, 355–74.

20. Vileisis, *Unknown Landscape*, 17–18.

21. Ibid.

22. Grunwald, *The Swamp*, 57. Grunwald also notes that Florida received an inordinate amount of rainfall, at least three times as much as did the Great Plains (55).

23. Ibid., 57. While the Armed Occupation Act of 1842 offered 160 acres to any homesteader willing to settle in the region for at least five years, in the 1840s settlement and cultivation were still distant achievements because the land was too wet to support crops.

24. John Lee Williams, *The Territory of Florida* (New York, 1837; Gainesville: University Press of Florida, 1962), 146, 34, 151. Such speculation on the erosive nature of the peninsula appears in numerous nineteenth-century guidebooks that circulated widely. For example, William Darby fashions the peninsula, "now irrevocably an integral part of the United States," an expanding mass of ocean detritus: "the whole peninsula owes its existence to mineral and animal deposition," he writes, and this "prodigious mound or wing dam" is growing still. "The land, although slowly, is evidently encroaching upon the sea along the whole south extremity of Florida. The same agents, which have formed the peninsula, are yet in unremitting activity." Darby, *Memoir on the Geography, and Natural and Civil History of Florida: Attended by a Map of That Country, Connected with the Adjacent Places: And an Appendix, Containing the Treaty of Cession, and Other Papers Relative to the Subject* (Philadelphia: Printed by T. H. Palmer, 1821), iii, 18, 8, 21. Other writers of early guides to Florida consider its physical connection to the continent recent and tenuous and deem watery land along the northern border with Georgia evidence that the peninsula was once an island. James Grant Forbes declares Florida "an integral part of the Union," yet also notes that the peninsula dissolves constantly: "owing to the agitation of the waters, which are driven against the southern extremity with continual violence, it is worn away, and divided

into many islands, keys, and rocks." *Sketches, Historical and Topographical, of the Floridas, More Particularly of East Florida* (Gainesville: University Press of Florida, 1964), v, 103.

25. Locke is not the only philosopher, of course, to ground identity in the possession of property: both David Hume and Lord Kames consider the intimate relationship between people and things fundamental to identity and society. Hume claims that civil law maintains "stability of possession," which is, "of all circumstances the most necessary to the establishment of human society." *Treatise*, 3.2.2.

26. De Brahm, *Report*, 33.

27. My source for information about the aims of the Board of Trade is De Vorsey's excellent introduction to De Brahm's *Report*, cited above.

28. De Brahm, *Report*, 5.

29. De Vorsey's 1971 edition of De Brahm's *Report* is the only complete, published reproduction; the British Library holds the original manuscript (Kings MS 210 & 211), and microfilm copies are available at some U.S. libraries. However, the portion of the *Report* to which I confine my analysis (*The Atlantic Pilot*) was published in 1772, and widely disseminated thereafter (see note 32).

30. For more on the Cape Florida Society, see Roland E. Chardon, "The Cape Florida Society of 1773," *Tequesta* 35 (1975): 1–36.

31. De Vorsey (De Brahm, *Report*, 298–99) cites the favorable reviews in *Critical Review* 34 (1772): 73–4 and *The Monthly Review; Or, Literary Journal* 46 (1772): 536–37 respectively. *The Atlantic Pilot* is a small section of De Brahm's *Report* and appears in De Vorsey's edition (241–52). While the *Report* was not published in full until the twentieth century (see note 29 above), the *Atlantic Pilot* portion was published upon completion (London, 1772), and De Vorsey discusses the reception, distribution, circulation, and influence of the *Pilot*, noting a French translation (Paris, 1788) and U.S. readership (*Report*, 298–99). Of particular relevance to *Liquid Landscape* is the *Pilot's* influence on Bernard Romans's *Concise Natural History* (1775) of Florida, which circulated widely during the first half of the nineteenth century, particularly among those interested in U.S. Territorial Florida (1821–45; see my Chapter 2). Thus Romans preserved De Brahm's reflections on Florida and disseminated them to a U.S. readership. Buckingham Smith, who was commissioned by Congress to survey the Everglades in 1848, reports that Romans's work inspired him to find De Brahm's maps and charts at the Washington, D.C., library of Peter Force, known today as the *American Archives* and held by the Library of Congress. Buckingham Smith and James D. Wescott. *Report . . . to Authorize the Drainage of the Ever Glades, in the State of Florida*. 30th Cong., 1st sess., Senate Report 242 Washington, D.C., 1848. Additionally, Romans is the likely source of Charles Blacker Vignoles's interest in De Brahm in *Observations upon the Floridas* (New York, 1823; Gainesville: University Press of Florida, 1977), discussed below.

32. De Brahm, *Report*, 298–99.

33. Ibid., 242.

34. As Braund explains, "The term [Tequesta] actually derives from the name of a sixteenth-century chiefdom located on the Miami River and Biscayne Bay. The designation was regularly employed by Spanish cartographers." In Romans, *Concise Natural History*, 48–49. See my Introduction for more on Florida's early populations and their demise.

35. De Brahm, *Report*, 244; emphasis added.

36. Ibid., 244–45; emphasis added.

37. De Brahm, *Report*, 10.

38. Romans, *Concise Natural History*, 263.

39. On the details of De Brahm's education, see Charles L. Mowat, "That 'Odd Being,' de Brahm," *Florida Historical Quarterly* 20, 4 (1942): 323–45.

40. De Brahm, *Report*, 10.

41. Martin J. S. Rudwick, *Bursting the Limits of Time: The Reconstruction of Geohistory in the Age of Revolution* (Chicago: University of Chicago Press, 2005), 6, 133–34.

42. James Hutton, "Theory of the Earth; or, An Investigation of the Laws Observable in the Composition, Dissolution, and Restoration of Land upon the Globe," *Transactions of the Royal Society of Edinburgh* 1 (1788): 209–304, 288.

43. Ibid., 296.

44. The English historian of science William Whewell coined the terms "catastrophism" and "uniformitarianism" after Lyell's publication of *Principles of Geology*. For more on the meaning of these terms, see Martin J. S. Rudwick, *Worlds Before Adam: The Reconstruction of Geohistory in the Age of Reform* (Chicago: University of Chicago Press, 2008), 358.

45. Rudwick, *Worlds*, 315–30.

46. Hutton, "Theory," 293.

47. De Brahm, *Report*, 244–45.

48. Brückner, *Geographic Revolution*, 20–25, 45. Lord Dartmouth specifically requested "plats" of his holdings. For useful facts about De Brahm's surveys of Dartmouth's land grants, see Chardon, who explains that De Brahm completed Dartmouth's plats in 1773 ("I have finished also the plots, which are to be joined to Your Grants," writes De Brahm, May 4, 1773); that Dartmouth owned land near Cape Florida, but that the grant can only be "approximately located" ("Cape Florida Society," 14); and that Dartmouth planned to settle twenty families on six thousand acres, though the colony never materialized and the land soon became known as the "Indian Hunting Grounds" (18).

49. Brückner, *Geographic Revolution*, 46. Brückner further encourages us to see the plat as a "continuation of the early modern emergence of what Richard Helgerson has called 'a cartographically and chorographically shaped consciousness of national power'" that emerged during the 1570s when, "'for the first time [Englishmen] took effective visual and conceptual possession of the physical kingdom in which they lived'" (20).

50. De Brahm, *Report*, 229.

51. Carman et al., *American Husbandry*, 364, 365.

52. Sir William Blackstone, *Commentaries on the Laws of England* (Oxford: Clarendon, 1765–69), 2.16.26. New islands always belong to the owner of the water in which they form (usually the sovereign), while expanding shores may belong either to the private individual or to the state, depending on how quickly the shores expand. As nineteenth-century legal writer Joseph K. Angell explains, if the increase of land is "slow and secret . . . and is so gradually and insensibly occasioned as to render impossible to perceive how much is added in each moment of time, it then belongs to the riparian proprietor to whose land the accession is made." Angell, *A Treatise on the Right of Property in the Tide Waters and in the Soil and Shores Thereof* (Boston: Harrison Gray, 1826), 249. The identification and legal definition of these watery lands, known as *maritima incrementa*, originate in Roman law. When describing *maritima incrementa*, both Blackstone and Sir Matthew Hale draw heavily on Bracton's *On the Laws and Customs of England*, a medieval treatise that attempts to achieve a standard formulation of English common law in terms of Roman and canon law.

53. Hale, *A History of the Foreshore and the Law Relating Thereto*, ed. Stuart J. Moore (London: Stevens & Haynes, 1888), 381–82.

54. Bartram, *Travels*, 88–89. See my Introduction for a discussion of the publication history and influence of *Travels*.

55. Bartram, *Travels*, 89–90.

56. Gregory A. Waselkov and Kathryn E. Holland Braund, *William Bartram on the Southeastern Indians* (Lincoln: University of Nebraska Press, 1995), 209.

57. Ibid., 210. As Gordon M. Sayre shows, the idea of the Mound-Builders "contributed to the myth of an American antiquity." Sayre, "The Mound Builders and the Imagination of American Antiquity in Jefferson, Bartram, and Chateaubriand," *Early American Literature* 33, 3 (1998): 225–49, 230, 235, 240. Waselkov and Braund concur.

58. Waselkov and Braund, *William Bartram*, 210–11. Waselkov and Braund note that Bartram's contemporaries may not have understood that he rejected the Mound-Builder myth in favor of the theory that ancestors of present-day Indians built the mounds (201).

59. Bartram, *Travels*, 516, 368, 520–21. Subsequent references cited in text.

60. For a discussion of the political implications of the Mound-Builder myth, and how debunking that myth did not always serve Indian populations favorably as one might expect, see Annette Kolodny's discussion of "the politics of American prehistory": *In Search of First Contact: The Vikings of Vinland, the Peoples of the Dawnland, and the Anglo-American Anxiety of Discovery* (Durham, N.C.: Duke University Press, 2012), 40–43.

61. Randolph J. Widmer, Introduction to Cushing, *Exploration of Ancient Key-Dweller Remains*, xviii. For more on Cushing's methodological innovations, also see Phyllis E. Kolianos and Brent R. Weisman, *The Lost Florida Manuscript of Frank Ham-*

ilton Cushing (Gainesville: University Press of Florida, 2005), 2. For more on Cushing's references to Bartram, see Waselkov and Braund, *William Bartram*, 137–38.

62. Cushing's method, which Kolianos and Weisman describe as an "ethnographically informed archaeology," involved interpreting the use and meaning of artifacts, rather than their date and function alone, as many of Cushing's peers did. This innovative method required consulting descriptions of land and people penned by earlier visitors. Accordingly the *Report* cites a variety of English, French, and Spanish narratives about early Florida, including Bartram's *Travels*; Bartram's "Observations," a text penned in 1788, though unpublished until 1853; Jonathan Dickinson's *God's Protecting Providence*, printed in Philadelphia in 1699 (35); René de Laudonnière's *L'histoire notable de la Floride*, penned during the 1560s and translated into English by Hakluyt in 1586 (52–53); Charles de Rochefort's *The History of the Caribby Islands*, translated into English by John Davies in 1666 (75); and Hernando de Escalante Fontaneda's *Memoria*, translated into English by Buckingham Smith in 1854 (118).

63. Cushing, *Exploration of Ancient Key-Dweller Remains*, 34. Subsequent references cited in text.

64. Cushing's remarkable theory of mounds has received little scholarly attention outside of biographies of Cushing and histories of the Calusa. Even Kolodny's recent and thorough discussion of the Mound-Builder myth overlooks Cushing's contributions.

65. Whereas buoyant water lettuce roots stabilize plant communities by remaining unanchored so that the structures do not capsize "when the river is suddenly raised," mounds stabilize human communities by serving as a temporary point of retreat when land turns to water (Bartram, *Travels*, 89, 326).

Chapter 2

1. Jedidiah Morse, *Geography Made Easy: Being a Short but Comprehensive System of That Very Useful and Agreeable Science* (New Haven, Conn.: Meigs, Bowen & Dana, 1784), iv; quoted in Brückner, *Geographic Revolution*, 114. Brückner records that Doolittle's map reached a large audience: appearing in "the most widely read geographical book ever written in and about America," it was broadly disseminated long after the year of its initial appearance and was embraced by "thousands of students for several generations" (116).

2. Morse, *Geography Made Easy . . . Calculated Particularly for the Use and Improvement of Schools in the United States of America*, 3rd ed. (Boston: Hall, 1791), 38.

3. See Brückner for more on how to decipher maps from this period. Martin Brückner, "Introduction: The Plurality of Early American Cartography," in *Early American Cartographies*, ed. Brückner (Chapel Hill: University of North Carolina Press, 2011).

4. Brückner, *Geographic Revolution*, 80. Brückner explains that before the mid-eighteenth century it was not uncommon for mapmakers to represent North America

as a "fragmented, elusive territory" that consisted of multiple islands, peninsulas, or other landmasses (80).

5. Jehlen, *American Incarnation*, 3. More recent studies of the rhetorical, conceptual, and political importance of the solid and self-contained continent include Brückner, *Geographic Revolution*; Price, *Dividing the Land*; Onuf, *Jefferson's Empire* and *Statehood and Union*; Drake, *The Nation's Nature*; and Baker, *Heartless Immensity*.

6. Brückner, *Early American Cartographies*, 19.

7. Brückner usefully reminds us that not all eighteenth-century maps of North America led to the nation-state. Brückner, *Early American Cartographies*, 12–13.

8. As Rifkin explains, the image of an evenly shaded map of North America belies a complicated colonial world of many peoples and polities with their own concepts and practices of space, place, and belonging. Many populations who did not seek "to belong to, or to be superintended by, the United States" challenged the "imagined map of the republic" by asserting sovereignty over some of the same land that proponents of U.S. expansion designated as "domestic space." Rifkin, *Manifesting America*, 5–6.

9. Romans, *Concise Natural History*, 257; emphasis added.

10. Charles Brockden Brown, trans., *A View of the Soil and Climate of the United States of America* (Philadelphia: Published by J. Conrad & Co., 1804), 316. Brown's endorsement of Romans's work appears in Brown's 1804 English translation of Constantin-François de Chassebœuf, comte de Volney's *Tableau du climat et du sol des États-Unis d'Amérique* (Paris 1803). Volney's work includes excerpts from Romans's natural history, but Brown's translation expands those excerpts for an American audience because "the country [Romans] speaks of is rapidly growing into an object of extraordinary interest and curiosity to the people of the United States" (Brown, *View*, xxv). While Brown was correct to note the limited availability of Romans's text in early America, the work was published in New York in 1775. Romans promoted it in major cities throughout the Northeast, and his list of subscribers includes professional navigators, U.S. political figures, and naturalists in America and England (Braund, 22). And during the nineteenth century—as U.S. interest in acquiring, then nationalizing, Florida grew—Romans's work provided information to Florida travelers, naturalists, and surveyors, including Buckingham Smith, first surveyor of the Florida Everglades in 1848 (Smith and Wescott, *Report*, 12). All five of the published guidebooks to Territorial Florida that I discuss in this chapter cite Romans's *Natural History*, and the text almost definitely served these guidebook authors as an important guide to even earlier sources about Florida's land and populations. The guidebooks cite many of the same British and Spanish colonial accounts of Florida that Romans cites, including Garcilaso de la Vega's chronicle of Hernando de Soto's Florida expedition, *La Florida del Inca* (1605) (Romans, 391; Williams, *Territory of Florida*, iii); De Brahm's maps and charts (Romans, 261 ff.; Vignoles, *Observations upon the Floridas*, 10); and early British promotional accounts such as William Stork's *Description of East Florida* (1769) containing John Bartram's Florida journal of 1765–66 (Romans, 244 ff.; Williams, iii). Thus Romans's *Natural History* probably helped preserve and transmit

earlier accounts of Florida to a nineteenth-century audience. For more detailed information on the publication, reception, and influence of Romans's work, see Kathryn E. Holland Braund's edition of the *Natural History*.

11. Vignoles, *Observations upon the Floridas*, 51. The work was originally published in New York in 1823. Its publication and reception history are discussed below.

12. Bartram, *Travels*, 25.

13. Brückner, *Geographic Revolution*, 80.

14. Gallay, *Indian Slave Trade*, 128. For the incredible story of Nairne in particular, see Chapter 5.

15. According to Gallay and other scholars, Nairne based his depiction of Florida on his experiences there in 1702, but he probably did not actually see the Everglades or Lake Okeechobee himself (Gallay, *Indian Slave Trade*, 127–28). Though the original of Nairne's map has been lost, the version of Florida Nairne drew on his map of the Southeast in 1708 appeared as an inset to Edward Crisp's *Compleat Description of the Province of Carolina in 3 Parts* (1711), which is one reason that Nairne's image of Florida circulated so widely, as I explain below. For the full story of Nairne's map, see Louis De Vorsey, "Maps in Colonial Promotion: James Edward Oglethorpe's Use of Maps in 'Selling' the Georgia Scheme," *Imago Mundi* 38 (1986): 35–45. While I have been unable to find evidence that Florida was cartographically represented as multiple islands prior to Nairne's map, Florida was sometimes thought to be a single "fabulous isle" during the sixteenth and seventeenth centuries, as Brückner explains (*Geographic Revolution*, 91).

16. Nairne to Charles Spencer, July 10, 1708, in Thomas Nairne, *Nairne's Muskhogean Journals: The 1708 Expedition to the Mississippi River*, ed. Alexander Moore (Jackson: University Press of Mississippi, 1988), 75.

17. Brückner, *Early American Cartographies*, 19; De Vorsey, "Maps in Colonial Promotion," 36.

18. Romans, *Concise Natural History*, 257.

19. Ibid., 256.

20. Guidebooks to Florida published in the United States during Florida's Territorial period (1821–45) aimed to satisfy American curiosity about Florida in the wake of annexation, though most also had an additional purpose of guiding travelers and settlers, promoting real estate, or luring investors and purchasers. Charles Blacker Vignoles, *Observations upon the Floridas* (New York, 1823), lix. Five of these guides have proven particularly important for *Liquid Landscape*. These include William Darby, *Memoir on the Geography, and Natural and Civil History of Florida* (Philadelphia, 1821); James Grant Forbes, *Sketches, Historical and Topographical, of the Floridas* (New York, 1821); William Hayne Simmons, *Notices of East Florida* (Charleston, 1822); Vignoles, *Observations upon the Floridas*; and John Lee Williams, *The Territory of Florida* (New York, 1837; reprinted 1839). The University of Florida has reproduced all but Darby's guide.

Of the five guides discussed, Williams's *Territory* had the most robust circulation history: contemporaries considered it *the* history of Florida, and it remained the only widely available one for almost thirty-five years, until the publication of George R. Fairbanks's *History of Florida* (1871) (Williams, *Territory of Florida*, iii, viii). The text proved a valuable source for Joshua Reed Giddings, the subject of Chapter 4. Giddings, *The Exiles of Florida* (Baltimore: Black Classic Press, 1997), 53. While the other four guides discussed—all published during the 1820s—circulated less widely, they were far from unknown. They shaped Williams's more popular account, for he cites all four in his Preface. Many of these guides were mentioned or reviewed in nationally circulating periodicals (the *North American Review* reviewed both Forbes's and Darby's works, for example), and many are mentioned in nineteenth-century literary histories or anthologies. For example, William Gilmore Simms, a friend of Simmons, read Simmons's book, misremembering the title as *History of the Seminoles*, its name in Evert and George Duyckinck's *Cyclopaedia of American Literature* (1866; Simmons, *Notices of East Florida*, xv, xvii). And many authors of these guides knew and borrowed from one another, as their citations indicate.

Through guidebooks to Territorial Florida, many accounts of the region under British and Spanish colonial rule reached a nineteenth-century readership eager for information on the recent annexation, for the authors relied on a combination of firsthand experience and existing accounts of Florida, sometimes penned as early as the sixteenth century. The natural histories of John Bartram and William Bartram are cited by all but Vignoles. Likewise, all five authors drew heavily on Romans's *Natural History*, and on many of the earlier accounts Romans cites (Vignoles likely owes his awareness of De Brahm's work to Romans, while Williams quotes at length from several other of Romans's sources, including Vega and Stork; Vignoles, *Observations upon the Floridas*, 10; and Williams, *Territory of Florida*, iii). Other works of importance to Williams in particular include William Roberts's *Account of the first discovery, and natural history of Florida* (London, 1763) and "a rare and ancient manuscript in the Spanish language," which Williams never identifies (iii, viii) and that a nineteenth-century reader of Williams suspects is a "forgery." Daniel G. Brinton, *Notes on the Floridian Peninsula: Its Literary History, Indian Tribes and Antiquities* (Philadelphia: Joseph Sabin, 1859), 52.

21. Simmons, *Notices of East Florida*, 24. The publication and reception history of this text and other guides to Florida from this period is discussed above.

22. Williams, *Territory of Florida*, iv. Williams proceeds to write that "the descriptions of the Indian inhabitants is at best imperfect," and that, finally, he is unable to "fill up" the drawing.

23. Verner W. Crane, *The Southern Frontier, 1670–1732* (Durham, N.C.: Duke University Press, 1928), 93; Cumming, *Southeast in Early Maps*, 21; De Vorsey, "Maps in Colonial Promotion," 36.

24. Cumming, *Southeast in Early Maps*, 203.

25. Lloyd A. Brown, *The Story of Maps* (Boston: Little, Brown, 1949), 242.

26. Cumming, *Southeast in Early Maps*, 73.

27. Guy Benson, William Irwin, Heather Moore, and John Allen, eds., *Lewis and Clark: The Maps of Exploration, 1507–1814,* University of Virginia, Special Collections Exhibit (Charlottesville, Va.: Howell Press, 2002), 34.

28. As Cumming explains, de l'Isle's map, particularly "In its detail of the Gulf-region continent from Mexico to Florida . . . is of historical importance. It was soon copied widely and frequently by French, Netherlands, German, and even English map-makers" (*Southeast in Early Maps*, 38–39).

29. Based on my research, I would speculate that, of all island maps discussed in this chapter, the following three circulated most widely in early North America: Crisp's *Compleat Description of the Province of Carolina* (1711; Figure 9) (bearing Nairne's im-age); de l'Isle's *Carte de la Louisiane et du cours du Missisipi* (1718; Figure 10); and Gib-son's *A Map of the New Governments, of East & West Florida* (1763; Figure 13) (or its copy by Jefferys in 1768). The configuration of islands on Gibson's map was the one most widely available to North Americans during the eighteenth century. Gibson's map appeared in *The Gentleman's Magazine* (London), November 1763, accompanying an article titled "Some Account of the Government of East and West Florida . . ." (552–54). However, a nearly identical map circulated widely under a different title, "Florida from the latest authorities": it appears in Roberts's *Account*, a source for Williams's *Territory* (see above, note 20) and in a collection of maps by Thomas Jefferys and Rob-ert Sayer, *A General Topography of North America and the West Indies . . .* (London, 1768).

Yet other maps of Florida as islands also circulated in published works, and thus were probably not unknown to early Americans: Homann's *Mississippi* (1717?; Figure 11) appeared in his work *Neuer atlas über die Gantze Welt* (1714) and in Homann Erben's *Atlas geographicus major* (1759 or 1763?; Beinecke bibliographic notes); Isaak Tirion's *Algemeene Kaart van de Westindische Eilanden* (1769; Figure 15) appeared in vol. 3 of Thomas Salmon's *Hedendaagsche historie of tegenwoordige staet* (Amsterdam, 1769) and the Library of Congress holds a version of this map titled *Kaart van de onderdon-ingschappen van Mexico en Nieuw Granada in de Spaansche West-Indien* (Amsterdam, 1765). The following maps discussed exist in manuscript form alone, however, and thus their circulation histories are difficult to determine: Antonio Arredondo's *Descripcion Geografica* (1742; Figure 12), which contests British expansion into the region, exists in at least two original versions (Library of Congress bibliographic note); and Thomas Wright's *Map of Georgia and Florida* (1763; Figure 14) is a pen-and-ink copy, probably from an original in London (Cumming, *Southeast in Early Maps*, 290) (thanks to S. Max Edelson for bringing this map to my attention).

30. See circulation histories of these maps (above) for a sense of how and where early North Americans may have encountered them.

31. John Aikin, *Geographical Delineations . . .* (Philadelphia, 1807), 371.

32. Ibid. Aikin's text was published originally in Great Britain in 1806, but the one-volume American edition of 1807 was advertised as "greatly superior" to the British

one because it included more on geographical terms and principles, an expanded section on the United States, and a contracted section on Europe. Stephen Daniels and Paul Elliott, "'Outline maps of knowledge': John Aikin's Geographical Imagination," in *Religious Dissent and the Aikin-Barbauld Circle, 1740–1860,* ed. Felicity James and Ian Inkster (New York: Cambridge University Press, 2012), 94–125. The book remained popular enough in the United States that in 1819 John Lauris Blake, a well-known American clergyman and author, published a companion text, *Questions Adapted to Aikin's Geography* (Salem, Mass.: John D. Cushing, 1819).

Aikin's use of the term "terraqueous" to describe a specific region is unusual. It usually meant "consisting of, or formed of, land and water," and was most often used to designate the entire planet, as in the "terraqueous globe" (*Oxford English Dictionary,* s.v. "terraqueous," a). Yet here Aikin borrows the term for Florida, perhaps because this word seems one of the best available ways to make sense of and describe a region formed when land gave way to water.

33. Jedidiah Morse et al., *The American Universal Geography . . .* (Boston, 1805), 1:85. The enormous popularity of Morse's many geography textbooks has been well established (see above).

34. Jefferson included several of Thomson's appendices in the first French and English editions of *Notes* (1787).

35. Thomas Jefferson, *The Writings of Thomas Jefferson . . . ,* vol. 2, ed. Albert Ellery Bergh (Washington, D.C., 1903), 25.

36. Ibid., 266.

37. As early as 1808 Jefferson formally expressed interest in annexing Florida, writing that "the sand bank of East Florida" was desirable for the purposes of "peace alone," since the region contained no arable land that could be sold to prospective American inhabitants. Jefferson to Monsieur Du Pont de Nemours, February 1, 1808, *Writings,* 10:350. For discussions of how such reflections on the U.S. annexation of Florida elicited both concern and fascination about North America's vexed intertwinements with Caribbean populations, culture, and economy, see Iannini, *Fatal Revolutions*; Goudie, *Creole America*; and Parrish, *American Curiosity.*

38. For a discussion of early American "seriality," see White, *Backcountry and the City,* pt. 2.

39. The provision that townships be "six miles square" is first stated in the Land Ordinance of 1785, though this idea informs the Northwest Ordinance, which set the pattern for western settlement.

40. Onuf, *Statehood and Union,* 4. As Onuf further explains, clear state boundaries and land titles would ostensibly create federal income while "rationalizing settlement patterns and providing the basis for social order in the national domain" (53).

41. Brückner, *Geographic Revolution,* 88.

42. Montesquieu, *The Spirit of Laws* (1748), 1:5.

43. James Madison, Alexander Hamilton, and John Jay, *The Federalist Papers,* ed. Isaac Kramnick (Harmondsworth: Penguin, 1987), 117.

44. Ibid., 94.

45. Ibid., 101, 268.

46. Seelye usefully explains that "Connecting lines of communication are essential to imperial design, a kind of closure promoting consolidation while permitting further expansion, which in turn justified further extension of the diagram." Seelye, *Beautiful Machine*, 6. For a discussion of narratives of U.S. character that emerge from places that challenge this diagram, such as riverine zones and deserts that disrupt narratives of continental nationhood, see LeMenager, *Manifest and Other Destinies*.

47. Benton, *A Search for Sovereignty*, 2. On this topic, also see Rifkin, *Manifesting America*.

48. The U.S. publication history of "The Florida Pirate"—after the tale's first appearance in *Blackwood's* (1821)—attests to the story's enduring popularity long after the early months of Florida's official U.S. annexation in 1821. According to Daniel Williams, a New Hampshire printer quickly issued the tale as an independent text in 1821, a New York printer issued three editions in 1823, a separate New York printer issued two editions in 1828, and in 1834 Pittsburgh printers issued the work. Williams, "Refuge upon the Sea: Captivity and Liberty in 'The Florida Pirate,'" *Early American Literature* 36, 1 (2001): 72. I have found that the text was also issued in Thomas and Talbot's Ten Cent Novelettes series in 1863.

49. The Adams-Onis Treaty of 1819, also called the Transcontinental Treaty, secured Spanish cession of Florida to the United States, though the treaty was not fully ratified until February 22, 1821. The official transfer of flags at Pensacola occurred on July 17, 1821, and "The Florida Pirate" was published the next month. See above, note 20, for a discussion of the publication and circulation of guidebooks to Florida during the 1820s and 1830s.

50. Gretchen Woertendyke, "John Howison's New Gothic Nationalism and Transatlantic Exchange," *Early American Literature* 43, 2 (2008): 309–35, 313; John Howison, "The Florida Pirate," *Blackwood's Magazine* 9 (August 1821): 519, 523.

51. For a more detailed discussion of wrecking along the Florida Reef, see Chapter 3.

52. Howison, "The Florida Pirate," 518, 516.

53. Howison's three accounts are *Foreign Scenes and Travelling Recreations* (Edinburgh: Oliver & Boyd, 1825); *Tales of the Colonies* (London: H. Colburn and R. Bentley, 1830); and *European Colonies, in Various Parts of the World*, 2 vols. (London: R. Bentley, 1834). Each of these texts appears to have been published only once. However, as Woertendyke observes, Howison was a prolific and popular writer whose work appeared frequently in *Blackwood's Edinburgh Magazine*.

54. Howison, *European Colonies*, 2:430.

55. Ibid., 433, 303, 430.

56. Ibid., 446.

57. Ibid., 311. Howison's observations accord with historical accounts of late Spanish Florida. While nominally part of the Spanish borderlands during the early nineteenth

century, the region, with its "weakened government and state of near anarchy, appeared to be a natural port of entry for those who had lived for so long by the sword." Inhabited by "belligerent Creeks and Seminoles" and runaway slaves, it was "a perfect base from which adventurers could seek their fortunes." Owsley and Smith, *Filibusters and Expansionists,* 103–4. Indeed, Spain exercised little control after 1815; as Snyder shows, if Florida belonged to anyone by the early 1820s, it was to the Seminoles and their allies, escaped slaves armed and trained by the British during the War of 1812. Snyder, *Slavery in Indian Country,* 224.

58. Howison, *Foreign Scenes,* 1:236–37.

59. Ibid., 237–38.

60. Ibid., 242.

61. Ibid., 243.

62. Ibid., 247.

63. According to Onuf, these benefits would accrue as a result of federal land ordinances. Onuf, *Statehood and Union,* 53.

Chapter 3

1. James Fenimore Cooper, *Jack Tier; or, The Florida Reef.* New York: Burgess, Stringer, 1848. Rpt. in *Works of J. Fenimore Cooper,* vol. 7 (New York: Peter Fenelon Collier, 1892), 436–679, 499. Subsequent references cited in text. There is no scholarly edition of *Jack Tier,* although the text is under preparation as part of *The Writings of James Fenimore Cooper* (the Cooper Edition), which has already established much of Cooper's work. See below for a discussion of the novel's complex publication history.

2. As Dan Walden observes, Cooper's "coastscapes" remain generally neglected in most scholarly discussions of the novelist, even though many of the novels by Cooper that we consider "sea novels" are, in fact, set on coasts rather than "in the vast expanses of the open ocean" (147). Walden, "'A False Phantom': The Coastscape in James Fenimore Cooper's *The Pilot,*" *Studies in American Fiction* 42, 2 (2015): 147–66.

3. The novel most scholars now refer to as *Jack Tier* has a complicated, transatlantic publication history, during which it appeared many times under many different titles. It first appeared in two major periodicals—serially, simultaneously, and transatlantically, although with different titles: in *Graham's Magazine* (Philadelphia) an American audience read the work from November 1846 through March 1848 under the title *The Islets of the Gulf; Or, Rose Budd,* while during the same period British readers of *Bentley's Miscellany* (London) encountered the work as *Captain Spike; Or, Islets of the Gulf.* Then, during 1848, the work was issued by three separate publishers: Bentley of London published it in three volumes under *Captain Spike; Or, The Islets of the Gulf;* Burgess and Stringer of New York issued it as a two-volume work titled *Jack Tier; Or, The Florida Reef;* and Hodgson of London used the same title when issuing the text as three volumes. There were also many nineteenth-century reprints in England and the United States, as the catalog of the American Antiquarian Society suggests, and in 1849 the work was translated and published in Germany as *Capitän Spike, oder, die*

Golf-Inseln (a text that appears to have been reissued by German publishers at least once during the nineteenth century). For more on *Jack Tier*'s publication history, see Jeffrey Walker, "Reading Rose Budd; Or, Tough Sledding in *Jack Tier*," *James Fenimore Cooper Society Miscellaneous Papers* 27, ed. Steven Harthorn and Shalicia Wilson (2010): 11–14. Despite this robust publication history, *Jack Tier* receives only passing mention in biographies of Cooper, and remains mostly neglected within the large body of Cooper scholarship. In general, Cooper's *Leatherstocking Tales* continue to receive far more scholarly attention than does his "sea fiction," as Margaret Cohen demonstrates, even though the latter works were in many cases more intriguing to Cooper's contemporaries. Cohen, *The Novel and the Sea* (Princeton, N.J.: Princeton University Press, 2010), 134.

4. Writing in *The Albion* (New York) this writer also noted that readers would find "An added interest" in the novel's temporal setting, "the commencement of the present Mexican war" ("New Works," *The Albion: A Journal of News, Politics and Literature*, March 11, 1848).

5. Gerald Horne, *Race to Revolution: The United States and Cuba During Slavery and Jim Crow* (New York: New York University Press, 2014), esp. 100–122.

6. For more discussion of this central claim of *Liquid Landscape*, see my Introduction. See also Bibler, who discusses in particular this fantasy of southern exceptionalism that many scholars continue to share, whether intentionally or not ("Introduction: Smash the Mason-Dixon! Or, Manifesting the Southern United States" *PMLA* 131, 1 (2016): 153–56.).

7. I focus on the *Biography*'s second volume (Edinburgh, 1834; Boston, 1835) and third volume (Edinburgh, 1835). All five volumes of *Ornithological Biography* were marketed in the United States, as I explain in a fuller discussion of their publication and circulation history in Chapter 1.

8. As Streeby explains, 1848—the year of *Jack Tier*'s publication as an independent volume—marked a "watershed year" in the history of U.S. empire-building, which would now be a matter of establishing control over sites beyond the continent's shores and would thus require the country to assume a geographic form other than that of continental contiguity (*American Sensations*, 9).

9. In this way, antebellum ruminations on coral terrain and its inhabitants at the continent's southern edges offer a perspective on the changing nature of U.S. territorial sovereignty that we cannot get from fictions of more familiar frontiers, such as the West of Cooper's own better-known *Leatherstocking Tales*. Such ruminations also show that we need not always turn away from popular genres of writing for evidence that what Rifkin calls "extant regional spatial logics" persisted on ground that many popular works of antebellum literature portrayed as fully domesticated U.S. geography (*Manifesting America*, 95).

10. The novel thus appears to exhibit a well-established convention of mid-nineteenth-century American novels of the sea, including some of Cooper's own works. Yet here I seek to complicate Cohen's argument that Cooper inaugurates a new

kind of sea fiction shaped by the era's "maritime nationalism" that celebrates the U.S. capacity to supersede Great Britain's worldwide empire of the seas (*Novel and the Sea*, 9). Certain aspects of *Jack Tier* conform to the conventions Cohen identifies as "Cooper's poetics": the novel's heroes, Mulford and the U.S. marines aboard the *Poughkeepsie*, use "mariner's craft" to defy obstacles; display a winning professional ethos; risk their lives in the service of their country; and remain sharply focused on their patriotic mission. Yet the novel also calls into question certain key strategies of U.S. mastery of the Gulf, as my analysis indicates.

11. The full passage reads: "The consequence was that [Spike] did not fall in with the *Poughkeepsie* at all, which vessel was keeping a sharp look-out for him in the neighbourhood of Cape St. Antonio and the Isle of Pines [Cuba], at the very moment he was running down the coast of Yucatan" (497).

12. The "Loggerhead Key" Cooper intends is not the one in the Dry Tortugas, but rather "Loggerhead Key, El Contoy," an islet in the bay of Honduras near the Yucatan coast. For more on the names of places in this region during the nineteenth century, see Bishop Davenport, *A New Gazetteer: Or Geographical Dictionary, of North America and the West Indies . . .* (Baltimore: George M'Dowell & Son; Providence, R.I.: Hutchens & Shephard, 1832). Davenport (317) locates Loggerhead Key at "Lon. 87°45' W; Lat. 21°25' N."

13. It seems odd that Mulford remains with Spike, given the treachery of the latter. However, even though at this point in the narrative the virtuous Mulford realizes Spike is not selling flour at Key West, loyalty to the *Swash* (and concern for the passengers, including Rose) compels him to continue piloting the brig rather than escaping and allowing the navy to sink it.

14. Manucy, "Gibraltar of the Gulf of Mexico," is my primary source for this brief history.

15. The Pharos of Alexandria stood from 280 BC to 1480. Like De Brahm's "Pharus," this structure was inscribed with names (not of men, but gods) and was topped by a burning furnace.

16. De Brahm, *Report*, 197–98. De Brahm's drawing of the Pharus is not included in the published version of *The Atlantic Pilot* (1772), but it is part of the manuscript *Report of the Survey of the Southern District of North America* in which the *Pilot* also appears. For information on the publication and reception of De Brahm's works, see Chapter 1.

17. "Reflections on the Importance of Florida, &c, to Great Britain," *The Universal Museum; Or, Gentleman's and Ladies Polite Magazine*, 1763. This article appears to have been reprinted, at least in part, as "On the Present State of Florida" in another London periodical, *The Tradesman; Or, Commercial Magazine*, October 1813.

18. Caroline F. Levander discusses the phrase in "Confederate Cuba," *American Literature* 78, 4 (2006): 821–45.

19. "Thompson's Island," *National Advocate*, Saturday, July 17, 1824, col. D.

20. The 1829 report is cited by Joseph Gilbert Totten, *Report of General J.G. Totten, Chief Engineer, on the Subject of National Defences* (Washington, D.C.: Printed by A. Boyd Hamilton, 1851), 13.

21. "Pensacola.—Navy Yard.—Fortifications.—Dry Dock, &c.," *The Floridian* (Tallahassee) Saturday, November 1, 1845, col. D.

22. Joel Roberts Poinsett, *Notes on Mexico, made in the autumn of 1822* (London: John Miller, 1825), 294. Supporters of annexation and filibustering during the 1840s and 1850s argued that the geographic position of Cuba, so close as to be nearly visible from the United States, dictated annexation. According to the editor and owner of the New York *Sun*, "The possession of Cuba will complete our chain of territory. It is . . . the key to the Gulf . . . Cuba must be ours!" Moses Y. Beach, "Cuba Under the Flag of the United States," *Sun*, July 23, 1847.

23. Cora Montgomery (Jane McManus Storm Cazneau), "Cuba: The Key of the Mexican Gulf," in *A Series of Articles on the Cuban Question* (New York: La Verdad, 1849), 12.

24. Manucy, "The Gibraltar of the Gulf of Mexico," (306) briefly describes antebellum interest in Fort Jefferson as interest in control over the Americas, citing historical use of the phrase "Gibraltar" for the Fort (314).

25. Today remnants of Fort Jefferson still stand on Garden Key and are managed by the National Park Service. The quotation in this paragraph is from Manucy, "Gibraltar of the Gulf," 311.

26. J. B. Holder, "The Dry Tortugas," *Harper's New Monthly Magazine* 37, 218 (1868): 260–62.

27. This print is one of many images of Fort Jefferson that were published during the nineteenth century. Many more remarkable images of the fort, including nineteenth-century drawings and a number of early twentieth-century photographs, are available at the Library of Congress, Prints & Photographs Division.

28. U.S. Congress, "Florida Canal," 19th Cong., 1st Sess. (February 14, 1826).

29. U.S. Congress, Executive Documents, 23rd Cong., 2nd Sess. Letter from Joseph M. White to William Hendricks (January 18, 1826). The canal debate continued for several decades, and proponents claimed this geopolitical power for other Floridian sites as well. The writer of an 1859 article entitled "A New 'Key' to the Gulf of Mexico" calls for a ship canal across Florida on the grounds of "national policy" and "commercial development": "If once completed it would remove all those grounds of apprehension which . . . are founded on the position held by the Island of Cuba as the 'key' of the Gulf of Mexico. . . . By such a stroke of policy the Island of Cuba would, to all intents and purposes, be drifted, as our correspondent says, entirely outside the path of our national progress." In other words the canal would allow us to "forgo the acquisition" of Cuba and "ignore that island altogether." C. K. Marshall, *Daily National Intelligencer*, April 5, 1859.

30. Matthew Fontaine Maury, "The Maritime Interests of the South and West," *Army and Navy Chronicle* 2, 22 (November 30, 1843), 647–62. 653, 681, 647; emphasis added.

31. Matthew Fontaine Maury, "The Maritime Interests of the South and West—Concluded," *Army and Navy Chronicle* 2, 22 (November 30, 1843), 673–88. 683–4.

32. LeMenager, *Manifest and Other Destinies*, 1–2.

33. Ibid., 1.

34. Dodd, "The Wrecking Business on the Florida Reef," 171–72. The conflicting definitions of the term "wrecker" attest to the ambiguity that has historically surrounded wreckers: a wrecker is both "One who causes shipwreck, esp. for purposes of plunder by showing luring lights or false signals; a person who makes a business of watching for and plundering wrecked vessels; also, one who wrongfully seizes or appropriates wreck washed ashore" *and* "a person engaged in salving wrecked or endangered vessels or cargo; a salvager, salvor" (*OED*, s.v. "wrecker, n.").

35. Dodd, "The Wrecking Business on the Florida Reef," 172.

36. William Marvin, *A Treatise on the Law of Wreck and Salvage* (Boston: Little, Brown, 1858), 2; Dodd, "The Wrecking Business on the Florida Reef," 173. For more on the perils of the Florida Straits, see Marvin, 3.

37. Horne discusses Key West's role in slave smuggling during the antebellum period (*Race to Revolution*, 54–55). Key West's particular reputation as a harbor for slavers coming from Africa, via Cuba, figures centrally in Martin Robison Delany's *Blake; or, the Huts of America, a Novel* (Boston: Beacon, 1859), 194, 214. Awareness of this problem surfaces briefly in *Jack Tier* when Spike expresses his wish to avoid being mistaken for "a slaver" (43) and admits that the cargo he sells to Montefalderon may be used to fuel the Cuban slave trade (177).

38. The novel does contain one reference to plans for a somewhat permanent U.S. military presence at the Dry Tortugas: the narrator describes the islets as "the very spot in the contemplation of government for an outer man-of-war harbor" (501).

39. For more on the cartoon as satire of the Confederacy, see The Library Company of Philadelphia's bibliographic note on this image.

40. In reality, Mallory advocated for a coastal survey because he felt that the safety of the commodities passing over the Reef was essential for the United States at large. Emphasizing the value of such a survey to all citizens, he stated that "Upon this great highway of commerce, where the property of every section of the Union is afloat, the object of those familiar with the peculiar perils which beset it should be not only to make the route thoroughly safe, but to remove every *excuse* for shipwrecks." S. Doc. 30, 30th Cong., 2nd Sess. [531], 12; quoted in Dodd, "Wrecking Business on the Florida Reef," 198.

41. "Governor DuVal to the Secretary of State," Nov. 29, 1825, *Territorial Papers of the United States*, ed. Clarence Edwin Carter, 23: 364.

42. John Simonton, "Key West," *United States Telegraph*, May 9, 1826. Simonton had a personal interest in the salvage court, since he owned the island of Key West, which he purchased from a Spaniard *after* the province of Florida had been annexed by the United States. Many similar reflections on the Reef as "conduit" can be found in

nineteenth-century newspapers and congressional debates. See, for example, "Key West," *Pensacola Gazette*, Sept. 8, 1826, col. E; U.S. Congress, "Florida Wreckers," 19th Cong., 1st Sess. (January 11, 1826).

43. "Listner," *Natchez Gazette*, November 13, 1807; emphasis in original.

44. Emphasis in original. The wrecker's total lack of regard for common decency evidently extends to the rules of grammar, as his run-on sentence and incorrect spelling of the name of his own profession suggest.

45. *New Orleans Gazette and Commercial Advertiser*, July 13, 1819; reprinted from *National Advocate*.

46. Vignoles, *Observations upon the Floridas*, 125, 118. Vignoles offers many fascinating reflections on Florida wrecking in a section titled "Observations upon the Florida Keys and Wreckers" (117–28).

47. E. Z. C. Judson (Ned Buntline), "Sketches of the Florida War—Indian Key, Its Rise, Progress, and Destruction," *Western Literary Journal and Monthly Review* 1, 5 (March 1845): 281. This essay is one of Judson's five-part series titled "Sketches of the Florida War," which appeared monthly from December 1844 through April 1845 in the *Western Literary Journal*, the Cincinnati-based periodical that he edited. Under the name Ned Buntline, Judson also wrote a novel set in sixteenth-century Florida, *The Red Revenger, or, The Pirate King of the Floridas. A Tale of the Gulf and Its Islands* (New York, 1847). It was reprinted several times during the nineteenth century.

48. "Wrecking on the Florida Keys," *Harper's New Monthly Magazine* 107, 18 (April 1859), 577–86. 578. Although this hypothesis about the cause of the shipwreck is never proven, the narrator records that he overheard a conversation between the lighthouse keeper and the wrecker in which the two "rejoiced heartily" (580) that, because of their sinister trick of preventing the crew from seeking more help from other wreckers at Key West, they will be able to lay sole claim to a high percentage of the salvage. According to wrecking law, the first salvor is awarded the highest percentage of salvage—and the highest possible percentage of it, if no one else shows up to help.

49. John James Audubon. In *Audubon in Florida: With Selections from the Writings of John James Audubon*. Ed. Kathryn Hall Proby. Coral Gables, Fla.: University of Miami Press, 1974. 337–38. Subsequent references cited in text.

50. Audubon's acquaintance is Dr. Benjamin Strobel, who lived at Key West and published his own accounts of wreckers and wrecking. See John Viele, *The Florida Keys*, vol. 3, *The Wreckers* (Sarasota, Fla.: Pineapple Press, 2001).

51. It seems likely that Audubon was one of the sources for Cooper's descriptions of the Dry Tortugas.

52. Vignoles, *Observations upon the Floridas*, 127.

53. *History of the Navy of the United States of America Continued to 1853 from the Author's Manuscripts and other Authentic Sources* (1853) is a continuation of Cooper's *History of the Navy of the United States of America* (1839). The 1853 text carries the naval history past 1815—where the 1839 *History* and other editions of the *History*

published during Cooper's lifetime conclude—by drawing from "unfinished manuscripts, documents, etc., left by Mr. Cooper, and from other most reliable and authentic sources, published, documentary, and personal" ("Preface to the Continuation," vol. 1, New York: Putnam, 1853: xii). It remains uncertain whether Cooper himself authored the description of Porter in the 1853 continuation. Cooper did write much of what was eventually included in the text, and editor's notes indicate that he dictated other portions. For a detailed discussion of the authorship of the 1853 *History* see Wayne Franklin, *James Fenimore Cooper: The Later Years* (New Haven: Yale University Press, 2017), 530, 634 n. 48, 768 nn. 83–85.

54. Streeby considers 1848 a "a watershed year, a year when the boost to U.S. power in the world system provided by the U.S.-Mexican War, combined with the distracting social upheavals in Europe, made the United States into a major player in the battles for influence in and control of the Americas" (*American Sensations*, 9). My analysis of *Jack Tier* suggests that Cooper was less concerned with the specific details of the U.S.-Mexican War than with how to build on the "boost to U.S. power in the world system" the war would provide.

Chapter 4

1. Washington Hood, *Map of the Seat of War in Florida. Compiled By Order Of The Hon. Joel R. Poinsett, Secretary Of War, under the Direction of Col J.J. Abert U.S. Topt. Engineer, from the reconnoissances of the Officers of the U.S. Army* (Washington, D.C.: Bureau U.S. Topographical Engineers, 1838). Hood's map is the precursor of another, nearly identical map with the same title, the MacKay/Blake map of 1839, which does not acknowledge Hood as a source (David Rumsey bibliographic note).

2. "Florida," *Army and Navy Chronicle* 9, 6 (August 8, 1839): 88–9. This publication notice refers to the MacKay/Blake map.

3. For a discussion of the arenas of conflict in Florida during the First Seminole War, see Mahon, *Second Seminole War*, 18–28. For a discussion of the small number of non-military Americans in the antebellum United States who traveled to the Everglades, see Grunwald, *The Swamp*, 24–39. As I explain in Chapters 1 and 2, even firsthand observers of Florida from the antebellum United States rarely saw the Everglades; rather, much of their information on this area probably came from Indian informants or other locals.

4. For locations of the major conflicts in the Second Seminole War, see "Exploring the Seminole Wars through Maps" (*Florida Memory*, State Library & Archives of Florida): https://www.floridamemory.com/onlineclassroom/seminoles/sets/maps5/.

5. Wallace E. McMullen, "The Origin of the Term Everglades." *American Speech* 28, 1 (1953): 26–34. Many nineteenth-century observers comment on the seeming interminability of the Everglades and adjacent swamps. For example, in 1826 Audubon describes "eternal labyrinths of waters and marshes, interlocked, and apparently never ending" (Audubon, in *Audubon in Florida*, 26). Another visitor records that "the wet

prairie seems to be unlimited, extending off Southward beyond the reach of vision." Electus Backus, "Diary of a Campaign in Florida, in 1837–8" *Historical Magazine* 10 (September 1866): 279–85. 282. Some sense of this feeling about the region is captured by Marjorie Stoneman Douglas's famous term, "river of grass," which Jack E. Davis discusses in *An Everglades Providence: Marjorie Stoneman Douglas and the American Environmental Century* (Athens: University of Georgia Press, 2009).

6. Vileisis, *Unknown Landscape*, 17; Smith, *Report of Buckingham Smith*, 28–29. Smith was speaking largely from his personal experience surveying the Everglades for Congress in 1848.

7. "Florida," *Army and Navy Chronicle*, 88.

8. Captain John MacKay and Lieutenant J. Blake, *Map of the Seat of War in Florida* (1839); emphasis added. While both the original map (Hood 1838) and the reproduction (MacKay/Blake 1839) contain the label "Pay-hai-o-kee," only the latter map—not pictured here—features the dotted line.

9. See Snyder, *Slavery in Indian Country*, especially chap. 8. Additionally, see the Introduction to *Liquid Landscape* for a historical overview of who lived in Florida during this period.

10. Cusick (*Other War of 1812*) discusses adventurers and profiteers in late Spanish Florida, as do Owsley and Smith (*Filibusters and Expansionists*). For discussions of how slave smugglers used coastal and peninsular Florida, see Jonathan Walker, *Trial and Imprisonment of Jonathan Walker, at Pensacola, Florida: For Aiding Slaves to Escape from Bondage . . .* , preface by Maria W. Chapman (Boston: Published at the Anti-Slavery Office, 1846); and Richard Drake and Henry Byrd West, *Revelations of a Slave Smuggler Being the Autobiography of Capt. Rich'd Drake, an African Trader for Fifty Years-from 1807–1857 . . .* (New York: R.M. DeWitt, 1860). Abolitionists in other parts of the country who sympathized with Africans in Florida include Joshua Reed Giddings, the subject of this chapter, and Frederick Douglass, who published a number of essays on the Seminoles and their African allies in the early 1850s in *Frederick Douglass' Paper*. See Campbell, "The Seminoles," for more on abolitionist interest in Florida in the nineteenth century.

11. Concern over Florida's proximity to African populations of the Caribbean was voiced frequently during the antebellum period. I address one particularly clear instance—that of John T. Sprague—below.

12. Grunwald discusses the landscape challenges that U.S. military troops faced in Florida, where Seminoles managed to function on ground that troops found impossible to master (*The Swamp*, chap. 3, "Quagmire," 40–54). The landscape excuse was one way of boosting public and political support for U.S. troops in Florida, which understandably waned from time to time. This rhetorical strategy portrayed the military as blameless, thereby paving the way for requesting additional resources and troops to fight Florida wars that an empire built on slavery and Indian removal had no choice but to continue to try to win.

188 Notes to Pages 94–96

13. *An Authentic Narrative of the Seminole War* (Providence, R.I.: D.F. Blanchard, 1836). Reproduced in Kathryn Zabelle Derounian-Stodola, ed. *Women's Indian Captivity Narratives.* (New York: Penguin, 1998): 217–34.

14. "Opinion of the Court in Reference to the Failure of the Campaign in Florida, Conducted by Major General Scott, in 1836." *American State Papers* 7 (Washington: Gales and Seaton, 1861), 461–3. Cited in Grunwald, *The Swamp*, 44.

15. John T. Sprague, *The Origin, Progress, and Conclusion of the Florida War* (Gainesville: University Press of Florida, 1964; orig. 1848), 309.

16. Martha Schoolman demonstrates that abolitionists frequently used "geography as a key discourse of political intervention." Giddings, like many of the authors Schoolman describes, encourages readers to perceive "The image of escaping slaves not simply as refugees in need of guidance but as persons technically as well as physically capable of self-liberation" because of their keen geographic knowledge. Schoolman, *Abolitionist Geographies* (Minneapolis: University of Minnesota Press, 2014), 1, 13.

17. Rifkin, *Manifesting America*, 7. Rifkin complicates this spatial construction by turning to the "less conventionally literary" writings of the colonized that affirm the persistence of locally specific spatial practices and social formations on ground that many popular genres of antebellum literature portrayed as domestic. However, here and in the previous chapter, I show that we need not always turn away from popular genres to find evidence of such persistence.

18. The annexation of Texas in 1845, the Missouri Compromise of 1850, and the Kansas-Nebraska Act of 1854 significantly fueled the national debate over slavery leading to the Civil War, but Giddings's work turns south to introduce Florida directly into this debate. Upon first publication in 1858 Giddings's work was reviewed and widely praised in several nationally circulating periodicals, as I discuss below. Follett, Foster, & Company reissued *The Exiles of Florida* twice—in 1863 and again in 1868—under the title *The Florida Exiles and the War for Slavery*, and there are a few somewhat recent reprints. Attention to this work enriches our understanding of the U.S. geographies and populations that played a critical role in the national debate over slavery. The text also provides excellent evidence of Schoolman's claim that, for many abolitionists, "the South" included Florida and the Caribbean more broadly (*Abolitionist Geographies*, 12–13). Throughout, I refer to Joshua R. Giddings, *The Exiles of Florida: Or, the Crimes Committed by Our Government against the Maroons, Who Fled from South Carolina and Other Slave States, Seeking Protection Under Spanish Law* (Baltimore: Black Classic Press, 1997).

19. The advertisement for Giddings's *Exiles* appears as the second page of the prefatory matter (before the title page) of *Political Debates Between Hon. Abraham Lincoln and Hon. Stephen A. Douglas, In the Celebrated Campaign of 1858, in Illinois* (Columbus: Follett, Foster, and Company, 1860).

20. To my knowledge, no literary scholar or historian mentions this work other than in passing. Even Giddings's biographer, James Brewer Stewart, devotes just a

paragraph to *Exiles* in *Joshua R. Giddings and the Tactics of Radical Politics* (Cleveland: Press of Case Western Reserve University, 1970) and in his more recent revision of this material in *Abolitionist Politics and the Coming of the Civil War* (Amherst: University of Massachusetts Press, 2008).

21. The italics and capitalization are Giddings's. Here Giddings gets a few details wrong: the letter is dated September 2, 1821 (not 1822), and Jackson writes "runaway negroes" not "runaway slaves." Nonetheless, Giddings's point stands. Jackson's letter is reprinted as "Extract of a letter from General Jackson to the Secretary of War, dated September 2, 1821," *American State Papers: Indian Affairs* 5, 2 (1821): 414. For the earlier report from Pénières, see Jedidiah Morse, *A Report to the Secretary of War of the United States on Indian Affairs* . . . (New Haven, Conn.: Printed by S. Converse, 1822), Appendix Y: manuscript report of Morse, Picolata, July 15, 1821 (150).

22. Giddings, *Exiles*, 71.

23. Alvin O. Thompson, *Flight to Freedom: African Runaways and Maroons in the Americas* (Kingston, Jamaica: University of the West Indies Press, 2006), 67.

24. Schoolman, *Abolitionist Geographies*, 161.

25. Some of these persisting local versions of space and subjectivity are the subject of the analysis that follows.

26. Indeed, as Giddings recognizes, "The Spanish population called the Exiles 'Maroons,' after a class of free negroes who inhabit the mountains of Cuba, Jamaica, and other West Indian islands" (*Exiles*, 97–98). Yet Giddings chooses "exiles" as a safer term because there can be no confusion as to their status as free.

27. As Landers explains, the word Seminole is "a corruption of the Spanish word cimmaron, or runaway" (*Atlantic Creoles*, 179). On this term, see also Richard Price, *Maroon Societies: Rebel Slave Communities in the Americas* (1979; Baltimore: Johns Hopkins University Press, 1996). In Price's preface to the 1996 edition of *Maroon Societies* he explains that "Since the original publication of *Maroon Societies*, the Cuban philologist Jose Juan Arrom has pushed back the origins of the word *maroon* beyond the Spanish *cimarron* that was first used in Hispaniola to refer to the Spaniards' feral cattle, then to enslaved Amerindians who escaped to the hills and, by the early 1530s, mainly to the many Africans who were escaping from slavery on the island. That New World Spanish word—which spawned English *maroon*, as well as French and Dutch *marron* (and English *Seminole*)—actually derives, he now argues, from an Amerindian (Arawakan/Taino) root, making it one of the earliest linguistic coinages in the post-columbian Americas (Arrom 1986)" (xi–xii). Some historians speculate that the term also comes from a Creek word (Thompson), which Giddings also seems to suggest: he writes that some "Exiles were by the Creek Indians called 'Seminoles,' which in their dialect signifies 'runaways,' and the term being frequently used while conversing with the Indians, came into almost constant practice among the whites" (*Exiles*, 3). But whether deriving from the Spanish or Creek or both, "maroon" seems rooted in the concept of runaway.

28. Today the opposite is frequently true, as contemporary historians of African and Seminole ethnogenesis explain. See especially Kevin Mulroy, *The Seminole Freedmen: A History* (Norman: University of Oklahoma Press, 2007).

29. The U.S. government tried to force the Seminole to surrender Africans, and applied federal policies to both groups as one (and, as a further complication to this story, the Seminole had to fight for their own ethnogenesis, since they were sometimes legally viewed as Creek). Of course, some Seminoles did hold African slaves; see Snyder, *Slavery in Indian Country*, chap. 8, for a clear discussion of the actual relationship between the groups and why outsiders perceived this relationship as a threat to the plantation economy.

30. Upon first consideration this suggestion seems strange because of the context in which the phrase first appears. Giddings records that in 1776 General Charles Lee, commander of the southern colonies during the Revolutionary War, alerted Congress that "slaves belonging to the planters [of Georgia] fled from servitude and sought freedom among the '*Exiles of Florida*'" (*Exiles*, 4). Here Lee claims that the "exiles of Florida" welcome escaping slaves from Georgia, a claim intended to convince Congress to support an invasion of Florida. However, what appeals to Giddings is not the explicit purpose of the claim, but rather its implication that a community of Africans had established themselves successfully on Floridian ground long before the origin of the United States. At the time of the American Revolution, in other words, Africans already had a long history in Florida as a distinct group that was well known to slaves in North America interested in finding freedom. Thus, despite Lee's intended purpose in calling Congress's attention to the "exiles of Florida," Giddings embraces the phrase as suggestive of the long history of African possession sustained by networks beyond the plantation, and thus as a powerful way to undercut a plantocratic perspective on Florida's Africans even more certainly than would the term "maroon." And Giddings also perceives that the phrase has the added advantage of emphasizing the group's self-determination by rooting them in a specifically Floridian origin. So even though "maroon" appears in Giddings's subtitle for the work, he rejects it and titles the work *Exiles*.

31. Giddings is invested in African ethnogenesis. According to him, these Africans, though "forcibly torn from their native land" of Africa, "became voluntary Exiles" from the Carolinas when they escaped to Florida from slavery during the early eighteenth century and "constituted a separate community" under protection of Spain (*Exiles*, 335, 2). For uses of the phrase "exiles of Africa" in abolitionist discourse, see Joseph Rezek, "The Orations on the Abolition of the Slave Trade and the Uses of Print in the Early Black Atlantic," *Early American Literature* 45, 3 (2010): 655–82.

32. Giddings, *Exile*, vi. While Giddings never uses the term *bricolage*, his own description of his sources and method suggests his self-conscious use of some aspects of the technique: he writes that "It may not be improper to state, that, in several of our recent chapters, we have quoted from official documents pretty freely, for the reason that many living statesmen, as well as many who have passed to their final rest, were

deeply involved in those transactions, and we desired to make them speak for themselves as far as the documents would enable us to do so" (252).

33. Robert Levine, Introduction, in William Wells Brown, *Clotel, Or, the President's Daughter: A Narrative of Slave Life in the United States* (Boston: Bedford/ St. Martin's, 2011), 7. Giddings uses a narrower range of sources than does Brown, and is also more inclined to interpret the texts he imports, at times even pointing out the gaps.

34. Giddings, *Exiles*, 20–21. Subsequent references from *Exiles* cited in text.

35. Note that "fugitives" is meant ironically in this context; Giddings's point is that they are clearly not "runaways" according to the meaning of this term in the antebellum United States.

36. Giddings more explicitly states these points throughout the text, such as when he records that "At a time of profound peace, our army, acting under the direction of the Executive, invaded Florida, murdered many of these free men, and brought others to the United States and consigned them to slavery. An expensive and bloody war followed; but failing to capture more of the Exiles, our army was withdrawn" (*Exiles*, v; emphasis in original).

37. Legal scholar Andrew Fitzmaurice explains that while the notion of "occupation" actually emerged in the late Middle Ages as a way of recognizing individual land rights, during the eighteenth and nineteenth centuries Europeans and North Americans used the concept of occupation in the service of dispossession. Generally the concept justified imperial expansion, according to those who reasoned that people who "wandered" had not established individual proprietorship, and thus could not be considered to have dominion over the land. Fitzmaurice, "Discovery, Conquest, and Occupation of Territory," in *The Oxford Handbook of the History of International Law*, ed. B. Fassbender et al. (New York: Oxford University Press, 2012), 840–61.

38. For discussion of liberal conventions of personhood evoked in a racialized context, see Walter Johnson, "On Agency," *Journal of Social History* 37, 1 (2003): 113–24. See also Arthur Riss, *Race, Slavery, and Liberalism in Nineteenth-Century American Literature* (New York: Cambridge University Press, 2006).

39. "The Exiles of Florida," *Atlantic Monthly* 2, 11 (1858): 509–10.

40. "The Exiles of Florida," *Liberator* 28, 34 (August 20, 1858): 1.

41. "Art II. The Florida Maroons," *Methodist Quarterly Review* 12 (October 1860): 554. I have also located two additional positive reviews: "Violation of the Flag of Truce," *National Era* 13, 629 (January 20, 1859): 10; and "The Exiles of Florida, Letter from Hon. Josiah Quincy," *Liberator* 28, 30 (July 23, 1858): 118.

42. "Florida War" is an alternate popular name for the Second Seminole War.

43. Largely based on Sprague's firsthand observation as an army officer serving in Florida, *Origin* is the nineteenth century's only book-length account of the Florida War. Although the text was not reprinted during the period, an 1848 review of *Origin* in *The Literary World* (Boston) hails it as "one of the most interesting and valuable historical works that have appeared in this country for some time, and . . . one for which

there existed a widely felt necessity." The reviewer expresses particular "satisfaction" at Sprague's personal familiarity with and "candor" about the subject. "The Origin, Progress, and Conclusion of the Florida War," *Literary World* 3, 64 (April 22, 1848): 231. Nineteenth-century historians of Florida, including Brinton and Fairbanks, considered Sprague an authority on the Florida War. Giddings knew Sprague's work well, although the status of this text in *Exiles* is complicated: while in some places Giddings uses passages from *Origin* to support his alternate account of Florida's history, in other passages Sprague's work is one of the official accounts that Giddings seeks to dismantle.

44. At several points in this section Sprague heavily implies that the liberty of the United States as nation and empire is at stake, particularly when he appeals to "those who cherish our prosperity and the memory of those who bequeathed us our liberties" (*Origin*, 310).

45. Sprague, *Origin*, 310.

46. The Godfrey narrative was published only once during the nineteenth century, but it has been reissued by Kathryn Zabelle Derounian-Stodola in *Women's Indian Captivity Narratives* (New York: Penguin, 1998), 212–24. Subsequent references cited in text. Derounian-Stodola's introduction to the Godfrey narrative is the source of my information on its publication and circulation. This information is rather limited, and, according to Derounian-Stodola, the text's publisher, Daniel F. Blanchard, cannot be traced.

47. This claim surfaces in much extant commentary on the narrative. Snyder considers it "anti-Seminole propaganda" (*Slavery in Indian Country*, 219); Eric Gary Anderson calls it "Jacksonian propaganda" ("On Native Ground: Indigenous Presences and Countercolonial Strategies in Southern Narratives of Captivity, Removal, and Repossession," *Southern Spaces*, August 9, 2007); and Horne offers the most puzzling response of all when he uses the *Narrative* as an instance of the "ferocity of African fighters" in the Second Seminole War, overlooking that the *Narrative* prominently features an exceptionally nonviolent African (*Negro Comrades of the Crown*, 113). In the most extended treatment of the tale to date, Derounian-Stodola argues the opposite: she speculates that the text could be an "unusual example of abolitionist literature" (213–16). Ultimately I wish to address, then move beyond, a debate about whether the tale is pro- or anti-imperial.

48. Two examples of such narratives include Andrew Welch, *A Narrative of the Life and Sufferings of Mrs. Jane Johns, Who Was Barbarously Wounded and Scalped by Seminole Indians, in East Florida* (Charleston, S.C.: Burke & Giles, 1837); and *Massacre at Indian Key* (Philadelphia, 1841). News of the events described in both of these texts circulated in several U.S. periodicals, and the events of the latter text were particularly interesting to Americans in the United States during 1840, since one of the victims was Henry Perrine (1797–1840), a physician, botanist, and U.S. diplomat then living in Key West. This text has been reprinted in *Florida Historical Quarterly* 5, 1 (1926): 18–42.

49. "Troubles of Slaveholders," *The Emancipator* 4, 20 (September 12, 1839): 80.

50. Here I wish to show that the Godfrey narrative extends Christopher Castiglia's influential account of captivity narratives. Castiglia argues that narratives of white women's captivity offered white female readers an imaginative space of freedom: by portraying captivity as a state enabling "cultural crossings" denied by their culture's race and gender norms, these narratives exposed the colonialist nature and limitations of such norms. Castiglia, *Bound and Determined: Captivity, Culture-Crossing, and White Womanhood from Mary Rowlandson to Patty Hearst* (Chicago: University of Chicago Press, 1996), 10. However, while Castiglia focuses on accounts in which a white female captive experiences "cultural crossings," the Godfrey narrative is a unique example of an African who does so: after all, he participates in daily life among Indians and in new rituals, alliances, and institutions. Thereby the African takes center stage within the so-called Godfrey narrative; this narrative thus allows us to productively expand Castiglia's claims about free white women to enslaved African men: some readers of the story, whether white or black, may have perceived the African's tale as welcome evidence that the racial hierarchies sustaining slavery and empire were too restrictive for imagining the variety of roles that enslaved African men might assume.

51. For an extended discussion of wrecked goods, see Chapter 3 and below, where I discuss the career of Elizabeth Emmons.

52. Much of the paragraph from which this quote is taken is drawn almost verbatim from a military dispatch that had been printed in popular periodicals, including *The Globe* and *Niles' Register*.

53. For a discussion of the "female picaresque," see Cathy Davidson, *Revolution and the Word: The Rise of the Novel in America* (New York: Oxford University Press, 1986), 179–92.

54. *A Sketch of the Life of Elizabeth Emmons, or the Female Sailor: Who Was Brutally Murdered While at Sea, off the Coast of Florida, February 3d, 1841* (Boston: Graves & Bartlett, 1841). References from this work cited in text. This tale has not been republished since its initial publication. The only extant copy is held by the Library Company of Philadelphia, which offers a curator's note explaining that though the text presents itself as fact, it is "apparently fictitious": its publisher "Graves & Bartlett" is a false imprint, and there is no evidence that Elizabeth Emmons ever existed.

55. Many readers will note similarities between the story of Elizabeth Emmons and that of Lucy Brewer (1815).

56. Davidson, *Revolution*, 153, 185.

57. Brückner, *Geographic Revolution*, 183, 179. For a more extensive discussion of Brückner's analysis of how the idealized geographic form of the solid and integrated continent fostered a sense of the United States as both independent and culturally unified, see Chapter 2 of *Liquid Landscape*.

58. For more on Florida wreckers, see Chapter 3.

59. Davidson, *Revolution*, 185.

60. Ibid., 188.

61. A frontispiece features Emmons, glass eye and all, standing aboard a ship and holding a book. The book in this image emphasizes the opportunities Emmons finds by not returning home, including writing. The publisher's note further claims that "a description of the numerous places which [Emmons] had visited during her lifetime are found among her writings; and these, when published with a full history of her earthly career, and her numerous compositions, will make an interesting volume."

62. Emmons's 1841 narrative may be evidence of the need for more scholarship on the U.S. picaresque, post-1820. It is important to note that the scholarly sources on which I draw to establish the conventions of the picaresque examine the genre's pre-1820 development and role in the United States: Davidson's study focuses on early national writing before 1820, and Brückner focuses on the period from the 1680s through the 1820s. Similarly, in his provocative discussion of the "episode," Matthew Garrett focuses on "the two decades following the composition of the Constitution in Philadelphia" (ca. 1787–1807); Garrett, *Episodic Poetics*, 2. As D. Berton Emerson observes, however, post-1820 picaresque writers engaged related, but different, cultural and political challenges than did earlier U.S. writers. Emerson, " 'This is a strange book': Re-Membering Local Democratic Agency in Bird's *Sheppard Lee*," *ESQ: A Journal of the American Renaissance* 61, 2 (2015): 222–61.

63. For excellent information on what happened to the roughly six hundred Seminoles and Africans who remained in Florida during and after the conclusion of the Second Seminole War once an estimated 4,400 had been forcibly removed to Oklahoma, see William C. Sturtevant and Jessica R. Cattelino, "Florida Seminole and Miccosukee" in *Handbook of North American Indians*, vol. 14, *Southeast*, ed. Sturtevant and Raymond Fogelson (Washington, D.C.: Smithsonian Institution Press, 2004), 429–49.

64. For a discussion of the plantation economy that did develop in Florida, see Baptist, *Creating an Old South*.

65. Twentieth-century scholars have largely dismissed Goulding's work. A recent bibliography of southern writers describes Goulding's two Florida novels as "adventure books for the young" that "read as a kind of nineteenth-century scout handbook . . . salted with religious lessons, useful skills, and lore." "F. R. Goulding." in *Southern Writers: A New Biographical Dictionary*, ed. Joseph M. Flora, Amber Vogel, and Brian Giemza (Baton Rouge: Louisiana State University Press, 2006), 162–3.

66. The extended publication history of Goulding's works attests to their enduring interest during the nineteenth century. After appearing in Philadelphia in 1852 and 1853, *Young Marooners* was reissued in 1853 by two publishing houses in London. In 1855 a third London publisher issued the text, and 1858 saw its republication in both cities. In 1863 a publisher in Goulding's home state of Georgia issued a copy, and in 1864 Martien reprinted the text in Philadelphia, where a different publisher issued it in 1866. Copies were printed in London during the 1870s, and in Georgia and New York during the 1880s. In 1898 a Dutch translation, *De Jonge Avonturiers van Florida*, was printed in Amsterdam, and in 1902 a Russian translation, *V Liesakh Floridy*, appeared

in St. Petersburg. Although the sequel, *Marooner's Island*, was less popular, it nonetheless generated relatively high international demand in a competitive literary marketplace: after its serialization in a Georgia periodical in 1867, the novel was published as a single volume in 1869 in London and Philadelphia, and was subsequently reprinted on both sides of the Atlantic.

67. Harris hails *Young Marooners* as a "classic" in his Introduction to an 1887 U.S. edition. F. R. Goulding, *The Young Marooners on the Florida Coast . . .* , intro. Joel Chandler Harris (Uncle Remus) (New York: Dodd, Mead, 1887), iii. Additional praise is offered by Mildred Lewis Rutherford: Goulding "has done for American literature what Daniel De Foe [*sic*] has done for English literature"; and *Young Marooners* is like *Robinson Crusoe* in that it is so intriguing that one can "read it, and read it again with renewed interest." Mildred Lewis Rutherford, ed., *American Authors: A Hand-book of American Literature from Early Colonial to Living Writers* (Atlanta, Ga.: Franklin Printing and Publishing, 1894), 308. I draw figures of sale from James Wood Davidson, *The Living Writers of the South* (New York: Carleton, 1869), 229.

68. Amy Kaplan, *The Anarchy of Empire in the Making of U.S. Culture* (Cambridge, Mass.: Harvard UP, 2002), 25. Here I draw on Kaplan's influential discussion of "manifest domesticity," and particularly on her claim that "the discourse of domesticity was intimately intertwined with the discourse of Manifest Destiny in antebellum U.S. culture" (24). Kaplan demonstrates that, across a broad range of imaginative antebellum writing, the homesite frequently serves as "a mobile and mobilizing outpost" (25). Homemaking enacted empire-building, concealing "its origin in the violent appropriation of foreign land" and "colonizing specters of the foreign" (50).

69. Goulding was born in Georgia, worked as a Presbyterian minister, served as an unofficial Confederate chaplain during the Civil War, had two sons who served in the Confederate Army, and authored *The Confederate Soldier's Hymn-Book* (1864). Giemza in Flora et al., *Southern Writers*, 162–3. While Goulding was fascinated by American Indian culture (162), many of his novels sustain the myth of the vanishing Indian. See *Sal-o-quah; or, Boy Life Among the Cherokees* (1870); and *Sapelo; or, Child-Life on the Tide-Water* (1870).

70. F. R. Goulding, *Robert and Harold; or the Young Marooners on the Florida Coast* (Philadelphia: W.S. Martien, 1853), 75. "Devil Fish": a predatory anglerfish native to the eastern coast of North America, and known for its gigantic mouth. For readers skeptical that such a fish could snag a boat, Goulding's footnote relates that "There are hundreds of persons now living that recollect a similar adventure which took place in the bay of Charleston." This reader's skepticism remains undiminished by the note. *Young Marooners*, 75. Subsequent references cited in text.

71. Kenneth Wiggins Porter explains that a runaway slave called "Abraham or Abram, otherwise known as Yobly, was about forty-five or fifty at the outbreak of the war." Porter, "Relations Between Negroes and Indians Within the Present Limits of the United States, Chapter IV, Relations in the South," *Journal of Negro History* 17, 3 (1932): 321–50, 340.

72. Reflecting on Robert's poor shooting skills, the narrator relates that "Robert was not an expert artillerist" (464).

73. Streeby, *American Sensations*, 5, 7. While Streeby does not specifically discuss Goulding's work, its plotlines and publication history place it within the tradition of U.S. "imperial adventure fiction" produced around 1848, a "watershed year" in the history of U.S. empire-building (5, 7). Samuel Albert Link explains that Goulding began *Young Marooners* in 1847 and completed it in 1850. *Pioneers of Southern Literature* (Nashville: Publishing House, M.E. Church, South, Bigham & Smith, Agents, 1903): 277.

74. John Russell Bartlett, *Dictionary of Americanisms: A Glossary of Words and Phrases, Usually Regarded as Peculiar to the United States* (New York: Bartlett and Welford, 1848), 221. When Dr. Gordon acknowledges that the word is also "of West Indian origin" he echoes Bartlett's second edition (1859) and fourth edition (1877), which explain that the expression "marooning party" derives from the noun "maroon," "the name given to revolted negroes in the West Indies" who, "by taking to the forests and the mountains . . . rendered themselves formidable to the colonies and sustained a long and brave resistance against the whites" (1859: 264; 1877: 384).

75. Goulding, *Young Marooners*, 59; emphasis added.

76. For more on the use of bloodhounds in the Florida War and how they came to function as an abolitionist symbol, see Campbell, "The Seminoles," 259–302.

77. For a fascinating instance of the suggestion that Florida resembles Jamaica, see "Florida. Notes and Observations on its Present Condition," *Niles' National Register* 14, 23 (August 5, 1843): 359–61. 360. The author observes, "There is no war upon ancient or modern record sustained by savages against disciplined troops, in a manner more extraordinary than this of which I am now writing, except the maroon war of Jamaica, which may probably bear comparison." He attributes the similarity between these wars to a frightful correspondence of landscapes, for "Like Florida, the whole interior of this Island abounds with brush-wood and gigantic grass, capable of concealing any number of men, in which the maroons discovered sub-labyrinths, intricate, tortuous, and dangerous in the extreme." Campbell also cites other articles that suggest this similarity.

78. See Kaplan, *Anarchy*; Lora Romero, *Home Fronts: Domesticity and Its Critics in the Antebellum United States* (Durham, N.C.: Duke University Press, 1997).

79. Kaplan, *Anarchy*, 24. The frontier homesite Kaplan describes is supposed to lack "defining characteristics that would identify the landscape or settlers as specific to the region" (*Anarchy*, 24). Her lead example of "Manifest Domesticity," an essay called "Life on the Rio Grande" that appeared in the April 1847 issue of *Godey's Lady's Book*, depicts a white family "pic-nic-ing in the real gipsy style" in recently annexed Texas. "This family tableau," Kaplan explains, "evokes a larger domestic sphere," for it inspires the essay's writer to envision cities springing up, "'dwellings and villages dotting the wide prairies, and the school house and church rising side by

side, as on our New England hills they stand.'" According to Kaplan, then, the "family tableau" of "pic-nic-ing" prompted Americans to envision Texas as part of the U.S. because it signaled the territory's potential to support the same homes, villages, schools, and churches that New England did (23–25). This 1847 tableau of a family picnicking in territorial Texas appeared in the same year that Goulding began his story of a family "marooning" in recently incorporated Florida. However, by sharp contrast, as I show, Goulding's representation of Florida domesticity registers a failure to fully imagine Florida becoming an extension of the United States in the same way that other parts of the continent could, for Goulding's home evokes the specificity of Florida.

80. Goulding, *Young Marooners*, 29.

81. The home is called "Marooners' Home" in *Marooner's Island*. F. R. Goulding, *Marooner's Island: Or, Dr. Gordon in Search of His Children* (Philadelphia: Claxton, Remsen & Haffelfinger, 1869.), xi, 323. This same home appears in *Young Marooners*, though in a far less developed, more makeshift state: there are "sleeping apartments" (93), a "wing" for provisions, Sam's "shed-room" (388), and an "enclosure" around the tent made of "a double row of stakes" (291, 311).

82. This version of Goulding's Florida homesite is much closer to the "fit habitations" imagined in the Armed Occupation Act of 1842.

83. Kaplan, *Anarchy*, 26.

84. In this way the novel attests that some objects of U.S. empire are, in Rifkin's words, "absorbed but not entirely eliminated" (*Manifesting America*, 7).

85. Thomas Wentworth Higginson, *Army Life in a Black Regiment* (Boston: Fields, Osgood & Co., 1870), 248. For a discussion of Higginson's Civil War writings, see Christopher Looby's Introduction to *The Complete Civil War Journal and Selected Letters of Thomas Wentworth Higginson* (Chicago: University of Chicago Press, 1999).

86. Higginson, *Army Life*, 251. Higginson also discusses his interest in Florida's landscape in a February 15, 1863, diary entry that he does not include in *Army Life*. Writing in South Carolina, he records that "The more I become attached to this people, the more my desire grows to be transferred to some locality more permanently defensible than this. Should any peace, short of conquest, be adopted, it will be almost impossible to defend for freedom this mere fringe of islands & all these people must flee or be slaves again, in the event. But Florida is indefinitely more defensible and if that can be once reclaimed for freedom it could be held indefinitely; it cost the U.S. three hundred million, it is said, to subdue the Seminoles, & I am satisfied that these people, having once tasted freedom, could sustain themselves there indefinitely. Indeed the white loyalists of Florida say that black troops alone can regain the state & hold it forever. This conviction gives me great hope for this people, even should the worst occur" (*Complete Civil War Journal*, 102).

87. Harriet Beecher Stowe, *Dred: A Tale of the Great Dismal Swamp*, ed. Robert S. Levine (Chapel Hill: University of North Carolina Press, 2000), 210, 510.

Chapter 5

1. William Cullen Bryant, *The Letters of William Cullen Bryant*, ed. Thomas G. Voss (New York: Fordham University Press, 1992), 6: 107. For discussion of Bryant's Florida letters, see Charles I. Glicksberg, "Letters of William Cullen Bryant from Florida," *Florida Historical Quarterly* 14, 4 (1936): 255–74. "East Florida": the British name for peninsular Florida during the period of British rule (1763–83).

2. Bryant, *Letters*, 105. Subsequent references cited in text.

3. Facts about postbellum Florida's population, economy, and transportation infrastructure are drawn from the later chapters of Grunwald, *The Swamp*. For descriptions of plantation culture in the Florida Panhandle (also called Middle Florida) from the 1830s through the 1860s, see Baptist, *Creating an Old South*. For a discussion of the plantation culture that developed during the eighteenth century and flourished until the War of 1812 around Jacksonville and along the St. Johns River, see Landers, *Colonial Plantations*.

4. For more on popular travel narratives and settlers' guides that position postbellum Florida as a retrograde periphery of the nation, see Greeson, *Our South*, pt. 3, "The Question of Empire/The Reconstruction South." It is important, however, to note that Bryant's perspective on the South, slavery, and Reconstruction is more complicated than the views he expresses in the Florida letters, as Andrew Slap explains in *The Doom of Reconstruction: The Liberal Republicans in the Civil War Era* (New York: Fordham University Press, 2006).

5. Bryant, *Letters*, 106, 127. Stowe hosted many well-known visitors at her Mandarin home: Voss briefly describes Bryant's visit (*Letters*, 94), and many other visitors are discussed by Olav Thulesius, *Harriet Beecher Stowe in Florida, 1867 to 1884* (Jefferson, N.C.: McFarland, 2001); and John T. Foster and Sarah Whitmer Foster, *Beechers, Stowes, and Yankee Strangers: The Transformation of Florida* (Gainesville: University Press of Florida, 1999).

6. *Palmetto-Leaves* was first published in 1873 by James R. Osgood of Boston, although many of the letters therein had already appeared in the *Christian Union*, where Stowe began publishing letters on Florida in 1870 (Foster and Foster, *Beechers, Stowes, and Yankee Strangers*). Houghton, Mifflin reprinted *Palmetto-Leaves* twice (1873, 1900), and there is a Swedish translation of 1873. Upon initial publication the work was reviewed positively in *The Literary World* (Boston)—which praises Stowe's "enthusiasm" for Florida and the work's "pictures of luxuriant verdure" ("*Palmetto-Leaves,*" *The Literary World; a Monthly Review of Current Literature* 3, 10 [March 1, 1873])—and in the *Universalist Quarterly* (Boston), which deems the work "a delight to read" and a source of "truly valuable information" on "the question of Southern labor, the purchase and cultivation of Florida lands," and the climate and populations of the region. "Contemporary Literature." *Universalist Quarterly and General Review* 10 (July 1873): 384. Not all readers were captivated: a reviewer in *Appletons' Journal* (New York) writes that, while "whatever Mrs. Stowe writes will, of course, find many readers," *Palmetto-Leaves* is "dry" and almost entirely lacking in charm, value, and

freshness. "Literary Notes," *Appletons' Journal of Literature, Science and Art* 9, 213 (April 19, 1873): 540.

7. Joan D. Hedrick, *Harriet Beecher Stowe: A Life* (New York: Oxford University Press, 1994), 342; Matthews, "Southern Literary Studies," 297–98. For scholarly assessments of Stowe in Florida that echo Hedrick, see Powell, *New Masters*, 101; Paul Ortiz, *Emancipation Betrayed: The Hidden History of Black Organizing and White Violence in Florida from Reconstruction to the Bloody Election of 1920* (Berkeley: University of California Press, 2005); and Mark Howard Long, "Cultivating a New Order: Reconstructing Florida's Postbellum Frontier," Ph.D. dissertation, Loyola University, 2007. In general, scholars have summarily dismissed Stowe's postbellum Florida writings. Hedrick correctly observes that these works "have hardly been touched." Hedrick, "Harriet Beecher Stowe," in *Prospects for the Study of American Literature: A Guide for Scholars and Students*, ed. Richard Kopley (New York: New York University Press, 1997), 118. More recently, Cindy Weinstein suggests that this dearth is due to the inherent banality of these writings: Weinstein observes that Stowe "continued to write well into the 1880s," yet "it is difficult to imagine even the most devoted of Stowe readers making a compelling argument for the centrality or literary excellence of a text like *Palmetto Leaves*." Weinstein, introduction to *The Cambridge Companion to Harriet Beecher Stowe*, ed. Cindy Weinstein (New York: Cambridge University Press, 2004), 7.

8. Kaplan (*Anarchy*, 30–32) discusses household treatises by Stowe and Catharine Beecher as presentations of "imperial domesticity," which I discuss in more detail in Chapter 4.

9. As Christopher Hager and Cody Marrs observe, an "antebellum/postbellum framework" continues to structure American literary studies—including research, teaching, anthologies, and academic positions—even though nineteenth-century archives "carve out alternative trajectories." Hager and Marrs, "Against 1865: Reperiodizing the Nineteenth Century," *J19: The Journal of Nineteenth-Century Americanists* 1, 2 (2013): 259–84, 259–60. The scholarly neglect of Stowe's *Palmetto-Leaves*, and of a range of other postbellum works by Stowe, is one of Hager and Marr's key examples of one negative effect of "the 1865 divide": this divide encourages "a misplaced fealty to the 'antebellum' status of arguably 'postbellum' authors whose most canonical work happened to appear prior to the Civil War" (266, 270–71). My analysis of *Palmetto-Leaves* seeks to inspire more attention to Stowe's postbellum career.

10. Samuel Otter observes that many scholarly conclusions about Stowe's perspectives on race and slavery are based too heavily on *Uncle Tom's Cabin* (1852) alone. Otter, "Stowe and Race," in Weinstein, *Cambridge Companion to Harriet Beecher Stowe*, 15–38. Certainly the black characters of *Uncle Tom's Cabin* are, by and large, fixed representatives of certain racial stereotypes—direct products of Stowe's "romantic racialism," "the view that racial differences were essential and permanent but not hierarchical" (20). Yet, as Otter shows, Stowe's "confidence in a certain kind of representation" (28) faltered after she completed her best-known novel. Other and later writings demonstrate the "complexity—the characteristic peculiarity—of her thinking about race" (18): for

example, Dred, the eponymous hero of Stowe's 1856 novel, is "not merely an abstraction," but rather a character with a specific history and complicated genealogy (34). My analysis of *Palmetto-Leaves* builds on Otter's observation that a more complicated account of race and slavery emerges when we examine a fuller range of Stowe's work.

11. In this way this chapter furthers a central objective of *Liquid Landscape*, to suggest new ways of evaluating the conceptual importance, role, and influence of particular southern spaces and populations.

12. I thank Carrie Hyde for her insightful observation that Stowe is, after all, a theorist.

13. The cover of the first edition of *Palmetto-Leaves* features the leaves of the scrub-palmetto (or *Serenoa repens*) embossed in gold against red. This plant was first named by William Bartram. For more on the plant, see Daniel F. Austin, *Florida Ethnobotany* (Boca Raton: University of Central Florida Press, 2004), 1043–46.

14. S. Max Edelson explains that South Carolina's proindependence whites chose for the state's Revolutionary seal "a palmetto tree looming above 'an English oak fallen.'" Edelson, "Clearing Swamps, Harvesting Forests: Trees and the Making of a Plantation Landscape in the Colonial South Carolina Lowcountry," in *Environmental History and the American South: A Reader*, ed. Paul Sutter and Christopher J. Manganiello (Athens: University of Georgia Press, 2009), 120–21. The *Sabal palmetto* became the official state tree of both South Carolina and Florida during the twentieth century.

15. Harriet Beecher Stowe, *Palmetto-Leaves* (Boston: James R. Osgood, 1873), 254. Subsequent references cited in text.

16. Harriet Beecher Stowe, "Southern Christmas and New Year," *Christian Union* 13, 3 (January 19, 1876): 44.

17. Stowe also makes much of the fact that the orange tree "can be got from seed . . . and needs no budding" (146).

18. Here I complicate Hedrick's claim that Stowe always considered New England a "blueprint" for the rest of the nation (*Stowe*, 342).

19. "*Palmetto-Leaves*," *Literary World*, 146. The reviewer's observation that Stowe equally values all forms of Floridian flora, placing the orange tree "side by side" with more "vulgar" plants, foregrounds an almost democratic sensibility that emerges from time to time in *Palmetto-Leaves*. This sensibility supports the idea that Stowe may have intended her title, *Palmetto-Leaves*, to evoke that of another work, Walt Whitman's *Leaves of Grass* (1855), many editions of which appeared in print long after the Civil War and during the same decades when Stowe wrote letters from Florida that would appear in *Palmetto-Leaves*. In fact, Stowe may have been preparing *Palmetto-Leaves* for its 1873 publication while Whitman published the 1871–72 edition of *Leaves of Grass*.

20. Catherine Esther Beecher and Harriet Beecher Stowe, *The New Housekeeper's Manual: Embracing a New Revised Edition of The American Woman's Home; Or,*

Principles of Domestic Science (New York: J.B. Ford, 1874), 24. Subsequent references cited in text.

21. Stowe to George Eliot, May 11, 1872; cited in Annie Fields, *Life and Letters of Harriet Beecher Stowe* (Boston: Houghton, Mifflin, 1897), 339.

22. The Mandarin cottage no longer stands, although a historic marker designates the former site of the home on the present-day grounds of the Mandarin Community Club. There are many nineteenth-century photos, drawings, stereographs, and postcards of the home, and several of these may be viewed at the New York Public Library and the Library of Congress, Prints & Photographs Division. A short discussion and drawing of Stowe's home also appears in Edward King's monumental travel narrative, *The Great South: A Record of Journeys* . . . (Hartford, Conn.: American Publishing Company, 1875), 385–6.

23. Stowe to Charles, Winter 1877; in Fields, *Life and Letters*, 374.

24. For a comprehensive discussion of postbellum "local color" fiction, see Richard H. Brodhead, *Cultures of Letters: Scenes of Reading and Writing in Nineteenth-Century America* (Chicago: University of Chicago Press, 1993). For discussions of the cultural role of local color fiction about the postbellum South in particular, see Greeson, *Our South*, 259 ff. For the cultural role of picturesque descriptions of the South, see Rebecca C. McIntyre, "Promoting the Gothic South," *Southern Cultures* 11, 2 (2005): 33–61.

25. The essays that formed the two-volume *Picturesque America* (1872–74) appeared first in *Appletons' Journal* (New York) during 1870. Although Bryant provided a preface for *Picturesque America* and has been credited as the work's editor, his involvement was in fact rather limited; see Sue Rainey, *Creating Picturesque America: Monument to the Natural and Cultural Landscape* (Nashville: Vanderbilt University Press, 1994).

26. The phrase is Brodhead's (*Cultures*, 117); a classic example of such a text is King's *Great South*.

27. Brodhead, *Cultures*, 120.

28. Hedrick, *Stowe*, 340.

29. Stowe lived briefly at this plantation, Laurel Grove, from early 1867 through the end of April (Thulesius, 36–37). She had leased the property for her son, Frederick, and the family quickly hired over one hundred former slaves with Frederick as "superintendent" (Thulesius, 32–33). Her 1867 stay at Laurel Grove was her first visit to Florida, and the first time she saw the cottage at Mandarin across the river. She bought the cottage outright, Frederick left Florida in July 1867, and in 1868 Stowe first wintered at her Mandarin cottage, returning each winter for sixteen years until 1884. By 1870 she was publishing letters from Florida in the *Christian Union*, some of which are part of *Palmetto-Leaves*, and she continued writing many letters from Florida after the text's publication. She was still a frequent visitor of Florida when the Town of Orange Park was founded in 1877 and purchased by Washington G. Benedict's Boston-based Florida Winter Home and Development Co. in 1879, the year *Palmetto-Leaves* and Eunice

White Bullard Beecher's *Letters from Florida* were published. The year 1884 was Stowe's final winter in Florida, and she died in 1896.

30. The phrase is Powell's, but it resonates with Greeson's interpretation of Stowe (*Our South*, 256).

31. Harriet Beecher Stowe, "Our Florida Plantation," *Atlantic Monthly* 43, 259 (May 1879): 641–49, 641. Subsequent references cited in text.

32. Despite Winnah's refinement, she retains her way of laughing, for we later encounter her as she "cackled and crowed" (644).

33. Later Stowe hints at her involvement with Laurel Grove, yet she does so in a way that still obscures her role: "We have had in our own personal experience [of Southern negro laborers] pretty large opportunities of observation" (287). The strange locution of this sentence suggests that her "personal experience" may consist of mere "observation" of, rather than participation in, the postwar plantation enterprise.

34. Between February 1873 and April 1877 Stowe published eighteen essays on Florida in the *Christian Union*. "These additional articles lend support to the suggestion that she intended to write a second book about Florida" (Foster and Foster, *Beechers, Stowes, and Yankee Strangers*, 93). She also wrote many essays that were not published, as well as personal letters.

35. For a discussion of Howells and the regionalist commitments of the *Atlantic Monthly*, see Susan K. Harris, "American Regionalism," in *A Companion to American Literature and Culture*, ed. Paul Lauter (Chichester, Mass.: Wiley-Blackwell, 2010).

36. For specific discussions of antebellum plantation culture in Middle Florida, around the panhandle, see Baptist, *Creating an Old South*. For a discussion of the earlier plantation culture that flourished during the eighteenth and early nineteenth century around Jacksonville—and thus much closer to Stowe's home than Middle Florida—see Landers, *Colonial Plantations*.

37. Stowe, "Our Florida Plantation," 644.

38. Constructing a comprehensive history of Laurel Grove from Revolution to Stowe's arrival in early 1867 is challenging. I have relied on the following sources: Arch F. Blakey, *Parade of Memories: A History of Clay County, Florida* (Green Cove Springs, Fla.: Clay County Bicentennial Steering Committee, 1976); Clay County Clerk's Office; Foster and Foster, *Beechers, Stowes, and Yankee Strangers*; Landers, *Atlantic Creoles*; Mary Jo McTammany, "Clay County Memoirs: Street Names Provide Us a Glimpse of the Past," *Florida Times-Union*, August 24, 2005; Larry E. Rivers, *Slavery in Florida: Territorial Days to Emancipation* (Gainesville: University Press of Florida, 2000); Daniel L. Schafer, "Zephaniah Kingsley's Laurel Grove Plantation, 1803–1813," in Landers, *Colonial Plantations*, 98–120; Schafer, *Anna Madgigine Jai Kingsley: African Princess, Florida Slave, Plantation Slaveowner* (Gainesville: University Press of Florida, 2003); and Thulesius, *Harriet Beecher Stowe in Florida*. Anyone wishing to construct a fuller history of the property and its ownership prior to Stowe's arrival in

early 1867 should seek data in Florida state census records, Florida property and land records, Clay County records, the Family History Library, and other sources containing archival and unpublished material. To this end, it is crucial to note that Laurel Grove plantation, which no longer stands, is a different property than Kingsley's plantation to the north at Fort George Island, now called the Kingsley Plantation and managed by the National Park Service. For assistance with locating published and unpublished sources on Laurel Grove, my thanks are due to Daniel L. Schafer and Anne Toohey, a reference librarian at the Library of Congress.

39. Stowe, "Our Florida Plantation," 645. Greeson interprets the comment differently, maintaining that Stowe's discussions of Laurel Grove's former grandeur betray skepticism that the home was ever as cultivated by Southerners before the war as Stowe and her family made it after the war (*Our South*, 257).

40. In this way, Stowe's perspectives on labor and property in postbellum Florida may be productively compared to those of Constance Fenimore Woolson, whose Florida reflections are the subject of Sharon D. Kennedy-Nolle's recent study, *Writing Reconstruction: Race, Gender, and Citizenship in the Postwar South* (Chapel Hill: University of North Carolina Press, 2015). As Kennedy-Nolle explains, "Woolson's Reconstructive vision" involved "reconstructing the meaning of work to privilege the independence, dignity, and freedom of laborers in making their work arrangements" (2).

41. One possible path to property ownership open to black persons during the postbellum period was via the Southern Homestead Act of 1866, which opened 46 million acres of public lands in five Southern states including Florida, and specified that applicants could not be discriminated against on the basis of color. According to the act, homesteaders received 160 acres of land for a $10 registration fee, and were required to live on and improve the land for five years before receiving title. Nonetheless, it was extremely difficult for black persons to receive, pay for, and cultivate land in Florida, not least because of widespread white resistance to the act. Yet the act guaranteed black persons the right to apply for land, and Florida had more public land than any of the other four states covered under the act. The act was unfortunately repealed in 1876 under pressure from those who cited an economic advantage in the removal of restrictions on land ownership. For more on the act, see Michael L. Lanza, "'One of the Most Appreciated Labors of the Bureau': The Freedmen's Bureau and the Southern Homestead Act," in *The Freedmen's Bureau and Reconstruction: Reconsiderations*, ed. Paul A. Cimbala and Randall M. Miller (New York: Fordham University Press, 1999); and Paul Wallace Gates, "Federal Land Policy in the South, 1866–1888," *Journal of Southern History* 6, 3 (1940): 303–30.

42. For example, in the final letter of *Palmetto-Leaves* Stowe offers a regressive answer to the question "Who shall do the work for us?" when she responds that "black laborers," who toil "cheerfully" in the blistering heat that whites could not bear, will ensure the South's prosperity (280, 321). This conclusion has prompted more than one

reader to lament that in Florida the abolitionist author of *Uncle Tom's Cabin* reverted to the belief that blacks are incapable of self-directed labor, and thus ideally suited to work for whites (Greeson, *Our South*, 257).

43. For more on the many failures of Reconstruction in Florida, see Ortiz, *Emancipation Betrayed*.

44. Harriet Beecher Stowe, "Who Ought to Come to Florida?" *Christian Union*, May 7, 1870, 290.

45. Long, "New Order," 31.

46. According to Greeson, after Laurel Grove "Stowe's Reconstructors do not abandon their 'tragic' imperial project. Rather, they expand it, by taking it still farther south, buying an orange grove 'on the other side of the St. John's'" (*Our South*, 259). Geographically, however, Mandarin is no farther south than Laurel Grove, so Stowe's move to Mandarin took her directly east (see my "Map of Stowe's Florida," Figure 33).

47. Specifically, Stowe states that "the fine groves of Mandarin sprang up again from the root, and have been vigorous bearers for years since" (*Palmetto-Leaves*, 243).

48. "Who Ought to Come to Florida?" *Christian Union* 1, 19 (May 7, 1870): 290. On several occasions Stowe requests that readers abandon existing notions of growth and progress when considering Florida. For example, in *Palmetto-Leaves* she asks that we do not compare homes in Florida "with the finished ones of Northern States. They are spots torn out of the very heart of the forest, and where Nature is rebelling daily, and rushing back with all her might into the wild freedom from which she has been a moment led captive" (171). In the essay, "A New Palmetto Leaf," she explains that Florida's absence of northern winters means that "houses . . . do not need to be built as substantially as" in New England, and that "a house here can be simple and inexpensive, and yet very charming." *Christian Union* 9, 18 (May 6, 1874): 343.

49. Scrub-palmettos, too, provided an economic resource, as Stowe knew, for she writes that both Sabal palms and scrub-palmettos contain at their center "the bud from whence all future leaves spring. This bud is in great request for palmetto-hats," which locals and laborers make, wear, and sell (*Palmetto-Leaves*, 80).

50. Eunice White Bullard Beecher, *Letters from Florida* (New York: D. Appleton, 1879), 45. Subsequent references cited in text. Beecher's work was favorably reviewed in *The Literary World* (Boston) upon publication, although it has not been republished. "Minor Notices," *Literary World: A Monthly Review of Current Literature* 10, 10 (May 10, 1879): 154.

51. It is worth stressing that, instead of approaching the plants as obstacles to be cleared so that real progress can begin, Beecher and Stowe take them on their own terms, so to speak, looking closely for what can be learned about the nature of successful progress in these regions.

52. Black homesteaders came to Florida under the Southern Homestead Act and with the assistance of the Freedmen's Bureau (see note 41). Poor whites—often referred to as "crackers"—came from adjoining states and constituted a majority of the popu-

lation making a living in Florida by subsistence agriculture and cattle grazing. Although there is no consensus on precisely which white persons were and were not "crackers," the term seems to refer to those who exhibited certain cultural characteristics, mobility predominant among these, as James M. Denham and Canter Brown, Jr., explain in *Cracker Times and Pioneer Lives: The Florida Reminiscences of George Gillett Keen and Sarah Pamela Williams* (Columbia: University of South Carolina Press, 2000).

Coda

1. Zora Neale Hurston. *Their Eyes Were Watching God* (New York: HarperPerennial Modern Classics, 2006), 131. Subsequent references cited in text.

2. Martyn Bone, "The (Extended) South of Black Folk: Intraregional and Transnational Migrant Labor in *Jonah's Gourd Vine* and *Their Eyes Were Watching God*," *American Literature* 79, 4 (2007): 753–80.

3. For more on Hurston's awareness of the unequal effects of environmental disaster, see Susan Scott Parrish, "Zora Neale Hurston and the Environmental Ethic of Risk," in *American Studies, Ecocriticism, and Citizenship: Thinking and Acting in the Local and Global Commons*, ed. Joni Adamson and Kimberly N. Ruffin (New York: Routledge, 2013), 21–36.

4. Stewart E. Tolnay and E. M. Beck, "Racial Violence and Black Migration in the American South, 1910 to 1930," *American Sociological Review* 57, 1 (1992): 103–16; cited in Bone, "South of Black Folk," 763.

5. Hurston, *Dust Tracks on a Road* (New York: HarperPerennial, 1996), 1. Subsequent references cited in text.

6. Jay Barnes explains that although the early 1880s "were an era of rapid economic growth" in Florida, strong hurricanes disrupted this growth. Barnes, *Florida's Hurricane History* (Chapel Hill: University of North Carolina Press, 1998), 66–69.

7. Hurston's account of the hurricane that ravages Florida in *Their Eyes Were Watching God* is based on the devastating event and aftermath of the hurricane of 1928 that killed thousands of people across Florida and the Caribbean. Barnes provides a description of this storm and many other and earlier severe ones.

8. Hurston, *Dust Tracks*, 7.

9. Hurston describes Polk County sites in *Dust Tracks*, 143–52. This description of the Everglades is from Hurston's letter about *Their Eyes Were Watching God*. Hurston to William Stanley Hoole, March 7, 1936, reproduced in Carla Kaplan, *Zora Neale Hurston: A Life in Letters* (New York: Doubleday, 2002), 366–68.

10. I do not wish to diminish the violence of the location for poor and black persons; as Parrish acutely observes, "The black laborers' cabins are not protected by the dike but were structurally a part of the dike's function of protecting white agricultural property" ("Environmental Ethic of Risk," 34). Yet this violence, racial oppression, and loss does not mean that Hurston failed to perceive the value and possibility Florida also offered.

11. Hurston, *Mules and Men* (New York: HarperPerennial, 2008), 1.

12. Hurston is responsible for the "Folklore" chapter of the guide, which was undertaken by the Federal Writers' Project of the Works Progress Administration for the State of Florida. *Florida: A Guide to the Southernmost State*, American Guide Series (New York: Oxford University Press, 1939), 128–35.

Bibliography

Adams, Willi Paul. *The First American Constitutions: Republican Ideology and the Making of the State Constitutions in the Revolutionary Era.* Trans. Rita Kimber and Robert Kimber. New York: Rowman & Littlefield, 2001.

Aikin, John. *Geographical Delineations: Or, A Compendious View of the Natural and Political State of All Parts of the Globe.* Philadelphia: Printed for F. Nichols, by Kimber, Conrad &, no. 93, Market Street, 1807.

Allewaert, Monique. *Ariel's Ecology: Plantations, Personhood, and Colonialism in the American Tropics.* Minneapolis: University of Minnesota Press, 2013.

Anderson, Eric Gary. "On Native Ground: Indigenous Presences and Countercolonial Strategies in Southern Narratives of Captivity, Removal, and Repossession." *Southern Spaces* (August 9): 2007.

Angell, Joseph K. *Treatise on the Right of Property in Tide Waters and in the Soil and Shores Thereof.* Boston: Harrison Gray, 1826.

"Art II. The Florida Maroons." *Methodist Quarterly Review* 12 (October 1860): 554.

Audubon, John James. *Audubon in Florida: With Selections from the Writings of John James Audubon.* Ed. Kathryn Hall Proby. Coral Gables, Fla.: University of Miami Press, 1974.

———. *The Birds of America.* Octavo edition. London: by author, 1827–38; Philadelphia: John T. Bowen, 1839–44.

———. *Ornithological Biography; or, An Account of the Habits of the Birds of the United States of America . . . .* Edinburgh: Adam & Charles Black, 1831–39.

Austin, Daniel F. *Florida Ethnobotany: Fairchild Tropical Garden, Coral Gables, Florida Arizona-Sonora Desert Museum, Tucson, Arizona: With More Than 500 Species Illustrated by Penelope N. Honychurch.* Boca Raton: University of Central Florida Press, 2004.

Axtell, James. *The Indians' New South: Cultural Change in the Colonial Southeast.* Baton Rouge: Louisiana State University Press, 1997.

Backus, Electus. "Diary of a Campaign in Florida, in 1837–8." *Historical Magazine, and Notes and Queries Concerning the Antiquities, History, and Biography of America, 1857–1875* 10 (September 1866): 279–85.

Baker, Anne. *Heartless Immensity: Literature, Culture, and Geography in Antebellum America*. Ann Arbor: University of Michigan Press, 2006.

Baptist, Edward E. *Creating an Old South: Middle Florida's Plantation Frontier Before the Civil War*. Chapel Hill: University of North Carolina Press, 2002.

Barnes, Jay. *Florida's Hurricane History*. Chapel Hill: University of North Carolina Press, 1998.

Bartlett, John R. *Dictionary of Americanisms: A Glossary of Words and Phrases, Usually Regarded as Peculiar to the United States*. New York: Bartlett and Welford, 1848.

Bartram, William. *The Travels of William Bartram: Naturalist's Edition*. Ed. Francis Harper. New Haven, Conn.: Yale University Press, 1958.

———. *Travels through North & South Carolina, Georgia, East & West Florida....* Philadelphia: Printed by James & Johnson, 1791.

Bauer, Ralph, and José Antonio Mazzotti, eds. *Creole Subjects in the Colonial Americas: Empires, Texts, Identities*. Chapel Hill: Published for Omohundro Institute of Early American History and Culture by University of North Carolina Press, 2009.

Beach, Moses Y. "Cuba Under the Flag of the United States." *Sun*, July 23, 1847.

Beecher, Catharine Esther, and Harriet Beecher Stowe. *The New Housekeeper's Manual: Embracing a New Rev. Ed. of The American Woman's Home; Or, Principles of Domestic Science*. New York: J.B. Ford, 1874.

Beecher, Eunice White Bullard. *Letters from Florida*. New York: D. Appleton, 1879.

Benson, Guy, William Irwin, Heather Moore, and John Allen, eds. *Lewis and Clark: The Maps of Exploration, 1507–1814*. University of Virginia, Special Collections Exhibit. Charlottesville, Va.: Howell Press, 2002.

Benton, Lauren. *A Search for Sovereignty: Law and Geography in European Empires, 1400–1900*. New York: Cambridge University Press, 2010.

Bibler, Michael P. "Introduction: Smash the Mason-Dixon! Or, Manifesting the Southern United States." *PMLA* 131, 1 (2016): 153–56.

Blackstone, Sir William. *Commentaries on the Laws of England*. Oxford: Clarendon, 1765–69.

Blake, Nelson Manfred. *Land into Water—Water into Land: A History of Water Management in Florida*. Tallahassee: University of Florida Press, 1980.

Blakey, Arch Fredric. *Parade of Memories: A History of Clay County, Florida*. Green Cove Springs, Fla.: Clay County Bicentennial Steering Committee, 1976.

Bone, Martyn. "The (Extended) South of Black Folk: Intraregional and Transnational Migrant Labor in *Jonah's Gourd Vine* and *Their Eyes Were Watching God*." *American Literature* 79, 4 (2007): 753–80.

Braund, Kathryn, and Charlotte M. Porter, eds. *Fields of Vision: Essays on the Travels of William Bartram*. Tuscaloosa: University of Alabama Press, 2010.

Brickhouse, Anna. *The Unsettlement of America: Translation, Interpretation, and the Story of Don Luis De Velasco, 1560–1945*. New York: Oxford University Press, 2015.

Brinton, Daniel G. *Notes on the Floridian Peninsula, Its Literary History, Indian Tribes and Antiquities.* Philadelphia: Joseph Sabin, 1859.

Brodhead, Richard H. *Cultures of Letters: Scenes of Reading and Writing in Nineteenth-Century America.* Chicago: University of Chicago Press, 1993.

Brown, Charles Brockden. Trans., *A View of the Soil and Climate of the United States of America.* Philadelphia: J. Conrad & Co., 1804.

Brown, Lloyd A. *The Story of Maps.* Boston: Little, Brown, 1949.

Brown, William Wells. *Clotel, Or, the President's Daughter: A Narrative of Slave Life in the United States.* 1853. Boston: Bedford/St. Martin's, 2011.

Brückner, Martin. *Early American Cartographies.* Chapel Hill: University of North Carolina Press, 2011.

——. *The Geographic Revolution in Early America: Maps, Literacy, and National Identity.* Chapel Hill: Published for Omohundro Institute of Early American History and Culture by University of North Carolina Press, 2006.

Bryant, William C. *The Letters of William Cullen Bryant.* Ed. Thomas G. Voss. New York: Fordham University Press, 1992.

——. *Picturesque America, Or, the Land We Live in. . . .* New York: D. Appleton, 1872.

Buntline, Ned. *The Red Revenger: Or, the Pirate King of the Floridas: A Romance of the Gulf and Its Islands.* New York: S. French, 1847.

Bushnell, Amy Turner. "Ruling 'The Republic of Indians' in Seventeenth-Century Florida." In *American Encounters: Natives and Newcomers from European Contact to Indian Removal, 1500–1850,* ed. Peter C. Mancall and James Hart Merrell. 311–23. New York: Routledge, 2000.

——. "The Sacramental Imperative: Catholic Ritual and Indian Sedentism in the Provinces of Florida." In *Columbian Consequences,* vol. 2, *Archaeological and Historical Perspectives on the Spanish Borderlands East,* ed. David Hurst Thomas, 475–90. Washington, D.C.: Smithsonian Institution Press, 1989.

——. *Situado and Sabana: Spain's Support System for the Presidio and Mission Provinces of Florida.* New York: American Museum of Natural History, 1994.

Byrd, William. *The Westover Manuscripts: Containing the History of the Dividing Line Betwixt Virginia and North Carolina; A Journey to the Land of Eden, A.D. 1736: And a Progress to the Mines.* Ed. Edmund Ruffin. Petersburg: Printed by E. and J.C. Ruffin, 1841.

Campbell, John. "The Seminoles, the 'Bloodhound War,' and Abolitionism, 1796–1865." *Journal of Southern History* 72, 2 (2006): 259–302.

Carman, Harry J., John Mitchell, Arthur Young, and Richard Oswald, eds. *American Husbandry.* New York: Columbia University Press, 1939.

Carter, Clarence Edwin, and John Porter Bloom, eds. *The Territorial Papers of the United States.* Washington, D.C.: U.S. Government Printing Office, 1934.

Castiglia, Christopher. *Bound and Determined: Captivity, Culture-Crossing, and White Womanhood from Mary Rowlandson to Patty Hearst.* Chicago: University of Chicago Press, 1996.

Chardon, Roland E. "The Cape Florida Society of 1773." *Tequesta* 35 (1975): 1–36.

Chateaubriand, François-René. *Atala; René*. Berkeley: University of California Press, 1980.

———. *Travels in America and Italy*. London: Henry Colburn, 1828.

Cimbala, Paul A., and Randall M. Miller, eds. *The Freedmen's Bureau and Reconstruction: Reconsiderations*. New York: Fordham University Press, 1999.

Cohen, Margaret. *The Novel and the Sea*. Princeton, N.J.: Princeton University Press, 2010.

"Contemporary Literature." *Universalist Quarterly and General Review*10(July 1873): 384.

Cooper, James Fenimore. *History of the Navy of the United States of America*. New York: Putnam, 1853.

———. *Jack Tier; or, The Florida Reef*. New York: Burgess, Stringer, 1848. Rpt. in *Works of J. Fenimore Cooper*, vol. 7. New York: Peter Fenelon Collier, 1892. 436–679.

Crane, Verner W. *The Southern Frontier, 1670–1732*. Durham, N.C.: Duke University Press, 1928.

Crèvecoeur, J. Hector St. John de. *Letters from an American Farmer and Other Essays*. Ed. Dennis D. Moore. Cambridge, Mass.: Belknap Press of Harvard University Press, 2013.

Cronon, William. *Changes in the Land: Indians, Colonists, and the Ecology of New England*. New York: Hill and Wang, 1983.

Cumming, William Patterson. *The Southeast in Early Maps*. Rev. Louis De Vorsey. Chapel Hill: University of North Carolina Press, 1998.

Cushing, Frank Hamilton. *Exploration of Ancient Key-Dweller Remains on the Gulf Coast of Florida*. Ed. Randolph J. Widmer. Gainesville: University Press of Florida, 2000.

Cusick, James G. *The Other War of 1812: The Patriot War and the American Invasion of Spanish East Florida*. Gainesville: University Press of Florida, 2003.

Darby, William. *Memoir on the Geography, and Natural and Civil History of Florida: Attended by a Map of That Country, Connected with the Adjacent Places: And an Appendix, Containing the Treaty of Cession, and Other Papers Relative to the Subject*. Philadelphia: Printed by T. H. Palmer, 1821.

Davenport, Bishop. *A New Gazetteer: Or Geographical Dictionary, of North America and the West Indies. . . .* Baltimore: George M'Dowell & Son; Providence, R.I.: Hutchens & Shephard, 1832.

Davidson, Cathy N. *Revolution and the Word: The Rise of the Novel in America*. New York: Oxford University Press, 1986.

Davidson, James Wood. *The Living Writers of the South*. New York: Carleton, 1869.

Davis, Jack E. *An Everglades Providence: Marjory Stoneman Douglas and the American Environmental Century*. Athens: University of Georgia Press, 2009.

De Brahm, William John Gerard. *De Brahm's Report of the General Survey in the Southern District of North America*. Ed. Louis De Vorsey. Columbia: University of South Carolina Press, 1971.

Delany, Martin Robison. *Blake; or, The Huts of America, a Novel*. Boston: Beacon, 1970.

Denham, James M., and Canter Brown, Jr., eds. *Cracker Times and Pioneer Lives: The Florida Reminiscences of George Gillett Keen and Sarah Pamela Williams*. Columbia: University of South Carolina Press, 2000.

Derounian-Stodola, Kathryn Zabelle, ed. *Women's Indian Captivity Narratives*. New York: Penguin, 1998.

De Vorsey, Louis. "Maps in Colonial Promotion: James Edward Oglethorpe's Use of Maps in 'Selling' the Georgia Scheme." *Imago Mundi* 38 (1986): 35–45.

Dickinson, Jonathan. *Gods Protecting Providence Man's Surest Help and Defence. . . .* Printed in Philadelphia: by Reinier Jansen, 1699.

Dodd, Dorothy. "The Wrecking Business on the Florida Reef, 1822–1860." *Florida Historical Quarterly* 22, 4 (1944): 171–99.

Drake, James David. *The Nation's Nature: How Continental Presumptions Gave Rise to the United States of America*. Charlottesville: University of Virginia Press, 2011.

Drake, Richard, and Henry Byrd West. *Revelations of a Slave Smuggler Being the Autobiography of Capt. Rich'd Drake, an African Trader for Fifty Years-from 1807–1857. . . .* New York: R.M. DeWitt, 1860.

Dubcovsky, Alejandra. *Informed Power: Communication in the Early American South*. Cambridge, Mass.: Harvard University Press, 2016.

Edelson, S. Max. *The New Map of Empire: How Britain Imagined America Before Independence*. Cambridge, Mass.: Harvard University Press, 2017.

Ellicott, Andrew. *The Journal of Andrew Ellicott. . . .* Philadelphia: Printed by Budd & Bartram for Thomas Dobson, 1803.

Ely, James W. *The Guardian of Every Other Right: A Constitutional History of Property Rights*. New York: Oxford University Press, 1992.

Emerson, D. Berton. "'This is a strange book': Re-Membering Local Democratic Agency in Bird's *Sheppard Lee*." *ESQ: A Journal of the American Renaissance* 61, 2 (2015): 222–61.

"The Exiles of Florida." *Atlantic Monthly* 2, 11 (1858): 509–10.

"The Exiles of Florida." *Liberator* 28, 34 (August 20, 1858): 1.

"The Exiles of Florida, Letter from Hon. Josiah Quincy." *Liberator* 28, 30 (July 23, 1858): 118.

"Extract of a letter from General Jackson to the Secretary of War, dated September 2, 1821." *American State Papers: Indian Affairs* 5, 2 (1821).

Fagin, Nathan B. *William Bartram: Interpreter of the American Landscape*. Baltimore: Johns Hopkins University Press, 1933.

Fairbanks, George R. *History of Florida from Its Discovery by Ponce de Leon, in 1512, to the Close of the Florida War, in 1842*. Philadelphia: Lippincott, 1871.

Fields, Annie. *Life and Letters of Harriet Beecher Stowe*. Boston: Houghton, Mifflin, 1897.

Fitzmaurice, Andrew. "Discovery, Conquest, and Occupation of Territory." In *The Oxford Handbook of the History of International Law*, ed. Bardo Fassbender, Anne

Peters, Simone Peter, and Daniel Högger. 840–61. New York: Oxford University Press, 2012.

Flora, Joseph M., Amber Vogel, and Bryan Albin Giemza, eds. *Southern Writers: A New Biographical Dictionary*. Baton Rouge: Louisiana State University Press, 2006.

"Florida." *Army and Navy Chronicle* 9, 6 (August 8, 1839): 88–9.

"Florida. Notes and Observations on its Present Condition," *Niles' National Register* 14, 23 (August 5, 1843): 359–61.

Florida: A Guide to the Southernmost State. American Guide Series. New York: Oxford University Press, 1939.

Foner, Eric. *Reconstruction: America's Unfinished Revolution, 1863–1877*. New York: Harper & Row, 1988.

Fontaneda, Hernando de Escalante. *Letter of Hernando De Soto, and Memoir of Hernando De Escalante Fontaneda*. Trans. Buckingham Smith. Washington, D.C.: Priv., 1854.

Forbes, James Grant. *Sketches, Historical and Topographical, of the Floridas, More Particularly of East Florida*. Gainesville: University Press of Florida, 1964.

Foster, John T., and Sarah Whitmer Foster. *Beechers, Stowes, and Yankee Strangers: The Transformation of Florida*. Gainesville: University Press of Florida, 1999.

Franklin, Wayne. *James Fenimore Cooper: The Later Years*. New Haven: Yale University Press, 2017.

Gallay, Alan. *The Indian Slave Trade: The Rise of the English Empire in the American South, 1670–1717*. New Haven, Conn.: Yale University Press, 2002.

Garrett, Matthew. *Episodic Poetics: Politics and Literary Form After the Constitution*. New York: Oxford University Press, 2014.

Gates, Paul Wallace. "Federal Land Policy in the South, 1866–1888." *Journal of Southern History* 6, 3 (1940): 303–30.

Giddings, Joshua R. *The Exiles of Florida: Or, the Crimes Committed by Our Government Against the Maroons, Who Fled from South Carolina and Other Slave States, Seeking Protection Under Spanish Laws*. Baltimore: Black Classic Press, 1997.

Glicksberg, Charles I. "Letters of William Cullen Bryant from Florida." *Florida Historical Society Quarterly* 14, 4 (1936): 255–74.

Goudie, Sean X. *Creole America: The West Indies and the Formation of Literature and Culture in the New Republic*. Philadelphia: University of Pennsylvania Press, 2006.

Goulding, F. R. *Marooner's Island: Or, Dr. Gordon in Search of His Children*. Philadelphia: Claxton, Remsen & Haffelfinger, 1869.

———. *Robert and Harold; or the Young Marooners on the Florida Coast*. Philadelphia: W.S. Martien, 1853.

———. *V Lĩesakh Floridy: Prikliùcheniĩa Trekh Mal'chikov I OdnoĩDĩevochki*. Trans. M. Granstrem. St. Petersburg, Russia: Sobko, 1902.

———. *The Young Marooners on the Florida Coast, Or, Robert and Harold*. Intro. Joel Chandler Harris (Uncle Remus). New York: Dodd, Mead, 1887.

Goulding, F. R. *De jonge avonturiers van Florida*. Trans. J.F. Brunet. Amsterdam: N.J. Boon, 1898.

Greeson, Jennifer Rae. *Our South: Geographic Fantasy and the Rise of National Literature*. Cambridge, Mass.: Harvard University Press, 2010.

Gruesz, Kirsten Silva. "America." In *Keywords for American Cultural Studies*, ed. Bruce Burgett and Glenn Hendler. 16–22. New York: New York University Press, 2007.

Grunwald, Michael. *The Swamp: The Everglades, Florida, and the Politics of Paradise*. New York: Simon & Schuster, 2006.

Guterl, Matthew Pratt. *American Mediterranean: Southern Slaveholders in the Age of Emancipation*. Cambridge, Mass.: Harvard University Press, 2008.

———. "South." In *Keywords for American Cultural Studies*, ed. Bruce Burgett and Glenn Hendler. 230–33. New York: New York University Press, 2007.

Hager, Christopher, and Cody Marrs. "Against 1865: Reperiodizing the Nineteenth Century." *J19: The Journal of Nineteenth-Century Americanists* 1, 2 (2013): 259–84.

Hale, Matthew, Stuart A. Moore, and Robert G. Hall. *A History of the Foreshore. . . .* London: Stevens & Haynes, 1888.

Hart-Davis, Duff. *Audubon's Elephant: America's Greatest Naturalist and the Making of the Birds of America*. New York: Holt, 2004.

Hedrick, Joan D. *Harriet Beecher Stowe: A Life*. New York: Oxford University Press, 1994.

Higginson, Thomas W. *Army Life in a Black Regiment*. Boston: Fields, Osgood & Co., 1870.

———. *The Complete Civil War Journal and Selected Letters of Thomas Wentworth Higginson*. Ed. Christopher Looby. Chicago: University of Chicago Press, 2000.

Holder, J. B. "The Dry Tortugas." *Harper's New Monthly Magazine* 37, 218 (1868): 260–62.

Hood, Washington. *Map of the Seat of War in Florida. Compiled By Order Of The Hon. Joel R. Poinsett, Secretary Of War, under the Direction of Col J.J. Abert U.S. Topt. Engineer, from the reconnoissances of the Officers of the U.S. Army*. Washington, D.C.: Bureau U.S. Topographical Engineers, 1838.

Horne, Gerald. *Negro Comrades of the Crown: African Americans and the British Empire Fight the U.S. Before Emancipation*. New York: New York University Press, 2012.

———. *Race to Revolution: The United States and Cuba During Slavery and Jim Crow*. New York: New York University Press, 2014.

Howison, John. *European Colonies, in Various Parts of the World, Viewed in Their Social, Moral and Physical Condition*. London: R. Bentley, 1834.

———. "The Florida Pirate." *Blackwood's Magazine* 9 (August 1821): 516–31.

———. *Foreign Scenes and Travelling Recreations*. Edinburgh: Oliver & Boyd, 1825.

———. *Tales of the Colonies*. London: H. Colburn, 1830.

Hume, David, L. *A Treatise of Human Nature*. Ed. A. Selby-Bigge and P. H. Nidditch. Oxford: Clarendon, 1978.

Hurston, Zora Neale. *Dust Tracks on a Road*. New York: HarperPerennial, 1996.

———. *Mules and Men*. New York: HarperPerennial, 2008.

———. *Their Eyes Were Watching God*. New York: HarperPerennial Modern Classics, 2006.

Hutton, James. "Theory of the Earth; or, An Investigation of the Laws Observable in the Composition, Dissolution, and Restoration of Land upon the Globe." *Transactions of the Royal Society of Edinburgh* 1 (1788): 209–304, 288.

Iannini, Christopher P. *Fatal Revolutions: Natural History, West Indian Slavery, and the Routes of American Literature*. Chapel Hill: Published for Omohundro Institute of Early American History and Culture by the University of North Carolina Press, 2012.

James, Felicity, and Ian Inkster, eds. *Religious Dissent and the Aikin-Barbauld Circle, 1740–1860*. New York: Cambridge University Press, 2012.

Jefferson, Thomas. *The Writings of Thomas Jefferson*. . . . Ed. Andrew A. Lipscomb and Albert Ellery Bergh. Washington, D.C.: Thomas Jefferson Memorial Association, 1903.

Jefferys, Thomas, and Robert Sayer. *Florida from the Latest Authorities*. London: Printed for Robert Sayer & Thomas Jefferys, 1768.

———. *A General Topography of North America and the West Indies*. . . . London: Printed for R. Sayer, 1768.

Jehlen, Myra. *American Incarnation: The Individual, the Nation, and the Continent*. Cambridge, Mass.: Harvard University Press, 1986.

Johnson, Walter. "On Agency." *Journal of Social History* 37, 1 (2003): 113–24.

Judson, E. Z. C. (Ned Buntline). "Sketches of the Florida War—Indian Key, Its Rise, Progress, and Destruction." *Western Literary Journal and Monthly Review* 1, 5(March 1845): 281–82.

Kaplan, Amy. *The Anarchy of Empire in the Making of U.S. Culture*. Cambridge, Mass.: Harvard University Press, 2002.

Kaplan, Carla. *Zora Neale Hurston: A Life in Letters*. New York: Doubleday, 2002.

Kennedy-Nolle, Sharon D. *Writing Reconstruction: Race, Gender, and Citizenship in the Postwar South*. Chapel Hill: University of North Carolina Press, 2015.

King, Edward, and James Wells Champney. *The Great South: A Record of Journeys*. Hartford, Conn.: American Publishing Company, 1875.

Kolianos, Phyllis E., and Brent Richards Weisman, eds. *The Lost Florida Manuscript of Frank Hamilton Cushing*. Gainesville: University Press of Florida, 2005.

Kolodny, Annette. *In Search of First Contact: The Vikings of Vinland, the Peoples of the Dawnland, and the Anglo-American Anxiety of Discovery*. Durham, N.C.: Duke University Press, 2012.

Kopley, Richard, ed. *Prospects for the Study of American Literature: A Guide for Scholars and Students*. New York: New York University Press, 1997.

Landers, Jane G. *Atlantic Creoles in the Age of Revolutions*. Cambridge, Mass.: Harvard University Press, 2010.

———. *Black Society in Spanish Florida*. Urbana: University of Illinois Press, 1999.

———. *Colonial Plantations and Economy in Florida*. Gainesville: University Press of Florida, 2000.

Laudonnière, René G. de. *Three Voyages*. Trans. Charles E. Bennett. Gainesville: University Press of Florida, 1975.

Lauter, Paul. *A Companion to American Literature and Culture*. Chichester, Mass.: Wiley-Blackwell, 2010.

LeMenager, Stephanie. *Manifest and Other Destinies: Territorial Fictions of the Nineteenth-Century United States*. Lincoln: University of Nebraska Press, 2004.

Levander, Caroline Field. "Confederate Cuba." *American Literature* 78, 4 (2006): 821–45.

Levander, Caroline Field, and Robert S. Levine, eds. *Hemispheric American Studies*. New Brunswick, N.J.: Rutgers University Press, 2008.

Levine, Robert S. *Dislocating Race and Nation: Episodes in Nineteenth-Century American Literary Nationalism*. Chapel Hill: University of North Carolina Press, 2008.

Lincoln, Abraham, and Stephen A. Douglas. *Political Debates between Hon. Abraham Lincoln and Hon. Stephen A. Douglas, in the Celebrated Campaign of 1858, in Illinois: Including the Preceding Speeches of Each, at Chicago, Springfield, Etc.: Also, the Two Great Speeches of Mr. Lincoln in Ohio, in 1859, As Carefully Prepared by the Reporters of Each Party, and Published at the Times of Their Delivery*. Columbus: Follett, Foster, & Company, 1860.

Link, Samuel Albert. *Pioneers of Southern Literature*. Nashville: Publishing House, M.E. Church, South, Bigham & Smith, Agents, 1903.

"Literary Notes." *Appletons' Journal of Literature, Science and Art* 9, 213(April 19, 1873): 540.

Locke, John. *Second Treatise of Government*. Ed. C. B. Macpherson. Indianapolis: Hackett, 1980.

Long, Mark Howard. "Cultivating a New Order: Reconstructing Florida's Postbellum Frontier." Ph.D. dissertation, Loyola University, 2007.

MacKay, John and J. Blake. *Map of the Seat of War in Florida*. Smithfield, N.C.: Army of the South, Head Quarters, 1839.

Madison, James, Alexander Hamilton, and John Jay. *The Federalist Papers*. Ed. Isaac Kramnick. Harmondsworth: Penguin, 1987.

Mahon, John K. *History of the Second Seminole War, 1835–1842*. Gainesville: University Press of Florida, 1967.

Manucy, Albert C. "The Gibralter of the Gulf of Mexico." *Florida Historical Quarterly* 21, 4 (1943): 303–31.

Marshall, C. K. "A New 'Key' to the Gulf of Mexico." *Daily National Intelligencer*, April 5, 1859.

Marvin, William. *A Treatise on the Law of Wreck and Salvage*. Boston: Little, Brown, 1858.

Massacre at Indian Key, [Florida]. Philadelphia, 1841.

"Massacre at Indian Key, August 7, 1840 and the Death of Doctor Henry Perrine." *Florida Historical Society Quarterly* 5, 1 (1926): 18–42.

Matthews, John T. "Southern Literary Studies." In *Companion to American Literary Studies*, ed. Caroline Field Levander and Robert S. Levine. 294–309. Malden, Mass.: Wiley, 2011.

Maury, Matthew Fontaine. "The Maritime Interests of the South and West." *Army and Navy Chronicle, and Scientific Repository, being a Continuation of Homans'* 2, 22 (November 30, 1843), 647–62.

———. "The Maritime Interests of the South and West.—Concluded." *Army and Navy Chronicle, and Scientific Repository, being a Continuation of Homans'* 2, 22 (November 30, 1843), 673–88.

McCoy, Drew R. *The Elusive Republic: Political Economy in Jeffersonian America.* Chapel Hill: Published for Omohundro Institute of Early American History and Culture by University of North Carolina Press, 1980.

McIntyre, Rebecca C. "Promoting the Gothic South." *Southern Cultures* 11, 2 (2005): 33–61.

McMullen, Wallace E. "The Origin of the Term Everglades." *American Speech* 28, 1 (1953): 26–34.

McTammany, Mary Jo. "Clay County Memoirs: Street Names Provide Us a Glimpse of the Past." *Florida Times-Union*, August 24, 2005.

"Minor Notices." *The Literary World: A Monthly Review of Current Literature* 10, 10 (May 10, 1879): 154.

Montesquieu, Charles S. *The Spirit of Laws: A Compendium of the First English Edition.* Ed. David W. Carrithers. Berkeley: University of California Press, 1977.

Montgomery, Cora (Jane McManus Storm Cazneau). "Cuba: The Key of the Mexican Gulf." In *A Series of Articles on the Cuban Question.* 12–14. New York: La Verdad, 1849.

Morse, Jedidiah. *Geography Made Easy: Being a Short but Comprehensive System of That Very Useful and Agreeable Science.* New Haven, Conn.: Meigs, Bowen & Dana, 1784.

———. *Geography Made Easy . . . Calculated Particularly for the Use and Improvement of Schools in the United States of America.* 3rd ed. Boston: Hall, 1791.

———. *A Report to the Secretary of War of the United States on Indian Affairs: Comprising a Narrative of a Tour Performed in the Summer of 1820. . . .* New Haven, Conn.: Printed by S. Converse, 1822.

Morse, Jedidiah, Samuel Webber, John Arrowsmith, Enoch G. Gridley, John Scoles, Thomas K. Marshall, Aaron Arrowsmith, and Samuel Lewis. *The American Universal Geography . . . Calculated for Americans. . . .* Boston: J. T. Buckingham, for Thomas & Andrews. Sold at Their Store, No. 45 Newbury-Street, 1805.

Mowat, Charles L. "The First Campaign of Publicity for Florida." *Mississippi Valley Historical Review* 30, 3 (1943): 359.

——. "That 'Odd Being,' de Brahm." *Florida Historical Quarterly* 20, 4 (1942): 323–45.

Mulroy, Kevin. *The Seminole Freedmen: A History*. Norman: University of Oklahoma Press, 2007.

Nairne, Thomas. *Nairne's Muskhogean Journals: The 1708 Expedition to the Mississippi River*. Ed. Alexander Moore. Jackson: University Press of Mississippi, 1988.

"New Works." *The Albion: A Journal of News, Politics and Literature* (March 11, 1848).

Onuf, Peter S. *Jefferson's Empire: The Language of American Nationhood*. Charlottesville: University of Virginia Press, 2000.

——. *Statehood and Union: A History of the Northwest Ordinance*. Bloomington: Indiana University Press, 1987.

"The Origin, Progress, and Conclusion of the Florida War." *Literary World* 3, 64 (April 22, 1848): 231.

"Opinion of the court in reference to the failure of the campaign in Florida, conducted by Major General Scott, in 1836." *American State Papers* 7. Washington: Gales and Seaton, 1861. 461–3.

Ortiz, Paul. *Emancipation Betrayed: The Hidden History of Black Organizing and White Violence in Florida from Reconstruction to the Bloody Election of 1920*. Berkeley: University of California Press, 2005.

Otter, Samuel. "Stowe and Race." In *The Cambridge Companion to Harriet Beecher Stowe*, ed. Cindy Weinstein. 15–38. Cambridge: Cambridge University Press, 2004.

Owsley, Frank Lawrence, Jr., and Gene A. Smith. *Filibusters and Expansionists: Jeffersonian Manifest Destiny, 1800–1821*. Tuscaloosa: University of Alabama Press, 1997.

"Palmetto-Leaves." *The Literary World; a Monthly Review of Current Literature* 3, 10 (March 1, 1873): 146.

Panagopoulos, E. P. "Chateaubriand's Florida and His Journey to America." *Florida Historical Quarterly* 49, 2 (1970): 140–52.

Parrish, Susan Scott. *American Curiosity: Cultures of Natural History in the Colonial British Atlantic World*. Chapel Hill: Published for Omohundro Institute of Early American History and Culture by University of North Carolina Press, 2006.

——. "William Byrd II and the Crossed Languages of Science, Satire, and Empire in British America." In *Creole Subjects in the Colonial Americas: Empires, Texts, Identities*, ed. Ralph Bauer and José Antonio Mazzotti. 355–72. Chapel Hill: Published for Omohundro Institute of Early American History and Culture by University of North Carolina Press, 2009.

——. "Zora Neale Hurston and the Environmental Ethic of Risk." In *American Studies, Ecocriticism, and Citizenship: Thinking and Acting in the Local and Global Commons*, ed. Joni Adamson and Kimberly N. Ruffin. 21–36. New York: Routledge, 2013.

Poinsett, Joel Roberts. *Notes on Mexico, made in the autumn of 1822*. London: John Miller, 1825.

Porter, Charlotte M. "Following Bartram's 'Track': Titian Ramsay Peale's Florida Journey." Tampa: Florida Historical Society, 1983.

Porter, Kenneth W. "Relations Between Negroes and Indians Within the Present Limits of the United States, Chapter IV, Relations in the South." *Journal of Negro History* 17, 3 (1932): 321–50.

Powell, Lawrence N. *New Masters: Northern Planters During the Civil War and Reconstruction*. New York: Fordham University Press, 1998.

Price, Edward T. *Dividing the Land: Early American Beginnings of Our Private Property Mosaic*. Chicago: University of Chicago Press, 1995.

Price, Richard. *Maroon Societies: Rebel Slave Communities in the Americas*. Baltimore: Johns Hopkins University Press, 1996.

Rainey, Sue. *Creating Picturesque America: Monument to the Natural and Cultural Landscape*. Nashville: Vanderbilt University Press, 1994.

"Reflections on the Importance of Florida, &c, to Great Britain." *The Universal Museum; Or, Gentleman's and Ladies Polite Magazine*, 1763.

Reid, John Phillip. *The Concept of Representation in the Age of the American Revolution*. Chicago: University of Chicago Press, 1989.

Rezek, Joseph. "The Orations on the Abolition of the Slave Trade and the Uses of Print in the Early Black Atlantic." *Early American Literature* 45, 3 (2010): 655–82.

Rifkin, Mark. *Manifesting America: The Imperial Construction of U.S. National Space*. Oxford: Oxford University Press, 2009.

———. *Settler Common Sense: Queerness and Everyday Colonialism in the American Renaissance*. Minneapolis: University of Minnesota Press, 2014.

Ring, Natalie J. *The Problem South: Region, Empire, and the New Liberal State, 1880–1930*. Athens: University of Georgia Press, 2012.

Riss, Arthur. *Race, Slavery, and Liberalism in Nineteenth-Century American Literature*. New York: Cambridge University Press, 2006.

Rivers, Larry E. *Slavery in Florida: Territorial Days to Emancipation*. Gainesville: University Press of Florida, 2000.

Rochefort, Charles de. *The History of the Caribby Islands. . . .* Trans. John Davies. London: Printed by J. M. for T. Dring & J. Starkey, 1666.

Romans, Bernard, ed. *A Concise Natural History of East and West Florida*. Intro. and annotations Kathryn E. Holland Braund. Tuscaloosa: University of Alabama Press, 1999.

Romero, Lora. *Home Fronts: Domesticity and Its Critics in the Antebellum United States*. Durham, N.C.: Duke University Press, 1997.

Rosen, Deborah A. *Border Law: The First Seminole War and American Nationhood*. Cambridge, Mass.: Harvard University Press, 2015.

Rudwick, Martin J. S. *Bursting the Limits of Time: The Reconstruction of Geohistory in the Age of Revolution*. Chicago: University of Chicago Press, 2005.

———. *Worlds Before Adam: The Reconstruction of Geohistory in the Age of Reform.* Chicago: University of Chicago Press, 2008.

Rutherford, Mildred Lewis, ed. *American Authors: A Hand-book of American Literature from Early Colonial to Living Writers.* Atlanta: Franklin Printing & Publishing, 1894.

Salmon, Thomas, and Matthias Goch. *Hedendaagsche historie of tegenwoordige staet van alle volkeren, in opzigte hunner landsgelegenheit, personen, klederen, gebouwen, zeden, wetten, gewoontens, godsdienst, regering, konsten en wetenschappen, koophandel, handwerken, landbouw, landziektens, planten, dieren, mineralen en andere zaken tot de natuurlyke historie dienende,* vol. 3, Amsterdam: Isaak Tirion, 1769.

Sayre, Gordon M. "The Mound Builders and the Imagination of American Antiquity in Jefferson, Bartram, and Chateaubriand." *Early American Literature* 33, 3 (1998): 225–49.

Schafer, Daniel L. *Anna Madgigine Jai Kingsley: African Princess, Florida Slave, Plantation Slaveowner.* Gainesville: University Press of Florida, 2003.

———. *William Bartram and the Ghost Plantations of British East Florida.* Gainesville: University Press of Florida, 2010.

———. "Zephaniah Kingsley's Laurel Grove Plantation." In *Colonial Plantations and Economy in Florida,* ed. Jane L. Landers. 98–120. Gainesville: University Press of Florida, 2000.

Schoolman, Martha. *Abolitionist Geographies.* Minneapolis: University of Minnesota Press, 2014.

Seed, Patricia. *Ceremonies of Possession in Europe's Conquest of the New World, 1492–1640.* New York: Cambridge University Press, 1995.

Seelye, John D. *Beautiful Machine: Rivers and the Republican Plan, 1755–1825.* New York: Oxford University Press, 1991.

Shankman, Andrew. *Crucible of American Democracy: The Struggle to Fuse Egalitarianism & Capitalism in Jeffersonian Pennsylvania.* Lawrence: University of Kansas Press, 2004.

Shofner, Jerrell H. *Nor Is It over Yet: Florida in the Era of Reconstruction, 1863–1877.* Gainesville: University Press of Florida, 1974.

Simmons, William H. *Notices of East Florida: With an Account of the Seminole Nation of Indians.* Gainesville: University Press of Florida, 1973.

Simonton, John. "Key West." *United States Telegraph,* May 9, 1826.

A Sketch of the Life of Elizabeth Emmons, or the Female Sailor: Who Was Brutally Murdered While at Sea, Off the Coast of Florida, February 3d, 1841. Boston: Graves & Bartlett, 1841.

Slap, Andrew L. *The Doom of Reconstruction: The Liberal Republicans in the Civil War Era.* New York: Fordham University Press, 2006.

Smith, Buckingham, and James D. Wescott. *Report . . . to Authorize the Drainage of the Ever Glades, in the State of Florida.* 30th Cong., 1st sess., Senate Report 242. Washington, D.C., 1848.

Snyder, Christina. *Slavery in Indian Country: The Changing Face of Captivity in Early America*. Cambridge, Mass.: Harvard University Press, 2010.

"Some Account of the Government of East and West Florida. . . ." *Gentleman's Magazine*, London (1763): 552–54.

Sprague, John T. *The Origin, Progress, and Conclusion of the Florida War*. Gainesville: University Press of Florida, 1964.

Stagg, J. C. A. *Borderlines in Borderlands: James Madison and the Spanish-American Frontier, 1776–1821*. New Haven, Conn.: Yale University Press, 2009.

Stewart, James Brewer. *Abolitionist Politics and the Coming of the Civil War*. Amherst: University of Massachusetts Press, 2008.

———. *Joshua R. Giddings and the Tactics of Radical Politics*. Cleveland: Press of Case Western Reserve University, 1970.

Stork, William. *An Account of the First Discovery and Natural History of Florida*. London, 1763.

Stowe, Harriet Beecher. *Dred: A Tale of the Great Dismal Swamp*. Ed. Robert S. Levine. Chapel Hill: University of North Carolina Press, 2000.

———. "A New Palmetto Leaf." *Christian Union* 9, 18 (May 6, 1874): 343.

———. "Our Florida Plantation." *Atlantic Monthly* 43, 259 (May 1879): 641–49.

———. *Palmetto-Leaves*. Boston: James R. Osgood, 1873.

———. "Southern Christmas and New Year." *Christian Union* 13, 3 (January 19, 1876): 44.

———. "Who Ought to Come to Florida?" *Christian Union* 1, 19 (May 7, 1870): 290.

Streeby, Shelley. *American Sensations: Class, Empire, and the Production of Popular Culture*. Berkeley: University of California Press, 2002.

Sturtevant, William C., and Jessica R. Cattelino. "Florida Seminole and Miccosukee." In *Handbook of North American Indians*, vol. 14, *Southeast*, ed. William C. Sturtevant and Raymond Fogelson. 429–49. Washington, D.C.: Smithsonian Institution Press, 2004.

Sutter, Paul, and Christopher J. Manganiello, eds. *Environmental History and the American South: A Reader*. Athens: University of Georgia Press, 2009.

Thompson, Alvin O. *Flight to Freedom: African Runaways and Maroons in the Americas*. Kingston, Jamaica: University of the West Indies Press, 2006.

Thoreau, Henry D. *Collected Essays and Poems*. Ed. Elizabeth H. Witherell. New York: Literary Classics of the United States, 2001.

Thulesius, Olav. *Harriet Beecher Stowe in Florida, 1867 to 1884*. Jefferson, N.C.: McFarland, 2001.

Tolnay, Stewart E., and E. M. Beck. "Racial Violence and Black Migration in the American South, 1910 to 1930." *American Sociological Review* 57, 1 (1992): 103–16.

Totten, Joseph Gilbert. *Report of General J.G. Totten, Chief Engineer, on the Subject of National Defences*. Washington, D.C.: Printed by A. Boyd Hamilton, 1851.

"Troubles of Slaveholders," *The Emancipator* 4, 20 (September 12, 1839): 80.

U.S. Congress. "Florida Canal." 19th Cong., 1st sess. (February 14, 1826).

———. "Florida Wreckers." 19th Cong., 1st sess. (January 11, 1826).

Vedder, Lee A. *John James Audubon and the Birds of America: A Visionary Achievement in Ornithological Illustration.* San Marino, Calif.: Huntington Library, 2006.

Vega, Garcilasso. *La Florida del Inca: Historia del Adelantado Hernando de Soto governador y capitan general del reyno de la Florida y de otros heroicos cavalleros españoles e indios.* Lisbona, Espana, 1605.

Viele, John. *The Florida Keys.* Vol. 3, *The Wreckers.* Sarasota, Fla.: Pineapple Press, 2001.

Vignoles, Charles Blacker. *Observations upon the Floridas.* Gainesville: University Press of Florida, 1977.

Vileisis, Ann. *Discovering the Unknown Landscape: A History of America's Wetlands.* Washington, D.C.: Island Press, 1997.

"Violation of the Flag of Truce." *National Era* 13, 629 (Jan. 20, 1859): 10.

Volney, Constantin-François C. *Tableau du climat et du sol des États-Unis d'Amérique.* Paris,s.n., 1803.

———. *A View of the Soil and Climate of the United States of America: With Supplementary Remarks upon Florida, on the French Colonies on the Mississippi and Ohio and in Canada, and on the Aboriginal Tribes of America.* Trans. Charles B. Brown. Philadelphia: Conrad, 1804.

Walden, Dan. "'A False Phantom': The Coastscape in James Fenimore Cooper's *The Pilot.*" *Studies in American Fiction* 42, 2 (2015): 147–66.

Walker, Jeffrey. "Reading Rose Budd; Or, Tough Sledding in *Jack Tier.*" In *James Fenimore Cooper Society Miscellaneous Papers* 27, ed. Steven Harthorn and Shalicia Wilson (2010): 11–14.

Walker, Jonathan. *Trial and Imprisonment of Jonathan Walker, at Pensacola, Florida: For Aiding Slaves to Escape from Bondage. . . .* Pref. Maria W. Chapman. Boston: Published at the Anti-Slavery Office, 1846.

Walls, Laura Dassow. "Literature, Geography, and the Spaces of Interdisciplinarity." *American Literary History* 23, 4 (2011): 860–72.

Waselkov, Gregory A., and Kathryn E. Holland Braund, eds. *William Bartram on the Southeastern Indians.* Lincoln: University of Nebraska Press, 1995.

Weinstein, Cindy, ed. *The Cambridge Companion to Harriet Beecher Stowe.* New York: Cambridge University Press, 2004.

Welch, Andrew. *A Narrative of the Life and Sufferings of Mrs. Jane Johns Who Was Barbarously Wounded and Scalped by Seminole Indians, in East Florida.* Charleston, S.C.: Printed by Burke & Giles, 1837.

Welch, Margaret Curzon. "John James Audubon and His American Audience: Art, Science, and Nature, 1830–1860." PhD dissertation, University of Pennsylvania, 1988.

White, Ed. *The Backcountry and the City: Colonization and Conflict in Early America.* Minneapolis: University of Minnesota Press, 2005.

———. "Crèvecoeur in Wyoming." *Early American Literature* 43, 2 (2008): 379–407.

Williams, Daniel. "Refuge upon the Sea: Captivity and Liberty in 'The Florida Pirate.'" *Early American Literature* 36, 1 (2001): 71–88.

Williams, John Lee. *The Territory of Florida, Or, Sketches of the Topography, Civil and Natural History, of the Country, the Climate, and the Indian Tribes, from the First Discovery to the Present Time, with a Map, Views, Etc.* Gainesville: University Press of Florida, 1962.

Woertendyke, Gretchen. "John Howison's New Gothic Nationalism and Transatlantic Exchange." *Early American Literature* 43, 2 (2008): 309–35.

"Wrecking on the Florida Keys," *Harper's New Monthly Magazine* 107, 18 (April 1859), 577–86.

Index

Page numbers in italics refer to figures.

Acknowledgements

It is a privilege to thank the many people and institutions that have helped me complete this book. First and foremost I thank Elisa Tamarkin for sharing her rare ability to look and listen, without which I would have missed many extraordinary things. I am grateful to her beyond words. I am also grateful for the early and instrumental support of Michael Clark and Rodrigo Lazo, and for early and generous funding from the University of California, Irvine.

For the resources and community required to write this book, I have the good fortune to thank two English Departments. At Texas Tech University I am particularly grateful to Jen Shelton for her mentorship, and to Bryce Conrad, Julie Nelson Couch, Dennis Covington, Sam Dragga, Angela Eaton, John Poch, Jennifer Snead, and Bill Wenthe for support and spirited conversation. In more recent years, Miami University has been a wonderful place to teach and write. For mentorship that goes above and beyond, I thank Andrew Hebard. For astonishing collegiality, intellectual engagement, and enthusiasm, I thank all of my colleagues, and particularly Jim Bromley, cris cheek, Yu-Fang Cho, Mary Jean Corbett, Madelyn Detloff, Erin Edwards, Daisy Hernández, Cheryl Johnson, Katie Johnson, Cindy Klestinec, Tim Lockridge, Margaret Luongo, Anita Mannur, Timothy Melley, TaraShea Nesbit, Kaara Peterson, and Cathy Wagner. And for unfailing support and good cheer, I thank our excellent department chair, LuMing Mao.

As I wrote this book I received advice, assistance, and important suggestions from many individuals who spoke with me about my ideas, and read or listened to portions of the manuscript. I am grateful to Bill Brown, Martin Brückner, Drew Cayton, Louis De Vorsey, Alejandra Dubcovsky, S. Max Edelson, Adrian Finucane, Thomas Hallock, Karlos Hill, Steve Hindle, Christopher Hom, Renata Keller, Michelle McDonald, Roderick McDonald, Andrew Newman, Lindsay O'Neill, Roy Ritchie, Melissa Sanchez, Esther Na Schwartz, Jeremy Schwartz, Jason Sharples, Cameron Strang, Alan Taylor, and Gretchen Woertendyke. I particularly thank Jack Matthews, whose early mentorship at Boston University showed me a way forward, and who remained with me along the path, even reading every word of the manuscript in its nearly final form. And I owe deep gratitude to Cristobal Silva for always reading carefully and advising wisely.

Opportunities to present my work in a number of venues allowed me to rethink and refine. I am thankful to fellow panelists and audience members at conferences hosted by the following professional societies: the Society of Early Americanists, the Omohundro Institute of Early American History and Culture, the American Studies Association, and the Society for the Study of Southern Literature. I am also grateful to two writing groups. In the Southern California Americanist Group (II) supported by the Huntington Library I thank Michelle Chihara, Aaron DeRosa, Bert Emerson, Christopher Hunter, Thomas Koenigs, Sharon Oster, Stella Setka, Stefanie Sobelle, and Derrick Spires for carefully reading Chapter 5. And I thank all members of the Early Americanist Writing Group—Angie Calcaterra, Travis Foster, Greta LaFleur, Wendy Roberts, Kacy Tillman, Abram Van Engen, and Caroline Wigginton—for collectively enriching my work by being its most lively, demanding, and generous audience.

This book would not exist without support from the following institutions and fellowship programs: the University of Pennsylvania's McNeil Center for Early American Studies; the Barbara Thom Postdoctoral Fellowship at the Huntington Library; and the Kislak Fellowship in American Studies at the Library of Congress's Kluge Center. Each institution provided a scholarly community whose interdisciplinary expertise expanded and transformed my approach to literary studies. And support and research staffs at these and other institutions provided expert and generous assistance. I especially thank, at the McNeil Center, Amy L. Baxter-Bellamy; at the Huntington Library, Christopher Adde, Molly Gipson, Juan Gomez, Leslie Jobsky, Brian Moeller, Carolyn Powell, Stephen Tabor, and Catherine Wehrey-Miller; at the Library of Congress, Travis Hensley, Thomas Mann, Mary Lou Reker, and Jason Steinhauer; at the Harriet Beecher Stowe Center, Elizabeth G. Burgess; at the University of Florida Special Collections, James G. Cusick; and at the Library Company of Philadelphia, James N. Green and Nicole Joniec. A Fothergill Research Award from the Bartram Trail Conference provided support as well.

The stellar editorial process of the Early American Studies Series at the University of Pennsylvania Press also crucially shaped this book. In particular, I wish to thank Bob Lockhart for his early and continuing enthusiasm, and for steadfast care and professionalism at every stage. Max Cavitch and Dan Richter read and critiqued the manuscript at several phases, offering invaluable suggestions. Anonymous external readers gave constructive critique. And managing editors Alison A. Anderson and Lily Palladino read with precision as they prepared the manuscript for publication. Further, I am grateful to two journals for permission to reproduce portions of earlier versions of Chapters 1 and 2, significant elements of which originally appeared in "Liquid Landscape: Possession and Floridian Geography," *Early American Literature* 47, 1 (2012), 89–114; and "Island Nation: Mapping Florida, Revising America," *Early American Studies* 11, 2 (2013), 243–271.

A network of friends and supporters has sustained me across many years and thousands of miles, such that this space cannot hold the names of all to whom I am grateful. A special thanks to the Pasadena hospitality of Sarah Hanley and Malcolm Rohrbough, and the many others in that city who made summers and semesters at the Huntington possible and even more enjoyable, including Laurine Tuleja; Pat and Bob Smith; and Bruce Krohn and Linda Ross (and Greg and Lucy, too). For enduring friendship, I thank Tracie Ashe; Nick Carrabba; Lara and Tim Crowley; Katrina Harack; Cristi Kupstas; Marta Kvande; Carol and Julian Rice; Melissa Shim; Arden Stern; Erin Walsh and Paul Pender; and Aaron Winter and Susannah Rosenblatt. Rose Curtin, Lindsay Schakenbach Regele and Matt Regele, and Elizabeth Stockton and Ryan Brown make Ohio an excellent place to be; Ian and Kristine Crockett make Los Angeles truly awesome. I cannot imagine this profession without Cynthia Nazarian and Stefan Vander Elst; Christina Snyder and Jacob Lee; Scott Sowerby and Wayne Huang; and book club members Dominic Mastroianni and Michelle Neely. And for priceless love and laughter, there are no better than Christine, Marcello, Enzo, and Vincent Giuliano.

Finally, my most heartfelt thanks are for family. My mother, Dianne Currie, deserves more gratitude than can ever be shown or spoken for providing the foundation of my intellectual curiosity and sustaining me in countless ways at every stage of life, much as her mother, Elaine Munyer, did for her. Sharon and Bill Conley, Will Conley, and Dianne, Mike, Arden, and Lily Del Bueno continue to surround me with love and support. Marilyn Munyer is an adventure and inspiration all her own. Jeannine, EJ, Dylan, and Noah Shalaby bring endless joy. My husband's parents, Francine and Edward Navakas, emanate extraordinary love while modeling lives of compassion and intellectual engagement. Memories of Annette Glasberg and Adele Ginsburg burn brightly; Gabe, Lily, Isabella, and Samuel Navakas continually delight and surprise; and Myrna, Rich, Burton, and Jade Glasberg give unparalleled shelter from the storm. My father, Mitch Currie, was a bit late; but Dad, you arrived just on time. Always most of all, I thank Gene Navakas for the life and love we share: thank you for listening to every word with a mind that ranges widely, yet turns over each thing with infinite interest. This book has taken us to places strange and wonderful, and I could not imagine a better traveling companion.